Jeff Shaw

GENTLEMAN ON THE DOOR
a doormans story

JEFF SHAW

Jeff Shaw

GENTLEMAN ON THE DOOR
a doormans story

Acknowledgements

I'd like to give special thanks to the people who were with me as the events in this book unfolded. There's a lot of them, starting with my mum and late dad, Lloyd, Phil, Slim, Esau, Trevor, Coulton, Valentine, Nick, Louise, Sharon and Julie, twins Caroline and Nikki, Claire, Tony and Jill, Catherine, the Nana girls, Adelle, April, Nigel, Frances BB, John BB, Ross, Big M, Lew, Chris, Gay Mick, blond Julie, Brewin, Sadie, Chrissie, Helen and many, many more.

I'd like to thank the people who supported me during my last few weeks in Australia in 2008 and on my return to the UK in 2009 as I went on the worst roller coaster ride of my life. Particularly worthy of mention are Pepe who was kind enough to phone me every week without fail, Kris, Ronnie and Hattie, Peter and Liz and finally Shaun and Marian who let me stay with them for a few days as I saw my dreams evaporate. They all gave me the energy and motivation to keep going and to recognise that the future is there to be taken.

This book would be incomplete without acknowledging the fun and very real dangers of door work. Kudos to all the doormen I ever knew.

This book was originally published in black and white in 2009 as No Time to Cry and subtitled Tales of a Leicester Bouncer. Following a lot of feedback I've renamed it, updated it and republished.

© Copyright Jeffrey E Shaw, 2014
First edition February 2014

ISBN-13: 978-1494748524

ISBN-10: 1494748525

Preface

On one warm English summers evening of 1983 my life took a change in direction. A change that affected me forever. I often reflect on that night and the many that followed. It's more than a quarter of a century later, time to tell the story. My life as a doorman.

I much prefer being called a doorman than a bouncer. It suits me and my story better. In my opinion a bouncer of the 80's conjures up images of thickset, limited vocabulary men in bow ties. My story isn't so much like this, or even along the lines of the Geoff Thompson (and many others) style of gruff, aggressive stuff which I've casually browsed through in Borders and Waterstones, but never really read. No, it's more the me of now reflecting on the me of then.

It's about the innocent, shy, naïve Jeff who once said he'd NEVER work on the doors and who spent nearly all of his spare time at the gym who morphed into an extremely well built, often scared but friendly doorman, who slowly became a sullen, shaven headed, uncaring pig until he finally saw the light, no – not in any sort of religious sense – and who became an assertive, confident and well rounded individual with enough confidence to spend some years living alone on the other side of the world.

Despite my assertion that I would never work the doors I eventually spent 15 years working all over the place in my "security" career but most of my experiences took place in my home town of Leicester and especially at a couple of joints that were around in those days: the Helsinki Bar and the Centre Bar.

First thing: I haven't always been small, fat and balding with sagging muscles. Nope. When I first started to work as a doorman I'd been training for over 10 years and was already pretty muscular, although not very big. Sadly I was also **VERY** short of money. I was just finishing an apprenticeship in the steel industry and, with the encouragement of my parents – especially my dad – had just gone out and bought a brand new, sand coloured 'A' registration Talbot Samba for about £3000 on the Never Never. What a car!

A guy called Coulton, who was my original boss at the Centre Bar and gets the odd mention here and there throughout this tale, may remember it very well because he was always helping me to get it going again. He even lent me his car one time while he spent all day hitting mine very hard with a blunt spanner. Even from the first day, the damn thing always had electrics that didn't work or was overheating or not starting or cutting out. Consequently in my early years the repayments and costs of repairs were completely draining me of any spare cash.

Now, when you're always at the gym, are aged about 21 or 22, short of money and surrounded by bouncers who seem to have lots of cash – and women – mustn't forget that part, what seems like a very, very good idea? A few months, pay off the car.

I have to say that getting a door job was easy. First off I decided I needed to make myself look tougher. I was renowned for having curly hair which not only made me look girly, but also gave me a very close resemblance to Marine Boy, so one Saturday I had it all cut into a short back and sides at Rons, the place in the city to go for a haircut, and then met up with a doorman agency my mum, of all people, had given me a tip-off about. They had named themselves Secure-A-Door and were based on a stall in the local market. I know. Secure-A-Door sounds like a company that sells padlocks or steel bars and having a market stall really didn't add to their image in my mind.

That Saturday afternoon I huffed and puffed up my courage and went down to the market to see them. They were expecting me. You have to understand. It was a big thing for me to go there by myself. Huge. There was one guy there. He looked amused when I strolled up and he casually asked me about my door experience, er... none. But after a few tough sounding comments of *'yeah mate'* in responses to his questions – which is hilarious when you consider my whiny, high pitched nasal accent, and a few dirty glares all around (a self defense method I honed over the years) he offered me a job on the spot. I said, inevitably, "yeah mate."

In truth Secure-A-Door were getting a lot of work and their presence in the city was growing. They were desperate for men and would probably have employed Marine Boy himself if he turned up. In hindsight I think he did!

By the next weekend I was standing and shivering with nerves outside a 'fun' pub in a rough part of Leicester. Okay, lets be clear. A rougher part of Leicester than the rest of it.

I must've looked a super treat. There I was with my nervous, pale face and shabby haircut, squeezed into a borrowed DJ (dinner jacket) that was two sizes too small, wearing a big purple bow tie – also borrowed – and my Doc Martin shoes. What a start.

1

The Early Me

I consider that I had a very conventional British upbringing. Born in early November 1960, my family would probably tell you I am a true Scorpio. According to the internet that's passionate, imaginative, determined, persevering, inflexible and self-confident. According to me it's more full of grit, drive and determination with a lot of intolerance thrown in for good measure.

I'm the youngest of two brothers, with less than 2 years between us and come from a white, middle class family living in a little village just outside Leicester, pronounced by the locals as "Lesta", which I often describe as a dull and grey industrial city in the East Midlands. It's a city once well known for knitting and shoes, but like all UK cities the face of industry has changed since the 80's and neither of those industries do well there now.

My parents were in their late 30's when I arrived which was pretty unusual for the late 1950's / early 1960's. In those days most couples started their families much younger.

My dad, Mark, was born in London and was a sixty a day Benson and Hedges Number 8 man. The strongest. As he aged – after much fuss from the schoolboy me and much effort from him – he stopped smoking overnight.

My mum, Kay, is also a reformed smoker. She also stopped cold through sheer will power when she was in her early forties. Perhaps that's where I get my own willpower from.

My dad worked hard and doted on me, in my mind more so than my brother. He was a medium height, balding, wide shouldered chap with a fairly swarthy complexion and his main forte was selling – anything. He spent a lot of his working life as a travelling salesman, often winning monthly and quarterly prizes for his efforts but, like me, he held down several part time jobs as well. Anything from egg farming to collecting loan repayments.

In the parlour of the 80's, he had the gift of the gab. In modern speak that's strong persuasive and influencing skills in certain situations – but he had come from a rough upbringing and suffered from many nervous breakdowns in his lifetime as a result. He eventually quit selling to work as a night shift petrol pump attendant before dying in 1988, aged 61. It was a very sad and unexpected death that I witnessed and the events of his death have left me with some serious mental scars that, even though I put them right back to the deepest recesses of my conscious mind, know I will carry to my own dying day.

Apart from looking after us, which I'm sure was a full time job, my mum worked part-time doing various clerical jobs at estate agents, small factories and local businesses. She comes from Coventry and was very good at what she did, quick, efficient and precise and kept up her work rate until her mid 60's.

She is a very, very caring person and would do anything for anybody. She is now 90 and still lives in the same house I grew up in. At less than 5' tall, my mum has wavy hair that has only gone a wiry grey in recent years and is the only daughter of Russian / Polish immigrants. Like me she is as blind as a bat without her glasses. She is also incredibly clever – much brighter than me or my brother. I wanted to write her biography but she wouldn't let me. All I've been allowed to say is that she represents a typical lady who grew up during the hardships of World War 2. She was even in the Land Army from the age of about 16 and was even strafed by a Meschersmitt fighter plane once. Apparently diving into a hedge was her only means of surviving the attack.

These days she suffers quite a few physical difficulties but grits her teeth, well, those few she has left, and gets on with it. Oh, and she likes to talk. Gawd. Does she like to talk! I inherited that too.

Neither of my parents drank and they didn't visit the pub on a Friday or Saturday night. They used to go to the occasional show but, mostly, seemed happy to spend time at home with the kids. Maybe they didn't have the money to do much else. I don't know.

I often tell people I'm second generation German-Russian and love to prattle on about a story of my ancestors fleeing Russia to go to America but not being able to read and ending up getting on the boat to England by mistake.

It sounds more exotic than reality which is; I'm the youngest son of English parents, one of which was abandoned by a German dad and the other had Polish blood. I know my fathers original surname was Schultz which he changed to Shaw by deed poll in the 40's a short time after he met my mum and that my mothers family name was anglicised to Fisher at some point in the family history. Mum has always maintained that the original family name was Fischerlovitz. Not long after I started writing the first version of this book she finally gave up and told me the Fischerlovitz part was a figment of her imagination. It was news to me. Damn. There goes any exotic part of my history!

I was always a good kid growing up. Pale faced with an awful short back and sides until I was about 9 or 10. We used to go down to the local village barber to have it cut. My mum called him the knife and fork man which gives you some idea. Eventually I was allowed to grow it longer – to about shoulder length, although it curled into big, thick rolls so it never actually reached my shoulders!

I was never very tall and even as I entered my teenage years was very skinny. I had also started to wear my glasses at about 10 when I realised I couldn't see the blackboard from where I cowered at the back of the classroom. I was never in any trouble and reasonably good to above average at school, but not exceptional. My report cards seem to show that I was seen as not quite as bright as my big brother, although I apparently "added zest and interest to each and every [French] lesson." Thanks Mr. Baldie or whatever your real name was. On top of that I was always getting comments about being quiet and shy, oh so very shy.

I am the total opposite to my brother, Barrie. Whilst he got himself tattooed at 15, was in a lot of school teams and was a real lady killer at a very early age I only dreamed of getting a tattoo, never really had any girlfriends as a youngster and preferred to stay at home and read science fiction books about Conan the Barbarian or watch action movies. The very few kids I hung out with at school were the same. I didn't hang around with the sporty or the brainy or the dumb. I had no gang to hide in. There was just... me. A bit of a loner if you like, likely to burst into tears if pushed too hard by a teacher or embarrassed or scared. Not one of the elite in any way, shape or form. Today they would call me a nerd. Then they called me a puff. A phrase to this day I still loathe and detest.

I always aspired to make the school teams like my big brother. I didn't care which sport. I just wanted to be bigger, better, more athletic. I never did. I simply wasn't good enough. Those bloody Conan books and Marvel comics! I daydreamed of having big muscles as I walked home across the fields from school and often imagined myself being bitten by a magic spider or injected with some magic potion. Oh how close I came to that!

One day one of my friends, Tony, walked by me. I noticed he'd put a lot of solid weight on. I was 11 and was impressed. "What have you been doing?" I asked in my squeaky, unbroken voice. "Weight training" he replied with a big smirk.

I left school in 1977 at sixteen with a few reasonable 'O' levels and the odd GCSE and somehow, despite my shyness, got an apprenticeship in the steel industry. It was the thing to do. I did 5 years day release studying Metallurgy. What you may ask? Nobody ever seems to know. It's the study of metals and materials and their properties.

The place I worked at went out of business a few years ago and I have since met and made friends with the man who was the MD when I was there. Something I never dreamed would even be possible. It was a big employer in its day and both me and my brother started our careers there. Me even doing the same course at the same Technical College as him.

We were so unalike that we didn't get along. Surprise, surprise. Hardly two peas in a pod. He must've viewed me as a nerd as well and left home at 17, getting married to Elaine at 18 and having two kids. I didn't. He's even long sighted and has fairly straight hair while I'm short sighted with my wonderful curls. Well, I had curly hair then. We're more similar now. Neither of us have much hair left.

Boring as it is, I learned to drive at 17 and passed my test the first time after about 9 months of once a week lessons with Mrs. Deeth from down the road. I bought my first car with financial help from my parents. Prior to that I'd been getting about on my inherited Honda SS50 moped. It had belonged to Barrie first and, lets be right about this. He had screwed the balls off it. It was knackered.

My first car was a rotting 15 or so year old red mini with a 7 digit registration that started JOE. I had no idea! It was as knackered as the moped and had big holes in the floor that made no pretence at keeping the rain out and ended up giving the whole car a constant sort of musky, sodden smell. I even had to remove the carpet and hang it on a radiator at work one day because it was so wet. The manager, Milne, found it hanging there – touching the soggy thing as though it was infected and giving me a bollocking for taking it into the offices to dry out. On top of that it was always breaking down. It got me around, sort of, but in the end I sold it to Barrie for peanuts and upgraded to a newer blue version. I can't remember what made him buy 'Joe' but it didn't last too much longer and he soon made sure it ended up at a scrap yard.

Looking back, I was nothing exceptional. Nothing particularly different from any other shy, bookish, nerdish kid except for one thing. The training. Always the training. Tony's muscles had really impressed me. He had stopped going. I had started. I was eleven. I weighed less than 7 stone.

Soon after I started training I had a life changing incident with one of the very few lads I used to hang out with at school.

His name was Keith and, bullied as he was himself, he used to delight in taking his frustrations out by twisting my arm up my back virtually every day. He was a small kid with almost white fair hair. I have no clue as to why I put up with this and stayed 'friends' with him for years, often going round to his house and playing soccer with him. My parents even took this 'friend' chocolates round when he broke his wrist. This one time he tried to twist my arm up my back and for the first time ever failed! He gave me a sour look. "You've got stronger" he groaned. My heart took a bit of a leap. He never tried the arm thing on me again.

Unfortunately another poor lad called Haydn, who I ended up working with 20 years later, took the arm twisting instead. I should've stepped in to help but I didn't. I think I was scared. Up until then it had been a steady stream of bullying from Keith. Because of my appearance and shyness I'd been bullied all my life until that point. I couldn't abide bullies then and I can't now.

Training. The gym. My release. My first real love. As my strength grew so did my enjoyment of life. The gym became my second home. In my early years I worshipped at the alter of 'the Schwarzenegger'. He was the hero of the magazines of the day. There was no one else in my eyes. Slowly though I woke up and realised what really made him tick. He may be driven but, to me, he has often revealed the underpinnings of a dislikeable man. I stopped my hero worship decades ago. Mind you, he still demonstrated an amazing physique in his prime.

My early training started with once a week sessions for about an hour at the local night school. I used to walk there and back. The exercises I did were completely unstructured and random. A set of curls here, a few calf raises there. My gains were poor but I loved the feel in my little muscles. It took a while but I eventually graduated to a pure bodybuilding gym called Granby Health Club 10 minutes walk from Leicester train station. There really weren't that many to chose from. By now I was about 14.

The bodybuilding gym was an eye opener for me. It was tiny but I was fascinated by the guys in there. Not only did my routines become more structured, to my untrained eye the men who worked out there looked like they were out of Health and Strength, the only UK bodybuilding magazine I was aware of and which I'd discovered by accident hidden on the top shelf next to the porn mags I was secretly eyeing in WH Smiths.

The gym was rapidly becoming the only place I felt at ease. The only place outside of school or, later, work where I had any real friends. A common bond. Bodybuilding.

A few years later I discovered the bodybuilding writings of an American named Mentzer, a man who ended up having a big influence on my thinking and, ultimately, my training. He was a sort of hero for years until I finally met him in California in 2001 a few days before he died of a heart attack at 49 and my views of him changed for the worse in twenty seconds.

Despite my early adoration and desire to meet him in the flesh I have never met Schwarzenegger. These days I don't want to. How times change.

2

Granby Health Club

My association with some of Leicesters hard men goes all the way back to my beginnings at Granby Health Club. I don't think the name has the allure of Golds Gym or Worlds Gym but it was called that because it occupied a small third floor office in Granby Street.

It was at the sparsely equipped Granby Health Club that I first met some well known Leicester characters such as Kingsley (aka Kingy or The King), T. P. (the gym owner), Jordie and Eagle. Like I said, these guys fascinated me.

After work my good old dad used to drive me there 3 times a week and wait patiently with a tea and a sandwich in a local café while I trained. The guys in the gym took me under their wing.

Kingy was a big guy with a few tattoos including a swan on his hand, jet black hair and a moustache and would've been in his mid to late 30's. I don't know what he did for a living. I liked him. I was always the kid to him which, as I got older, I started to find funny.

T. P. was sandy haired and Leicester born but is of Irish descent. He looked like a typical labourer. Rough, ready and able to work. I later learned he had his own roofing business. For some reason he didn't like me. I think he saw me as the kid like Kingy and gave me some workouts to follow, but I was occupying space in his gym so I was also a nuisance to him in some ways. Never mind. I was a paying member so he put up with it, although it's probably fair to say I took a few unnecessary insults from him and eventually grew to dislike him as much as he disliked me.

T. P. was in his late 20's at the time and I have vivid memories of him being fined for nicking bricks from a building site and also parking his tatty blue flatbed truck outside the gym. I also remember his forearms were covered in big red welts from where he'd tipped hot tar over himself from his work.

Jordie and Eagle were both teenagers, 18 or 19 at the most. Because they were closer to my age I got on well with both of them. Even at that age Jordie was a massive 16 stone, with a gap toothed grin and shaggy blond hair that gradually thinned over the years I knew him. He had arms like my legs and legs like tree trunks. It was hilarious whenever I stood my teeny 7 stone frame next to his. He used to wear a thick, pale blue angora jumper and drive around in a topless dark blue Spitfire with cream seats. I thought it was the bizz. About twenty years later I found out they were supposed to be notorious for having wheels come off them when you were driving along. I wonder if that ever happened to Jordie?

The funny thing is that I didn't hesitate to get competitive and used to compete in bodybuilding contests and he, this massive, muscular grinning guy didn't. I asked him why once and he told me he didn't think he was good enough.

Eagle was the younger of the two and had freckles, ginger hair and a thin ginger moustache. I don't think he was old enough to grow it properly. He was nowhere near as big or as muscular as Jordie but much, much bigger than me, well... everyone was. I do know that he was a scaffolder and painter and decorator by day and would often appear at the gym with paint in his hair and on his hands. I soon found out that he regularly donned a dinner jacket and a bow tie at night and worked as a doorman at the Fusion, a massive, popular place in Lee Circle.

It was Eagle that had offered me my first door job – way before Force 8. They were having trouble with a crowd who were coming in every week and causing mayhem. Eagle told me he used to keep part of a stool leg up his sleeve. Every time these guys started out came the leg. He showed me a couple of stitches he had in the top of his head one week. I didn't hesitate in turning down his kind offer.

Much later on there was another guy around who we all called Big John. John was very tall, had very greasy, short brown hair, an oval face and bright coloured dragon tattoos down both forearms. He was no older than me and liked to talk a lot when he was supposed to be training. An awful lot. I liked him as well and spent a few weeks training with him before, like a lot of guys, he just vanished over night. During that time he let me borrow some grease splattered books on bodybuilding written by Mentzer and then variously told me he was ex-army, a butcher, owned his own business, had been in prison. Who knows the truth.

John was incredibly strong and would juggle around 100lb dumbbells like they were nothing. I could barely get them off the floor. He also worked at some place called Topps as a doorman. I was so innocent I had no clue as to where that was or what it was like. In his view doorwork was all about 'bottle'. "As long as you've got more bottle than them" he told me one night. He suggested I worked with him at Topps for a bit of pocket money. The idea ticked in my head. I thought of the stitches I'd seen in Eagles head and the stool leg. I said no.

I've never considered myself a hard man like all these guys. Not then. Not now. I never wanted to be. In fact, the only thing that ever made me feel I could pretend to be hard enough to stand on any door was the fact that one of the regulars who turned up later at Sugars Gym, where I was destined to find myself, was a pale teenage matchstick by the name of Karl who also claimed to work the doors.

Funnily enough I was friends with him at first and it was with Karl that I would make my occasional trips out to nightclubs but towards the end of my association with him I thought that he was a complete prick. He had a pudding basin fringe with greasy brown hair that went down over his ears and worked next door to Sugars at a knitting factory as a junior something but always seemed to be in the gym, even during his lunch hour. Like me, he also competed in bodybuilding contests but even I looked big compared to him.

3

Known Associates

In the summer of 1977 I went away for my annual holiday with my parents. It was our first time abroad. I couldn't wait to get back to Granby Health Club and get going again. I felt so small after my break, even though I didn't really have much muscle to lose. When I came back T.P told me everything had changed. It appeared he had partially sold out to a big West Indian chap who was going to play a big part in my destiny. T.P. told me the West Indian's name was Sugar. He was standing there grinning.

At first I really didn't like him. He kept interrupting my workouts to ask for gym payments. Even in the middle of a set. I reported back to my parents. They knew nothing about the importance of completing a set. All they knew was that they had already paid T.P. for the year. I was getting fed up. My parents were getting fed up. They phoned up Citizens Advice.

Because of the ever increasing demands for the already paid fees I decided to leave Granby Health Club and in early 1977 I went to train at another place called Bradallens. My parents must have sighed. More money. It was here that I met Leicesters most infamous bodybuilder. A guy named Khachik.

Right by the clock tower in Leicester city centre, Bradallens was even more sparsely equipped than Granby Health Club. It was owned by a chap called Bradshaw who I later learned was known as Leicesters first Mr. Big. Yep. Knew him too. Shit – that was a LONG time ago.

The first time I went in Khachik was sitting there and looked massive to me. He was the manager. I was 16. I'm pretty sure my mum went with me. In those long distant days he had shoulder length light brown hair and along with another guy, by the name of Stevie, was Bradshaws protégé.

For those that are interested, Khachik is a squish nosed guy and as far as I can recall had an Arabic father and English mother, both now deceased. He's about my height (5' 10" ish) but, unlike me, was built like the proverbial, with fantastic abs, from a very young age. I think he had studied martial arts for a while before he took up bodybuilding and genuinely looked as tough as he was.

Stevie was a great guy, dead friendly and with short dark brown hair, teenager moustache and the best biceps I'd ever seen at that time. In comparison I was the shy kid with his mum, bum fluff, small muscles, glasses and girly, extremely curly hair who always stayed quietly in the background, wouldn't say boo to a goose and just got on with his training. An amazing difference between us when you realise that I am actually about the same age as the two of them, although probably 10 years less mature at the time.

I immediately liked Khachik and Stevie, maybe it was their similar ages, and Khachik was nothing but kind and polite and soon took me under his wing, helping me with my training and diet – although I kept getting his first name wrong and called him Ronnie for a while. It isn't. No wonder he gave me funny looks from time to time.

Bradshaw was rarely there but I heard the two of them talking about him and was intrigued. When I did discover him lurking one day I was surprised to see this geezer in his late thirties or so and with a shock of tightly curled, reddish hair and glasses. I didn't really find out he was a gangster for a long time. He hardly looked like one to me, not that I really knew what a gansgster was supposed to look like!

The gym move didn't last long mind because Bradallens went bust and shut down overnight. Bastards. In the end I had to go back to where I had come from but, by then, Granby Health Club had moved and was about to change to Sugars Gym. The dominance of Mr. Sugar was taking over from T. P. Most of the displaced Bradallens regulars ended up there as well.

4

Sugars Gym

The original Sugars Gym was Granby Health Club in disguise. It took up the entire second floor of an old building in Stamford Street, more or less in the city centre. It was mostly a men only environment and by todays standards it was still poorly equipped and dingy but back then I thought it was a great improvement from when T.P. owned it.

It had a tiny office and reception area, replete with a fuzzy colour TV and portable gas heater. The reception led you through to what must have been an old, oblong shaped knitting factory with white painted walls and big, black framed lever arch windows that ran down the length of the building. The windows let daylight flood in but they would never open or shut properly making it boiling in the summer and freezing in the winter, with rain and cold coming in and hitting you in the face.

A few more portable gas heaters were peppered around the place to try and keep us warm as we worked out during those cold, dark winter nights and served as a place to dump our sweaty shirts on during the summer.

As best as I can remember, over time, there was a squat rack at one end by the fire escape, a red painted leg extension / leg curl machine, a leg press machine, a rusty chinning bar, a pulldown machine with the weights attached to a rope that kept stretching and then snapping under the loads, a few cheap benches, some 5' and 6' bars, one sharply knurled Olympic bar permanently residing on the squat rack, plenty of weights painted black, bright yellow, red or blue depending on their size sitting on some home made big black stands and a big row of gold painted dumbbells along one wall.

It's fair to say that as it grew a lot of the stuff in there was homemade and badly welded. More than one piece of equipment broke under me. Why me? Who knows. Even if it wasn't me I seemed to get the blame. I have to say, it looked and felt like a torture chamber. I loved it.

By now I was at work and paying for the gym myself. I learned how to handle the demands for money from Mr. Sugar, always making sure I was paid up on time and often walking in with my subs visible in my hand to stop him asking for them the second I entered.

One thing I clearly remember about the place is the number of condensation covered mirrors all around. Believe me, we all spent time finding the most flattering one so that we could admire ourselves in front of it. I particularly spent a lot of time in front of my favourite, with my shirt off flexing my teeny muscles to melodious sax of Baker Street! What a poser! Nothing changed there then.

You had to walk the entire length of the gym to get to the minute changing rooms where we all used to heap our bags on top of one another – there were no private lockers – before entering our 'arena'.

By 1979 I was getting there at about 5pm, straight after work. By 6pm the place would be heaving. It was doing well with a loose membership of around a hundred and fifty or so. Everyone who was hardcore, which is where I now put myself, pretty much knew everyone. A lot of casuals came and went as well but despite the hotch-potch and changing faces, and it's fair to say that a lot of guys through there could easily be described as rogues, there was only ever petty theft and hardly any real trouble or strife. Having said that I did have my moments.

Training was now very serious indeed. I ended up having a major bust up with another big West Indian. How did it start? He didn't like the way I looked at his mate! I almost certainly gave his physique a jealous glare.

This guy had a scar along his face, given to him by some anonymous white guy one Christmas as he walked quietly round the city centre. Unsurprisingly he had a bit of a thing about white guys at the time. He gave me some pretty nasty verbal abuse. I retaliated, equally as nastily. It started to get really heated and racist from both of us. He grabbed a dumbbell and swung for me with it in his hand. It was a lazy swing. He missed. I think he missed on purpose. Fortunately I was rescued by Eagle who was now one of the bigger guys. Sugar came out. So did Kingy. T. P. was there. I had known these guys for some years now. Then they all went and had a major row in reception. I peeped in but they shooed me away. For some strange reason I was left out of it. No one ever said anything about it again. Odd. After that we were fine.

Rare incidents like this aside, the rogues were always pretty friendly to me and always helpful. For example – We never had to buy muscle magazines; all we had to do was put in an order and someone would casually stroll into WH Smiths and nick it. I guess they loved the challenge. The influence of these guys was so great they even convinced a bloke who worked at a warehouse to nick the latest magazines on their behalf.

Sadly this version of Sugars isn't there now. It hasn't been for a long time, closing down because of financial difficulties in about 1986 to be replaced by a much smaller version which I think was rather pretentiously entitled Sugars International Fitness Centre and which used to occupy a couple of floors of the building next door to the original. It's since moved again but as far as I know it's owned by Mr. Sugar. Let me introduce him a bit more: Sugar or, and he loves me for this, Dennis.

I didn't know his real name for ages. As we got past our initial differences I took the trouble to ask him where the name Sugar had come from. He looked at me. Little wrinkles formed around the corner of his eyes. I guess it wasn't the first time he'd been asked. "I'm sweet" he eventually replied, offering me a big, cheesy grin in the process.

After that I began to get on very well with him and my early reservations totally vanished. I was often a passenger in his various left hand drive BMW's if we all went off on a Saturday to watch a bodybuilding show. I thought it placed me in some sort of elevated position, even more so if I got to sit in the front seat.

In reality he just wanted someone to watch the oncoming traffic as he overtook because he couldn't see a damn thing! He'd often just say "okay?" in a deep twang and I'd say "yes" in my squeaky, nasal voice thinking he was asking about my health. He wasn't! It's a wonder we never had a major crash.

In the end I spent a short time between 1979 and 1980 working for him as the night manager of the gym but as I got to know him better and better and better he used to infuriate me because he had no sense of being on time for anything or any sense of urgency. When I wasn't working there I would stand outside the gym on Saturday mornings waiting for him to turn up and open the place, only to find myself the only one there – for at least an hour some weeks until he strolled up. No excuses – nothing.

In my young mind that made him a selfish bugger. After all – I HAD to train. Sugar was then, and still is now, very well known and a big name in the local community. He has many, many good qualities. Who knows what he thought of me. Perhaps he saw me as equally selfish. He did call me "his little white mate" to his West Indian friends which I thought was quite funny at the time. I don't think that I would be as amused by it today.

You just don't get gyms like the original Sugars today. They have much less charm and character and they're very certainly no longer mostly men only environments. I guess that last part has to be a good thing.

I'd started competing in bodybuilding contests way back. By my reckoning somewhere around 1973. This was even before I met Sugar. In fact, it was me that partially helped guide him through his first contest in Nottingham in August 1977 or so (he had some guy with him he kept referring to as his trainer). By that time I was a seasoned competitor so I thought I knew how to prepare backstage but I was tiny and had no place being on stage at any time. In the early contests

I didn't have a clue on what I was doing and just used to copy the big guys. I was so crap.

As you might imagine I never got anywhere but it didn't stop me and I had a massive collection of bodybuilding magazines and books by the time I was 20, even taking a lead part in a 1980 bodybuilding seminar that Sugar organised. Can you imagine that? Mr. Shy sitting behind a microphone and voicing his opinion on bodybuilding at 20. It was my life. It's still a big part of it. The longest lay off I've ever had in all that time was about 18 months as I made a stress filled transition back from Australia to the UK in late 2008 / early 2009.

Let me summarise and be abundantly clear; at the peak of my time at Sugars I didn't drink or smoke. It interrupted my training. I never went to the movies. It interrupted my training. I didn't go out for meals at restaurants. It interrupted my training. I had few friends outside the gym. I almost never went out to pubs or nightclubs, maybe once a year. I didn't even take an aspirin if I had a headache. I guess at that point I was boring. **Very**. There really isn't much else to say.

Training inside Sugars Gym (1984)
Picture Courtesy Jeff Shaw

5

Dave, Dave and Dave

Summer 1983. I had now been training at Sugars for 6 years. I was only about 13 stone but in the shape of my life. I had just come back from 2 weeks in Spain. It seems that a break of booze, sex and sun does wonders for your physique.

I had also just finished my Metallurgy course. Feeling inspired I decided that in the September I was going to buy a brand new car. A car that turned out to be the woeful Samba. Seems I had a Spanish theme going on in my head!

With all this in mind, it was pretty easy to overcome any reservations I had about door work. Within a week I'd been to see Secure-A-Door and they'd offered me a job. It was about to open up a whole new world.

I've never knowingly worked for an agency since those days, because I soon found out two things about them. One: the owners don't usually stay, letting their boys take all the heat which is one way for them to earn easy money and two: they can try every trick in the book to get a bigger slice of your pay. Very easy money.

As I said I didn't – and still don't – drink or smoke and I very rarely visited pubs or clubs. Thinking about it, I seem to have reverted back because I no longer visit pubs and clubs. I'm much more of a theatre guy now. I've even been to see Pirates of Penzance! Sophisticated or what?

My first door was a place called Force 8. What a venue. It was also called the Windmill and I think it was in a little village called Humberstone, although it's so long ago I'm not sure. I do remember it was a long drive from the village I lived in and I got pretty lost the first time I had to find it. I'm not the best of map readers. Another thing I inherited from my mum. There were no such things as Sat Navs in those days.

One of my older jokes was that the first time I went out to a pub and stayed out late was the night that I started working as a doorman. I admit it, it was a lie! I had been out with Karl. However, the truth was that it was still only the second or third time! I was so raw.

Over the years I learned that doormen are pretty much ten a penny, most of them constantly chopping and changing where they work, but on my very first night on the doors there was:

Dave – a big, beefy bloke in his early thirties with a scruffy 'tache and scruffy dark collar length hair. With there being 3 Daves I soon renamed him the tub of lard, behind his back of course. He was the guy off the stall and I soon discovered was one of 3 co-owners of Secure-A-Door.

Dave – a skinny West Indian. About the same age as tub of lard. He was the second of three owners of Secure-A-Door. Skinny Dave came across as more intelligent than the tub of lard and even claimed he had seen me training at Sugars. It may have been true. I didn't recognise him but there were so many guys coming and going back then.

Dave – The bespectacled Head Doorman. About 40, he always wore a rose in his lapel, liked fishing and loved to wear a cummerbund. In all my days since I NEVER saw another doorman wear either a rose or a cummerbund. Most, including me, would've thought it was ridiculous. Very odd things for him to wear.

He had all the physical presence, authority and assertiveness of a garage mechanic who couldn't find his favourite spanner. Much to my disgust, he also had what I call fisherman fingers – big and thick with an orange tinge at the tips as a result of handling his little fishy maggots. I do hope he never held them in his mouth. I've heard some tales about keen fishermen.

Cefus[1] – Another West Indian. At 17 he was a big guy and, I found out, the only really experienced doorman out of the lot

---

[1] Spelling could be very off here

of us. He had a bit of bum fluff on his chin and was one of three brothers who worked the doors all over town. He never said much to me – well – he never really said much to anyone but I learned a lot of early stuff from watching him in action. A few years later I was told he was seriously slashed around the legs and back and I never heard of him again.

Jan Cheese – a Dutchman living in Leicester. I can't remember his real name. He was another teenager and definitely thought of himself a bit of a 'hard man'. He claimed to be a martial arts expert and used to walk around with a 3" length of wooden dowel up his sleeve as his 'ultimate weapon'. It didn't do him much good. I met him again about a year later. I didn't recognise him at first. His nose had been pulverised.

The most I learned from Jan was not to stand with your hands clasped in front of your groin. "It looks like your holding your dick" he told me in some strange accent. After that, and for the rest of my career, when I wasn't slouching I always stood with my hands in my pockets or behind my back.

Paul – a former police sergeant who was never on the books of Secure-A-Door but liked to hang around for free in case there was any trouble. I guess he was just out for the night. I have no idea. He was very thin, about 30 and had long, very lank blond hair and was a mate of Dave, the Head Doorman.

A few years after I had left Force 8 I heard some tales about Paul and it made my blood run cold but he seemed okay with me. Either you can never tell or the stories we got to hear were pure bullshit. Probably the latter.

There was also another geezer who turned up later. I never did discover his name. Just because he was about 6 feet 10 tall he reckoned he was tough. My overriding recollections of him are that he was very grey, balding and must've been in his fifties or sixties. He was so tall had to turn his head sideways every time he walked through an archway.

There was a third owner of Secure-A-Door who went by the name of Simon who I never met. He worked with my mum at an estate agent in town and is who she'd found out about them from. Simon later became well known for trying to be the youngest person to sail solo across the Atlantic single handed and being sunk by a whale – twice!!

Although I never met Simon it was his dinner jacket that I borrowed! I can't remember but I bet my mum lugged it all the way back from Leicester for me.

Great crew. Tub of lard and skinny Dave soon buggered off leaving me, Bespectacled Dave, Cefus, Jan and Paul.

Dave's first ever words to me, and I'll remember this to the day I die, were "I want you to float up and down." What am I? A bleeding magician? I had NO IDEA what he meant so I asked Cefus. It turned out that floating up and down meant just walking from A to B and then back again. I hate these technical terms!

To give you some idea, Force 8 was a very small place with a capacity of about 90. Floating from A to B took about 2 seconds. Floating back the other way took another 2 seconds. In fact floating around the whole joint took about 10 seconds.

Later on at The Helsinki Bar, commonly known as Helsinkis or Stinkis, I covered the whole place by myself and at the Centre Hotel, where the Centre Bay lay, there were 4 of us. When the hotel was at full capacity it was occupied by somewhere in the region of 2000 to 3000 or more people, spread over 3 main function rooms and 2 restaurants each with their own bar, plus the Centre Bar itself. We never floated in there. I slumped and bumbled around, Lloyd, my big door buddy, slouched nearly as much as me and farted, and farted, and farted. The others sat and sipped orange juice. Smelly – gee, thanks Lloyd – but cool.

Even by the end of the night Force 8 had only filled to about half capacity. Forty-five people. I nervously 'floated' my 2 seconds up and 2 seconds down in my Doc Martin shoes, too small jacket and poor haircut. Bugger all happened, even though I got many looks from people as I passed them 15 times every minute. I was bored stupid and my feet hurt. Years later I realised some of those looks were pure aggression as many people seem to think you're intimidating them simply by walking past and I had more than one call to arms just because of the way I looked at someone.

At the end of that first night Dave told me to go around getting people out. I was pretty intimidated by it all. It seemed so hard. In the end I crept up to some tables and practically whispered to the occupants "... excuse me, please can you finish your drinks and make your way out now. Thank you." After 15 years it was more "Oi... haven't you got homes to go to? Bugger off and let me go home to mine."

I have to say that of all things being able to get several thousand drunken louts out of a pub / bar / club gave me more confidence in standing up in front of a crowd than anything else I have ever done. Since then I've had jobs where I've had to present to as many as 500 engineers at any one time. Never has it been as intimidating as that first time asking people to finish their drinks.

It was only about 10.45pm by the time the place was cleared. Fifteen minutes to get everyone out. Tub of lard and skinny Dave seem to mysteriously re-appear. Better than that, they then very generously gave me £12 cash in hand for my pathetic efforts. Remember, this was the early 80's. In one 4 hour session I'd earned double my hourly rate from my day job for doing nothing other than standing around and mumbling to get people out. Boy, I was so coming back next week.

The plan was I only worked on Saturdays so in-between my first and second nights I had plenty of time to think about being a doorman. The more time went on the more nervous I got. Early career thumpity-thumps set in. By the Saturday night I was pretty much shitting myself. What if this happened? What if that happened? Was it worth it for £12?

Being the good foot soldier I was, I took a deep breath, jumped in my car and off I went. I turned up early. Because I'd still only got the borrowed DJ and bow tie I decided not to put them on until the last minute. Not only were they stupid looking, I remember it was very hot and sticky. Combined, these made the second hand cigarette taste that these places had in those days overwhelming. The manager gave me a look, raised his eyebrows and sarcastically asked if that was how I was going to dress for work. I was irritated. I wasn't sure about the job and I didn't even know his name. There was absolutely no need for him to be like that. On top of that I didn't even have to be there for at least another 30 minutes. I mumbled something vague in return and went outside, out of the way.

Most people don't realise that other than the head doormen most guys can spend 99% of their time standing inside. It's a luxury to get fresh air when you're working. Those first few moments outside were the first time I'd ever actually 'stood' on a door and I reckoned that Dave had given himself the best job. It was summer, it was light, it was warm, the air was fresh. It was great.

Looking back, I guess it was then that I realised there was more to this job than money but I suppose I came to learn that the guy on the front door has a whole load of different issues to handle. You have about 2 seconds, or less, to decide if you're going to let someone in, you're often cramped for space and if anything happens either inside or outside you're the middle man so – no matter what, unless you're one of the less than enthusiastic doormen I met towards the end of my career – you have to get involved.

There are a few benefits though to having made so many quick decisions over the years – these days I'm still very good at sussing people up in a few seconds and I've never been scared or intimidated by any mans physical appearance or approach – big, small, fat, thin, arrogant, shy – since.

6

Lots of Bladder

There's no two ways about it. In those days a lot of doormen were full of shit and I would quietly laugh at some of their boasts in Sugars. These days they're often referred to as jacket fillers. They're not a new thing.

Anyone could do the job – there were no qualifications or requirements. All you had to do was pretend to be hard enough. A few would turn up at the gym every now and then with black eyes, a few stitches here and there and plenty of bladder.

The real tough ones never really bragged about their exploits and would be visibly annoyed if they got hurt. Even though doormen now have to pass an exam I assume that a lot of them still talk crap. Every tale the tosspots told you in my day was about how tough they were, how they fought off this mob, how they beat up this bloke. The Force 8 crew, apart from the silent Cefus, appeared to me to be absolutely no exception.

While I was standing outside that second night Head Doorman Dave appeared. I can't remember whether he was already there or arrived as I was marvelling at the summer air. It didn't take him long. I don't remember his exact words but in his thick Leicester accent it went along the lines of; "ere... Look at this." I looked. Nada. "ere" he pointed and jabbed the air with his stubby orange tipped finger. I looked again. There were faint pink stains around the sealant of small square windows in the door. "Some tosser head butted that last night. That's 'is blood." Thumpity-thump... thumpity-thump... thumpity-thump went my heart. "Soon chucked him out" he said with a knowing smile.

You come to learn in this job that anyone who head butts a window is really easy to chuck out. The glass in their forehead, their howls of pain and the blood streaming all over them gives it away. It's meaningless and stupid on their part. They hurt nothing but themselves and you're often left to pick up the pieces of flesh and glass.

In my time I've seen a guy hit himself over the head with a glass, someone repeatedly thump a door until their hand was mashed to bits, a skinhead girl with her leg almost in half after kicking a large pane of glass in (yuck) and every single lamp on a stairway smashed with drops of blood pointing towards the exit. BTW: This last wonderful bit of creativity was carried out by a bloke by the name of Ryan and some of his mates. Ryan is the guy from Leicester who won millions on the lottery and then went to prison for handling stolen cars.

Back to Force 8. "One of the local 'ard men" proclaimed Dave in his Leicester accent. "Twat."

I was worried. Scared really. I'd never encountered anything like that before. Sure – I'd had more than my fair share of schoolboy fights and lost a tooth at the front from one of them when I was about 13. I'd even had the incident at Sugars, but to see something that was obviously very violent and to then listen to some guy boasting about it was absolutely alien to me.

Never mind float inside. I nearly floated away on the gas that came out of a certain part of my anatomy. Not a good start. That night it got worse. Apparently the place had only just been done up. My first week had also been the first week the doors were open. It wasn't popular and was still only half full. I was getting bored again. One of the petty rules was that people couldn't smoke on the dance floor. Why? No idea.

Once or twice I had to go into the half a dozen or so people jigging around and ask them to put their cigarettes out. I got looks of death. Every time I stepped onto the dance floor, it was so quiet I felt like I could hear my Docs creaking and squeaking. I probably couldn't. I was so embarrassed by it all. In the end I just stopped 'floating' and starting leaning against the wall near the main door. My mind drifted in and out. I could hear a bell. I took no notice. The bell persisted. I took no notice.

Next thing was a frantic Asian face coming towards me. "Didn't you hear the alarm?" it screamed. Oh oh. Trouble. Apparently there was some drunk at the bar hassling the barmaids. The bell was the bar alarm. No one had bothered to tell me. I didn't have a clue what to do. Thumpity-thump... thumpity-thump... thumpity-thump. I looked around for some help. None! My next step? Go and get Dave. Bloody quick.

As usual he was outside talking to his mates. I grabbed him and told him there was trouble. I have to say – he stepped in without question, then tub of lard appeared from nowhere and between them the first of the many nameless, faceless drunks I came across in my career was bustled out. I watched in abject horror.

After they got him out Dave came back inside and gave me 'the look' and I knew my days as a doormen at Force 8 were numbered. Tub of lard was chuckling in the background. I think he expected me to react like that. I suppose I'd been 'bloodied' in a way. Luckily nothing else happened. I spent the rest of the night more scared than ever before getting cornered by some bespectacled, badly permed woman who went on and on about "having to have the whole lot out" (hysterectomy). I was shocked. At that time I had no idea how much some women will throw themselves at doormen. No wonder my pals at Sugars were so successful!!

Finally it came to last orders and round I went with my whispering act. I was so quiet that more than once somebody screamed "WHATTT?" as I asked them to drink up. In the end the place emptied. Cefus and Jan did far more than me for sure. Me? I was pretty glad it was all over. Pretty glad? Now there's an understatement.

Skinny Dave turned up soon after with some woman I'd never seen and they gave me £9 for my efforts. I asked why I got £12 the week before and they told me it was a mistake. I quit on the spot in a mixture of fear and disgust and vowed **never ever** to work as a doorman again. Too dangerous, too boring, too many scary women, too smoky and smelly and too many rip off artists. My mum probably lugged the dinner jacket all the way back into town again.

7

Establishing the Supply Chain

In the early 1980's me, training partner at the time, Ross, and a whole host of others used to finish our training at Sugars and walk round to the nearest coffee shop. We were a big gang.

Our regular haunt was Poppins on London Road. It was only 2 minutes walk away. Saturday was always the best day. We'd sit there boisterous and flushed and wolf down knickerbocker glories, ice cream and other delights. Funny. I've still got the taste for those. Wonder why?

An occasional part of this troop were a couple of French twins that were studying art at Uni. We'd nicknamed these guys the Honey Monsters because they, well, looked like the Honey Monster who starred in a cereal ad on TV. Course we were young, ignorant twits. Sorry. In reality they were both very nice guys and were massive compared to most of the crew in the gym with thick necks, torsos and arms and spoke with mixed English, Irish, French accents – a weird sound.

Today they own a chain of very popular restaurants in the heart of Paris, where they hail from, and are both successful artists having had several art exhibitions in various parts of the world. I guess that studying art in Leicester did nothing to harm their long term careers.

Briefly and unwittingly they were to become our steroid suppliers. The original steroid buying process was that we would get the damn things from whoever and wherever we could. It wasn't at all hard but it's not a great thing to do when you're dealing with drugs. Even steroids. These days there are loads of fakes on the market. Back then, all the drugs we got were the real deal.

Over time, as me and Ross got to know them, we realised that they were as heavily into bodybuilding as we were. Better than that, when they were at home they knew and trained at the gym of a very famous French bodybuilder called Nubret. Nubret had been runner up to the great Arnold at the 1975 Mr. Olympia. We all worked out that getting over the counter steroids through Nubret's connections was much easier and probably safer for any of us than using the black market that was available to us in the UK.

We built up trust between ourselves. We talked a lot. Things changed and eventually the process became that we would place an order, the brothers would give us a hand written receipt, often written with great flourish, and then head off to Paris, buy the stuff over the counter on our behalf and then give us our gear when they got back. We were taking so little at this point, about 2mg of Stromba a day and one injection of something called Trophobolene every 6 weeks that there was no need to do this very frequently and they ended up only ever doing it twice. I presume they made a small profit.

Every 6th week we went round to their dorm. The twins would then to inject and would occasionally squabble over who was going to 'do the deed'. Like many things, this was not planned, but it just seemed so simple and obvious to us. We were all so naïve. Injecting us was all part of the game.

I remember watching in horror one Saturday afternoon as we went round and one of the brothers got Ross to lay face down on his bed, pulled his trousers and pants down and jabbed him so hard in the arse that I'm sure he jerked 6" off the matress!!! Ouch. Oh my God. My turn next I thought. It didn't stop me though. Not for a second. Later, as we walked across town and back to my car I noticed that Ross had a big patch of blood spreading through the rear of his white coloured trousers. They'd obviously hit a vein. He later told me that his arse hurt for a week and he had a bruise the size of a football on his bum.

They could've killed him or both of us with this type of practise. We genuinely didn't care. We saw it as great fun... well... I did at least. I mean, it was so far from my upbringing!

In the end it all seemed so easy that we made our own trips to Paris which always ended up with a visit to Nubret's gym, then off to the chemists in Montmartre to place our order and finally back to the Honey Monsters house near the Sacre Coeur counting out boxes of steroids and needles before doing a bit of sight seeing, getting on the ferry and then strolling through customs and back towards Leicester.

I suppose it was marginally better than getting them to deliver the stuff to us.

8

Welcome to the Helsinki Bar

Now I had quit my job at Force 8 I was back to my cash strapped position and I'd started my long experiments with the steroids supplied by the Honey Monsters. That's why I'd been in such great shape after my summer holiday in Spain. I had got a lot bigger and stronger and very quickly but my pockets were emptying faster than I could fill them. Of course, I could've stopped using the 'stuff' to save some money, but after so many years of self inflicted torture without that much size to show for my efforts to get so big, so fast was extremely gratifying. Plus, when you're on them these things make you feel GOOD. The effects on what bodybuilders call 'the pump' are startling.

I remember training my back and it felt like someone had rammed hot shovels in there. Believe it or not that's a great feeling. Course, when you've been on them for a while or are coming off the effects aren't so good, but in the early days there was no way I was quitting. Now, before you think I am or was some sort of doped up drug cheat:

1. I haven't used any steroids for over 20 years
2. We all did it – and it was perfectly legal

What was I going to do? No money and big car repayment and growing steroid expenses. Three months after Force 8 and it was Christmas. I was completely broke. I could always go back to doorwork I suppose. As my desperation for money grew the ticking in my head grew.

First off I wandered into a nightclub called Mr. Kiesas a few nights before Christmas Eve on a Sugars Gym boys night out. Our regular once a year sojourn into the city where we all let our hair down. For those people who think that I've never drunk, think again. I was smashed that night. 2 pints and a sniff of the barmaids apron and I was legless. These days it's just the apron that gets me there.

Right by the clock tower in the centre of Leicester Mr. Kiesas was probably one of the major clubs in the city. Before being Mr. Kiesas it had been Baileys and had been there as long as I could remember. I didn't know it at the time but it was garnering a very notorious reputation.

Basically the doormen all worked for my old pal Khachik who had his own door agency called Unit Control (usually just called The Unit). They were so well known at one point that the entire tale of Khachik and his crew got a big write up in some trendy international magazine called The Face.

By this time I had fallen out in a big way with Khachik over some other stuff which had involved me going round to his house and, in front of his wife, accusing him of stealing a lot of money from me. What on earth was going on in my head?

He proclaimed innocence but, luckily, never made any move to harm me in any way, shape or form. Maybe he liked me! Up until then I'd always felt we'd been friends, often chatting or going for a coffee together.

Looking back I suppose he used me a bit. Now, it seems like I gave him lots of lifts for nothing in return but time changes perspectives. I even covered for him once when he went on a shop lifting spree in some health shop opposite Sugars. He just smirked and grinned as bottle after bottle of vitamins went in his jacket. He even asked the lady behind the counter where the Vitamin C were before looking at me, smiling and then shoving them in his pocket. I do remember smiling back. He had an infectious smile. He must've seen me as being quite the innocent or quite the fall guy.

After that night at his house whatever our friendship had been died an unsavoury death. I was furious. I knew he was lying. His eyes said it, his body said it. The words he used seemed forced from him. I never forgave him – part of my Scorpio nature I'm afraid.

I guess I was just a very minor player to him. He didn't seem that fussed one way or another so we were still cordial whenever we met in the gym, but we never really spoke to each other much from that day to this. In fact, the only time I had any real conversation with him after that was 7 or 8 years later in Los Angeles when him, my mum and me all bumped into each other. We were just sitting there soaking up the Californian sun and up he strolled so I said hello. We had a nice chat and a pleasant walk along Venice Beach for about an hour. I took some video footage of him with my brand new big, clunky camera that I was lugging around. He was jealous of it and made some remark. I raised my eyebrows but didn't respond.

When we got back to England, we found out he was supposed to be on the run for alleged involvement in gang warfare over, get this, hamburgers. I never found out if this was true, although two of his 'known associates' got life terms. Can you imagine the chances of randomly bumping into him pretty much halfway around the world? Why this sort of stuff happens to me I'll never know.

In 1983 / 84 the doormen at Kiesas were said to be running amok. Allegedly their favourite trick was to defecate and urinate in a communal bucket and then throw the contents over anybody who gave them hassle. **SURPRISE!** Lovely.

I never saw it myself but one guy told me he was there when they did it. Could have been all mouth for all I know. More likely it was all shite. Tee hee. C'mon. It wasn't that bad!

They were also rumoured to carry weapons. The story I got – and I have no idea how true this is – was that the Head Doorman, Lee – a thirty odd, blond haired guy with an upper body built like a gorillas and a Manchester United Red Devil tattoo on his arm, once hit someone with a spring loaded flick stick which caused so much damage that the blokes head went an instant shade of purple and looked ready to explode. A few weeks later he was supposed to have come back with his mates and, armed with a knife, said to Lee "do you remember me?" At which point Lee hit him again with the flick stick and then said "yes."

It was to come back and bite Lee though. Some years later we heard a story that his car had been bombed. Turned out someone had thrown a sparkplug through an open window, just missing his newborn baby who was in the back.

The hit 'em once, hit 'em hard trick didn't work for all of them though. Another guy, Luke, who I'd met at Bradallens when he was 15, tried the same trick at Le Chateau on London Road. Like me, Luke isn't that tall but he was truly, truly massive at the time. He was also a pretty good professional boxer at one point.

Apparently he was supposed to have become so annoyed with one guy that he smashed the barstool he was sitting on and used the chair leg to beat the bloke around the head. One of my later training partners, Big M, was working with Luke that night. He once told me he would never have dared to hit someone that hard. Sure enough the bloke came back a few weeks later complete with his mates and obligatory knife. Luke wasn't as fast as Lee and got sliced through the face from eye socket to chin.

Luke had an older brother. He was another huge bloke. I had bumped into him by accident in about 1981 when we were both studying for our respective careers. How did he treat me? When I wasn't looking he emptied the contents of at least two dirty ash trays into my bag. Thanks. I was too shy and introverted to say anything to him.

That drunken 1983 Christmas night I spoke to Lee. He had come back from 6 months in Australia earlier that year but I'd known him for about 6. "Any jobsh going?" I managed to slur. "Sure" said Lee looking at this tousle haired, bespectacled drunk in front of him, "we're looking for guys for Christmas Eve." "Count me in" I mumbled before staggering off into the night.

I remember I was with a guy called Roy who worked for Khachik at another place in town. His advice was don't do it. He knew about the Units special gift (shit surprise) and also how violent it could be there. I was still so naïve and so stupid. I kept saying "it'll be alright… it's Christmas. There won't be any trouble." I must've repeated it a dozen times or more. Roy kept shaking his head and telling me "don't count on it." He wasn't as pissed as me. Even in my drunken state I finally got it.

I saw Lee at the gym the next day. Bear in mind that training was so serious we never missed workouts no matter how we felt. I squirmed. "Sorry, mate... er... I was a bit drunk last night. It's not really for me." Lee looked hard at me. "Yeah... I noticed you were pissed." It was hard to miss really. And that was that. No Mr. Kiesas and no doorwork for Jeff.

What is really eerie though about that particular night is that me and Roy had wandered by my future workplace's windows and I clearly remember saying to him "look at that weird place" and him laughing in return before we wandered off. It was my first ever sight of the Helsinki Bar.

A couple of things have also come to mind. First is that Mr. Kiesas is the only nightclub I ever got asked to leave. The week I had started working as a doorman at Force 8 I'd gone in there straight from Sugars. It was the Thursday night, one night before my fated last Saturday. They'd just opened the doors. It was 9.30pm and empty. I wasn't alone though. With me was a guy called Ross, another one by the name of Wright and some bad breathed Scottish geezer they knew.

Ross was my training partner and my biggest buddy at the time. Wright came from Sugars too. I didn't know the Scottish bloke but the Kiesas doorstaff did – and they didn't like him.

To my surprise Luke, who worked there before he went to Le Chateau, and a big gang of others wandered up to us and asked us to go. "What's the matter?" I asked Luke, looking round at the absence of clientele or trouble. I was puzzled. I was surprised to see so many doormen hanging round the four of us. We hadn't done anything. Seems the Scottish geezer had a very bad rep and the manager wanted him out. I left quite willingly and happily, followed by Ross and Wright. The Scot trailed after us without a word. None of us wanted trouble. I never saw him again. I didn't want to smell his breath to be honest.

The second thing is that about six months after that Christmas Roy got himself into serious trouble for reportedly throwing someone through a window when he was working. The story I got was this guy was bad mouthing all the doorman and causing plenty of hassle. Roy supposedly crept up behind him and shoved – hard. It went to court but, luckily for him, he was found not guilty. It must've scared him though. Despite the usual doorman bravado Roy gave me after his day in court that "you could still see the scar", he never worked as a doorman again – even though I offered him a job more than once.

I struggled through that Christmas. I also took a break from the steroids. That's when I found out that they can have the most negative effects. Within days I was smaller, weaker and very, very depressed.

In the first week of January I had a big row with some guys in a shop over a brown jacket I'd bought. They were all the rage at Sugars but mega expensive. Everyone was getting a brown or a blue one. They were crap. I had no spare money, but, feeling a bit out of it, I still went out and bought one. The zip on mine broke after a couple of days. I took it back and played absolute bloody hell. The shop staff were shocked. I could see it in their eyes. So was I. This was so unlike me. It was probably the first time the effects of those things were evident in my personality.

Within days I got stuck in a tight parking spot in the Samba with Ross sitting beside me after we'd finished a night session at Sugars. An ampule of my injectable supplement that I had just bought had broken and I'd lost about £30 of contents – an awful lot of money for a man with none. When I found I was stuck I remember I just went ape. That and the jacket were too much. I couldn't get out no matter how hard I tried. Even Ross went white in the pale yellow lamplight. In the end he very calmly told me to just reverse back and I'd escape. Just as I screamed at him I'd tried that, two girls about our age arrived at the car in front that was causing me all the issues.

I frothed and screamed and snarled. They must have been scared shitless. In the end they jumped in their car and vamoosed and I drove forward and off in a screech of aggression. Could I have got out if I'd just reversed? Of course.

I now had absolutely nothing left. No money and no muscles. My fantastic physique of the summer was completely gone. I felt like I was cracking. I needed to get my body back at the very least. The money seemed so secondary. I needed ready cash for steroids though. It was all about buying in secret. What was the quickest way I could think of? Definitely doorwork. I've never been big on this imagination thing.

I didn't even consider an agency, just scoured the job ads and then, there it was. The second week of January 1984 and a small ad appeared for doormen at some place I'd never heard of in Rutland Street in Leicester. I guess it was fate.

I took a deep breath and phoned up on the Saturday morning, trying to use my Secure-A-Door tough guy voice. Some hopes! Never-the-less, I got an interview that afternoon but was so shy I didn't want to go by myself. Lucky me. I eventually talked a guy from the gym called Rob into going with me.

Rob was a year or so younger than me. He was a cocky, blond haired Londoner studying art or something at Uni. He wasn't taking as many steroids as me and, even in my post steroidal state, I always viewed him as smaller, fatter and weaker. I questioned him. He claimed to have had door experience at a pub in London, although I doubt this was true − or if it was − was similar to my Force 8 experience but I guess I thought he was more able and reliable than Dave or tub of lard and their mates, although that did prove to be wrong.

I was gob smacked when I walked into the far end of Rutland Street with Rob about noon for our interview and recognised this mystery place as the one I had staggered by with Roy a couple of weeks or so earlier.

We both took a deep breath and walked into a pretty empty Helsinki Bar for the first time. I asked a barman for the manager. He looked over in the direction of a thin lady and called her over. She looked at the two of us suspiciously. "It's about the door job" the barman told her.

The Helsinki Bar, Rutland Street (1984)
Picture Courtesy Jeff Shaw

I can't remember who did the talking for the two of us. Probably me. The managers name turned out to be Chrissie and she liked us enough to hire us on the spot. I was excited but as nervous as ever. This time I wanted a better experience than Force 8 so took the trouble to go and have a proper short back and sides, buy some expensive shoes, no more squeaky Doc Martins, a blue jacket and a tie in readiness.

Me and Rob started working there on Friday 20th January 1984.

9

Two Bars. One World. Part One.

You'll have noticed that I talk a lot about the Helsinki Bar and the Centre Bar. The majority of people reading this will probably have no clue as to what they were like. First off they were nothing more than drinking establishments.

In 1984 the doorways to these 2 places lay directly opposite each other at one edge of what was the quieter part of town. The Helsinki Bar was an isolated place, right off the street with nothing other than warehouses and offices either side but the Centre Bar was hidden in the variously named Centre, Penguin or International hotel. By the time I got there it was located in the basement of the hotel, although it had been moved around from function room to function room a few times. The same clientele moved from one to the other and back again all night long.

I've been told that Helsinkis was once a music factory. It became the trendy place it was in 1983 and was pretty much an instant hit. When I worked there it was open every night of the week (with the possible exception of Mondays) and had a shabbily white painted front with huge glass windows that would steam up making the innards invisible to anyone walking past. Once inside the place had an extremely high roof and was long and thin with minimal tables, a wooden floor, a lower level where the bar was and a small upper level peppered with a few crap tables and chairs that overlooked the bar. There was also a piano on a sort of low pedestal thing towards the back and a small back room with a Welsh Dresser standing against the wall. That room was where most of the druggies went for a smoke but was also used for private parties in the very early days.

The bar ran nearly the entire length of the place and had huge chalkboards on the wall behind it offering a bewildering array of exotic cocktails in various bright coloured chalks. It was mostly staffed by Uni students who wore white(ish) aprons tied round their waists and behind their necks and who all seemed to have red fingers. You always got a fresh glass when you ordered a drink at Helsinkis. Consequently the bar staff were constantly holding two upturned glasses on some sort of cleaner thing as they tried to keep up with demand. The thing left their hands wet and their fingers red.

The place also had huge lights hanging from the roof, yellow with nicotine stains that they flashed madly at last orders and as you walked in there was a coat stand on the right that was constantly covered in dozens of jackets. I often wondered if anyone had their coat nicked. I presume they did.

Happy hour went from 5pm to 7pm. I think drinks were half price. Yeah. I do know this is 2 hours. I asked once but got told not to ask.

During this slot they'd even serve you some hot stew if you were brave enough to order it.

That first night I made my way there from Sugars. I was supposed to have been training but felt too edgy and nervous and sat in the tiny reception of the gym for what seemed like hours waiting for the appointed time. In the end I took a deep breath, had a nervous cup of coffee with Ross, left him sitting there and then walked round for a 7.30pm start. Rob turned up a few minutes after me. Later I would pick him up from his girlfriends on my way in and we would arrive together. I don't think he owned a car. I'm not even sure he could drive.

My first night there was simply amazing. I just naturally stood to the left of the door as people entered and watched as they came in and came in and came in and came in. We didn't stop a soul. There were students, there were Punks, there were Goths, there were Rockabillys, there were Psychobillys, there were singers, there were druggies, there were gays, there were happy people.

The left of the door became my standard position. Me on the door. My door. Even if I were to go in Helsinkis today and that door was still there I would almost instinctively move to that same position. 25 plus years later, every time a Goth or Psychobilly walks past me in the street I turn and look to see if I know them. Weird isn't it? I'm probably just a bit soft in the head.

By about 9 – 9.30pm ish it was **seriously** about 3 or 4 or more times over the legal limit (of maybe a hundred or so). I'd never met people like this before. Everyone seemed to be having fun. Me and Rob were stunned.

Picture Courtesy Michelle Smith

Picture Courtesy Colin Bennett

Picture Courtesy Claire Palmer

Picture Courtesy Suzy Sissons

Picture Courtesy Erica Hooton

Picture Courtesy Erica Hooton

Jeff Shaw

Picture Courtesy Erica Hooton

Picture Courtesy Erica Hooton

Jeff Shaw

Picture Courtesy Erica Hooton

Picture Courtesy Erica Hooton

Picture Courtesy Erica Hooton

I don't think either of us really knew how to react so for everyone that walked through the door I simply said, "hello... good evening." It was what I'd seen Bespectacled Dave do at Force 8. Rob shrugged and followed suit.

Can you imagine? Some young guy or girl dressed up like the ones in the pictures with 2 doormen in suits and ties going Hello, Welcome. Good evening, Good night. We must've sounded like David Frost. They loved it. I loved it. I assume Rob loved it.

Chrissie told me later that loads of people had complimented her on her choice of doormen and that they really liked my friendly approach. In 1984 I had no idea if this was true, but it was just me being, well... me.

BTW: Chrissie happily took all the credit. Oh happy days. I wasn't the only one loving it. It didn't take long for me to find this on the internet: *... from the opening night circa 1983 [Helsinkis]... became the meeting place and musical melting pot for all of the city's disparate tribes... Full on NYE fancy dress parties, Alternative Miss Universe comps [and] gentlemen doormen... who firmly filtered out the townie twats!* [Barry Grogan].

At first me and Rob stood there ramrod straight with bulging chests stuck out but it got so packed we were literally crammed up against the door. The place filled up with smoke. If you were outside you couldn't see in. If you were inside you couldn't see across the room. There was a big, aluminium heater / cooler unit above our heads that made a lot of gurgling noises but it didn't seem to work. It got hotter and hotter. The coat stand filled up and this strange music blared out. It certainly wasn't pop or anything I'd heard before. I liked it. This was so far away from the hated and half empty Force 8 that it seemed surreal. There are certain tracks by the Thompson Twins (Doctor, Doctor) and Nina Simone (My Baby Just Cares for Me) that got played that night that still take me back if I hear them on the radio.

It was a turning point in my life. One of those key events that change you forever. In all my life I'd really avoided going out too much because I was too serious about training (for years I really wanted to win the Mr. Olympia competition) and also because I was quieter than most people I'd seen around city centres. Later I became a changed man but here, that night, I met people who appeared to have a similar nature to mine. From that first night I felt at home.

10

Learning the Ropes

Everything at Helsinkis was through the books. They even made us sign our names in a little register every time we turned up. It suited me. I wasn't bothered about paying tax. I was more nervous about getting caught for tax evasion. After a week in hand my take home pay was £10 a night. £20 for a weekends work. A bit more if we did the occasional Thursday night or the odd Saturday dinner time.

I soon found out that Rob had less idea than me. Two green boys together. I wonder if Chrissie ever realised. For the most part we stood on the door. My miniscule experience showed and I began to take the lead. Once in a while we'd take it in turns to 'float' round. Squeeze is a more appropriate term.

I always made it a habit to stand back and let other people go first if they were trying to get by me. After all – they were on a night out and could be rushing off anywhere, to meet anyone. I was working and had all night.

Occasionally, on my command, we'd move from the door and stand on the upper level and gaze around. People asked us what we were doing? Were we getting paid for that? I always answered with a smile. I never felt in any danger like I had at Force 8.

One time a high-heeled girl accidentally stood on my new shoes and left a hole in the toe. I'd not been working there long. I laughed. After that she tried to do it on purpose every bloody week. In the end I had more heel marks than I could count. I never tried too hard to stop her. Not once.

Jeff Shaw

Picture Courtesy Lorraine Smalley

Floating turned into wandering around, having fun whenever we got bored on the door, shaking hands with anyone who stuck theirs out. I even regularly fell for the old trick of someone offering you their hand only to snatch it away and thumb their nose at you at the last second. The trouble with me was that I fell for it again and again and again with one couple! Talk about frustrating! We all laughed every time.

People were mostly happy to drink up at the end of the night and my confidence in going around to herd them out increased and the volume of my voice went up proportionately although I still hesitated. I do recall asking one raven haired and tattooed girl to drink up who was being really slow. The bar was virtually empty. She was wearing skin tight, white riding jodhpurs. "I've only got a little tummy" she told me patting her teeny stomach. She sure had. I could have put one hand around it. I let it go, although I do remember thinking it won't stay that small if you keep drinking that stuff. Years later she tried the same trick in the Centre Bar. I was far less lenient. Mind you – a girlie drink up command – that's what I call funny. I never did learn to deepen my voice.

The toilets were rough as hell. You went through a door next to a little phone booth and then up a long, steep flight of very, very rickety stairs and then down a long corridor. The staff room and some offices were down there as well. How on earth anybody made themselves heard if they used the phone booth is beyond me.

Every so often we'd wander in to the toilets have a look and then wander back downstairs again. I started to learn my 'trade'. I started to learn how to talk to, flirt with, and influence people. I started to be able to feel danger and to know when to relax and smile. I was back on the gear, using my earnings to pay for it and getting bigger and bigger and stronger and stronger. By May that year I had gone from an emaciated 12 stone to 15 stone of solid muscle and was squatting over 600lbs and bench pressing 350lbs.

I've always been relatively strong and still am. At 14 I could squat 300lbs. Today, some 30 years later, 24 years without steroids and at 15 stone of not quite solid muscle I used 750lbs on the leg press. I can also still bench press 300lbs.

By that same May Rob was long gone. He had only lasted about 3 or 4 weeks. I assume he was scared off by a couple of 'fights' that happened, the appearance of Mr. Big and an incident in the toilets.

Toilet troubles. I still have them, but not like this. Henry, a long haired, scruffy looking barman with a posh voice (not like my Leicester accent) came racing up and told us that something was going on upstairs in the loo. How he knew is beyond me. Both me and Rob got up there straight away – which was a real no, no because we left the front door unattended. Hey we didn't know!

We kicked the trap door in. We could just have opened it, but where's the fun in that? Sitting and looking up at us in stunned silence were 3 blokes all sharing a needle. Great. I later told people we saw 3 blokes in the loo. One giving another a blow job and the third looking on, but that *may* have been an embellishment. Once we discovered them we just very politely asked them to leave and, without any fuss, they did. Down the stairs and out through the staff door that was directly in front of the stairs – literally leaving us trying to put the loo door back on and holding the virtually empty syringe. This was pre-AIDS. We stumbled down the stairs to the bar.

Chrissie came over. "What am I going to do with this?" I asked. Apart from being stick thin she had mousy brown hair and an off white, dead tooth right at the front. "Get rid of the fucking thing" she said. She had such a sweet way with words. They seemed to fit her profile. Mouth like a sewer one guy said to me a few weeks later. What words of wisdom she gave. I threw the thing in the street and stamped on it (needle, remnants of the contents, everything) and left it there. When I look back – we were so lucky.

The first of the fights was when Rob refused entry to a skinhead early one Friday night. The door used to open outwards away from us. At that time of night we still had room to move. Rob leaned across, opened it, saw this guy standing there and said "no." The bloke got all upset and mouthy so Rob took a step forward and shoved him in the chest. I suppose it was unnecessary but we really were green. He was a small bloke and Rob was hefty and, as a precaution, was also wearing a steel plate he'd invested in that was strapped to his forearm under his jacket. He'd offered one to me but I'd said no. Mr. Skinheads ribs must've met with steel and his back hit the pavement with a dull thud. Rob dived on top of him looking pretty much like a beached whale flapping around. I pulled him off before the skinhead was completely squished. You can get arrested for fighting in the street. You could get in even more serious trouble for suffocating someone to death with your belly.

Gasping for air Mr. Skinhead struggled to his little bootied feet and then, in front of everyone, threatened to get his big brother on us before running away down the street. Ahhh. Sweet. All over in twenty seconds.

It was the first time I'd ever been directly threatened as a doorman. After a while you do get more immune to it but that first time made us both fret a bit and we waited all night for the appearance of big brother. Nothing happened but we still weren't sure what to do. Our solution? Tell everyone at Sugars the next morning. That night there was an entire army of Sugars Gym guys hanging around waiting for something to happen. Mr. Skinhead never came back. Nor did his brother. Seems that some things aren't worth worrying about after all.

The second took place the following Thursday between a Psychobilly who went on to play guitar in a famous Psychobilly band and a guy I never recognised again with pink fluffy hair. The 'fight' was more a flicking of wrists and slapping contest at the foot of the stairs. It was over in a flash. I saw it out of the corner of my eye and dived in between the 2 of them before the thumpity-thump… thumpity-thump… thumpity-thumps could set in, while Rob stood there – steel plate at the ready I presume. I could feel the musician's ribs protruding out under his jumper. I think when he was in the band he played xylophone with those ribs. Fluffy fled for his life, crying and I was left with wispy pink bits of hair all over my lovely new blue jacket. Pink on blue – It didn't contrast well.

The musician had a flattop and a mean, thin face which he used to his advantage as he puffed himself up. I didn't know what to do. I was a little scared and very unsure, so I let him wander back to his table somewhere in the midst of the place. Chrissie came over a few minutes later and asked me what happened. Someone must've told her. I gave her my version of events. In her sweet way she said "fuck him off out" but it was too late, he had puffed himself up some more and left anyway. "He's already gone" I told her, trying to make out I'd ejected him. She seemed to buy it. Phew.

A few years later he boasted that I'd "seen him in action" and "backed off" and then proceeded to call me and the Centre Bar crew monkeys before trying to threaten us with CS gas. We all laughed at him and he left pronto without doing a thing, puffy chest all deflated never to be seen again.

That same night Bradshaw had appeared at the door. For some reason we'd been charging people a couple of pounds or so to go in. "Oh... I don't have to pay do I?" he asked. "I work the doors." Of course, he didn't recognise me. "It's Bradshaw isn't it?" I asked, even though I already knew. He gave me a quizzical look and nodded. You don't argue with those types of guys. I stepped back and in he went. Rob was aghast when I told him who and what he was. Much later I heard from someone else that Bradshaw had called me a pretty decent lad – I was pleased. Don't ask me why.

Anyway. It was all too much for Rob. The next night I turned up for work and he was nowhere to be seen. Apparently he'd quit without telling me and returned to London. Last I heard of him, he became a policeman. At least it saved me giving him a lift.

After Robs sudden departure I stood on Helsinkis door alone. My mates thought I was mad, my mum thought I was mad. A popular city centre venue, by myself on a Friday and Saturday night. There's no way I would do it now.

In the mid 90's I had an interview at some nameless pub in Leamington city centre. I was at my biggest, I was extremely experienced, had a bad attitude, a virtually shaven head, fresh facial and head scars and overall was pretty scary to look at and be around. Bless. I obviously looked like star quality! They offered me the job on the basis that I was the only doorman. I said no.

I soon found out that the Helsinki could be a right den of iniquity from a druggie point of view but it was very quiet trouble wise. Good job. I wasn't looking for trouble. I don't think I'd have lasted as long as I did as a doorman if I was fighting for my life every weekend. Some of the guys around in those days loved it. Looking back, even the altercations that seemed to drive Rob away were nothings. I got a bit of hassle from the odd person I wouldn't let in and the odd incident inside but nothing much really. The slow drink up girl got hassled by some twat and I asked her if she needed help. She didn't. One guy claimed he was an ex-Para and gave me the hard eyes.

Another tried to get in – all gap toothed, piano mouths we used to call them, and arms akimbo, trying to emphasise his slight stature. He looked a mess so there was no way.

Another told me I couldn't bounce a rubber ball. I turned someone else away because he had 18 lace Doc Martin boots. He went round the corner and told some other guys dressed the same way that there was no way I would let them in. They walked up to me. I knew them. "Do me a favour" I said. "Hang on 5 minutes 'till that guy has gone... then come back. I'll let you in." They did. I did. I became good friends with them. I spoke quietly. I was sweet. I was a gentleman. Well I think I was. Being polite and unthreatening seemed to be my forte. The truth? I didn't know what else to do. It became a part of my growing reputation and an important trademark.

Guys kept coming up to me and telling me they used to be the doormen there. There seemed to be a lot of them. None of them were much older than me. Maybe they weren't even as old. The thought went through my mind – had the whole of Leicester worked there?

First up in the procession was Romrig, a teeny-weeny bloke, with a scruffy beard and flattop who worked as a barber by day. Bearing in mind how massive I was now becoming, how he got a job as a doorman was beyond me.

Then there was Mark. He had a fully shaven pate and semi dressed as a skinhead. He seemed to fit the place well. Finally there was Kevin. He was a very tough Scotsman, with red hair and a port wine stain on his face who later went to prison with Bradshaw when they decided to kidnap a Norwegian businessman. Don't ask me. I'm only relating the tale.

All of three of them offered to help out at Helsinkis if there was any trouble. There wasn't. I was still saying "good evening" and "good night" to everyone. I was loving it, learning peoples names, getting to know what time they turned up, who their mates were, who avoided who. In the early evening there'd be a crowd of guys who I kept short-sightedly smiling at. They smiled back. In the end one of them came up to me and asked me if I had a brother who'd bought a brown jacket which had a problem with the zip. "That was me" I told him. "Now you know how lucky you were." His expression was priceless. He told me "I love it here. It's worth paying a few quid for a pint just to watch." I agreed.

As my early days standing there were in the midst of winter I kept the door firmly shut. If anyone came in and left the door dangling I'd reach out and pull it shut as fast as possible. I'd just closed it one Saturday night when this female vagrant appeared. She tried to open the door. It was obviously warm inside and freezing outside. I saw her reach for the door handle so grabbed my side and held on tightly. She tugged. No effect. She tugged a second time. No effect again. We stood and looked at each other. Some people came in, some people went out. She was still standing there. A few of the regulars cramped around me, saw her and looked at me. We had a little tug of war again. The regulars started to laugh. I wasn't budging. The vagrant started to laugh. I didn't really know how to react. In the end she shoved her fingers through the gold plated letterbox that was right in the middle of the door and tried to touch my hand. I jumped back. We all laughed. Then she just wandered away.

It didn't take long to learn that the Saturday night crowd was very different to the Friday night one. On Saturdays the place would fill very early. People would come in armed with tins and tins of Red Stripe. I wouldn't let them take the booze in so they'd dump it in a big heap under the coat stand and then leave their coats piled on top of each other on the stand before going inside for a short while. They'd then depart in their droves, complete with unopened tins at about 8.30pm. I found out later that there were organised trips to Rock City in Nottingham and that Helsinkis was pretty much the meeting place before everyone got on the coach and buggered off. After they'd gone a different crowd would come in.

Instructions from Chrissie were no townies so I'd do my best to filter them out but – what was a townie? I didn't really know so she was constantly complaining with her usual eloquence that I let too many in. Typically it went along the lines of "there's too many townie fuckers in here. What the fuck are you fucking about at you fucker?" In my defence I don't think I did because there was still no trouble.

One night another Scotsman, a dark brown haired bloke I think was called Ally or Angelo came up. I can't remember which one it was. They both went in there. He was a regular... "ayre ya be yersen tonai?" (Translation: Are you by yourself tonight?) "Dunya woree, I'll giv ya ei han if anythin gus ef" (Translation: Don't worry. I'll give you a hand if anything goes off). Guess who was the first one fighting that night? It was my first real bit of action by myself. Fortunately: 1. there was only him and one other geezer having a go and 2. They were right in front of the door. I turned round grabbed one in each hand and shoved them outside. Thumpity-thump... thumpity-thump... thumpity-thump. A few people came up to me and said well done, including Romrig and I calmed a little but that was it. After about 3 weeks of being alone I went to the owners of Helsinkis, two gays called Mel – a dark floppy haired, chubby guy with glasses and Tony – a tall, thin, grey haired balding guy and, in between my muted parps, told them that it was too dangerous to do this job by myself.

Chrissie was miffed. I'd gone over her head but she was having her own arguments with Mel and Tony and they eventually sacked her for – get this – going to the loo when she should have been in the bar. I was standing there when Tony demanded where she'd been. "Having a shit" was the response. "You're fired" was his.

A white / blond haired guy called Perry replaced Chrissie. I liked him but Tony fired him as well – falsely accusing him of stealing some of the takings (it went to court). Perry was replaced by another nice guy by the name of Thick – I kid you not. He must've suffered over that.

I never really liked either Mel or Tony. It didn't have anything to do with their sexuality. I just thought they were both rude in their own ways. There was a time before I worked there when the place had been broken into overnight. Apparently the bar staff hadn't fully dropped a latch on the staff door and someone had quite easily kicked it in. Mel and Tony's response? According to what I was told they sent a note to all the staff. It started "You Bastards...". Good job they didn't send a note like that to me.

Mel had run round one night when there had been a toga party in there. Apparently the police had been in contact and were on the lookout for one particular guy. This was during the time of the hunt for a murderer in my village who was thought to have been a Punk. The hunt later became known as the Blooding and was the very first time DNA testing had ever been used to track down a killer. In the search I'd been one of the very first ones in the world to give samples. One of the murders was very near where I lived. They'd been round to my house and asked me if I knew any Punks. They went round to everyone in the entire village. "I work at Helsinkis" I told them. "We know" they replied. "We've seen you there."

Anyway, the night of the toga party Mel went round all night with a little silver tray with a few cocktails on it – pretending to be delivering it to a table. In reality he was looking for this guy. He loved it. He was lording it up, down and around. It was so obvious to me. He carried on camping it here, there and everywhere before he eventually spotted the guy, presumably made a call and a plain-clothes policeman came in and arrested him right by me. The guy was a regular in there. Mel was in seventh heaven.

My views of Tony really became cemented after one of the bar staff told me that he liked to have sex in the rooms above the bar with his boyfriend, a glass collector called David, when the bar was in full swing on Saturday afternoons. It had nothing to do with me, but it hurt my personal sensibilities. Would I have felt the same if someone had told me that about a non homosexual relationship? I'm not at all homophobic, yet funnily enough, I doubt it. Strange.

Oh yeah. The funniest thing about the Ally / Angelo incident is that it was all over so fast I never really caught sight of the other guys face and – apparently – let him back in the next night. I didn't let Ally / Angelo in though because I knew him. If only he hadn't offered to help!

His mates told him that I'd let the other bloke back in straight away and Ally / Angelo came up to me as I leaned against the door jamb and moaned that I was being unfair to him. I wasn't really. I just hadn't realised. I eventually relented and let him back in about 3 weeks later.

11

Rapid Turnover

After Rob left a guy from Sugars called Renton, a white guy from Kendal in Cumbria despite his ethnic sounding name, had gone to see Chrissie behind my back to get the job. I must've mentioned it to him after Rob vamoosed. I don't remember. He didn't.

I quite liked Renton, he was the training partner of a ginger haired guy we all called Flash, but Chrissie didn't. Renton didn't directly tell me whether he had or hadn't got the job. I just know I was a bit surprised when I turned up at night and he wasn't there. Maybe he'd implied to me that he had been hired. I asked Chrissie when he was going to start and she said "fucking never."

I was frustrated so created a bit of a fuss about still being by myself. I probably went on and on about it at Sugars because a guy we all called "The Hunter" arrived at Helsinki at the start of one shift wearing a too big jacket, paint splattered Doc Martin boots and black framed glasses. The Hunter was a nice guy, but a bit on the slow side at the best of times. I'd been squatting in the gym when he was supposed to be spotting me in Ross' absence. In between my red faced, gasping reps with the knurling of the bar cutting hard into my shoulders I had glanced at him in the mirror facing me. You're not supposed to do that. Good job I did! The Hunter had taken off his shirt, was facing sideways to me and flexing his soft, pasty looking body in another mirror. Not the sort of thing you want to see when you've got a tremendous load on your back.

I didn't expect him to turn up at Helsinkis but he'd listened to me at the gym and was obviously expecting to work. He had no door experience at all. I seriously doubt that even Secure-A-Door would have hired him. As I was wondering what to say some faceless tosser came up to the door and gave me a bit of early evening hassle. I didn't want to let him in, purely because of his behaviour and was just using my smooth tongue to get him to bugger off when The Hunter stepped forward, taking off his glasses as he moved. I couldn't believe it. Neither could the tosser who took one look, laughed and wandered off of his own accord. I felt a bit trapped because I didn't really feel he was up to the mark so sidled over to Chrissie and asked if we could use him for the night. She read my face, took one look and shouted "fuck off" **VERY** loudly. Not very subtle but this was Chrissie. Sadly The Hunter still didn't get it so I had to tell him that there was no job there for him. He got it and went home looking more than a bit non plussed. The night went without any other incident and the next thing I knew, I turned up a week later and Chrissie had employed Daz, a guy who stepped up after Ross accidentally gave him a tip off.

Me and Ross had trained together for about five years by this time and had even gone on holiday together a few times, including the trip to Spain in the summer of '83. He worked at a factory that made wood turning machines as a fitter and would've been about 20 in 1984. Even compared to me he was a short arse, bow legged, with dirty brown hair, bitten up, grime filled nails and a fair few red headed little spots around his top lip. I used to think he was pretty strong for a short bloke, not that I was prejudiced. Of course not.

I'd tried hard to convince him to join me at Helsinkis rather than Rob and then join me once Rob had gone but he didn't want to know. I never discovered why, although I found out a few years later that he claimed he had worked there. Maybe he let Daz know on purpose about the job just to shut me up.

Ross and Daz worked together during the day, drank together during the week at the Tommie Cook, a pub on Narborough Road South which is on the outskirts of the city, and worked together on the doors at night. Their place of door employment was The Fusion. In those days pubs closed at 10.30pm and we didn't start until 7.30pm which must've seemed much more attractive to Daz than 9pm to 2.30am.

Daz was a blond, curly haired guy, not too dainty on his feet, with small, crafty eyes and a row of tiny milk teeth with a penchant for vodka and orange and chatting up women, any women. Ross had warned me that he was full of mouth and not to trust him in a fight but even then I was surprised when he decided to spend most of the night propped up against the coat stand secretively sipping his booze. Doormen aren't supposed to drink or smoke on duty. Didn't bother Daz.

At the end of most nights he was 3 sheets to the wind. I only ever saw him do anything once when he turned one teeny guy wearing a brown fedora away for being too young. The poor guys mouth turned down in disappointment. He went in there every week. "It's okay" I told Daz "I know him" which was sort of true at the time. Turns out it was much truer than I thought. He lived down the street from me. I even knew his very gay brother who went in there as well.

Chrissie came up to us at the end of the night once when Daz was there. We were both idling in the doorway. She looked cross and asked in her usual way "are you going to fucking walk round and get some of these fuckers out?" I was annoyed and told her. I was doing my bit. I'd only just been round. She just laughed. It was Daz just standing there leaning on the coat stand, sipping his booze.

In the end Daz only lasted a few weeks before he glumly declared to me that "you'll never pull in here" and to an astonished Chrissie that "the place had no atmosphere" (i.e. he was frustrated that he hadn't pulled) and went back to The Fusion and I was left by myself again. I'm sure Chrissie told him to fuck off if he didn't like it. A short time later the Baby Squad, a group of notorious local teenage thugs, caused a riot there. Daz ended up with 38 stitches in his back from a Stanley knife. Ouch. Funny how I remember the number.

Ross and Daz had a strange relationship really. Shortly before Daz was slashed they both made a road trip to Paris and bought a shit load of steroids (including some for me). It would've been some time around March 1984. Their rather perverse plan was to buy the gear, make a 100 – 200% mark up and then sell it around the country – making them the biggest steroid dealers around, starting in the Midlands. I have to say, this was something I was absolutely **NOT** interested in. I probably tried to talk them out of it. Marine Boy had a conscience.

Daz had a high spec, lime green Ford of some sort with an auto gearbox. They got the gear and loaded the car up to the gills, apparently filling every nook and cranny with everything from needles, to tablets and injectables. As they drove back towards the ferry they were late and rushing. With his right hand drive on the wrong side of the road Daz hit another car. Ross told me later than neither of them had seat belts on and his head hit the windscreen so hard it cracked it. I suppose his head is thicker than mine.

By the time they reached the ferry the car looked a mess and so did they. They made it out of France but, because it was off season, there were only a few vehicles and their appearance attracted the attention of UK Customs. With glowing eyes as he recounted this to me a few days after the events Ross said that the Customs officer pulled down the arm rest in the back seat, stuck his hand behind the cushion and pulled out a fist full of syringes. The next part of the saga was that Ross, Daz and the car were completely stripped. I assume the two guys had the full cavity search, who knows? He didn't tell me that bit!

Bringing steroids back in 1984 was perfectly legal but what was illegal was concealment and failure to declare. Both Ross and Daz received massive fines but not criminal records and the gear was confiscated. It took Ross ages to get the money to pay the fine, the import duty and to finally get all the gear back. I guess he then sold a lot of it to recoup his losses. I don't think he ever tried that trick again. Despite spilling the beans he never did give me my stuff. So much for best mates eh?

At Helsinkis I was now back to being alone. I'd been there for a grand total of 10 weeks and been through 2 other doormen already. I began to get there earlier. 7pm, then

6.30pm. On a Friday night I would go straight from Sugars and stand there erect and nearly always red eyed from the effects of my steroid driven workout. The news of Daz upset me, the steroids were having their negative effects on my personality and I was grumpy. I became fastidious about how I looked and dressed when I stood on the door. My hair had to be just right. I only ever wore black dress socks because coloured ones didn't look good with my suit and tie. I grew a moustache because I couldn't be arsed to shave. It came out bright red. I shaved it back off.

Poor old Sadie, a pretty teenage bar maid with brown hair sort of cut short in the neck but layered up like a walnut whip tried to cheer me up by throwing ice at me as a joke. I turned round and glared at her in return. She was shocked, not surprising and started to cry at me "that was out of order... that was really out of order..." She was very upset, also not surprising. It must have been an evil look. One of real malice. It took me weeks to apologise. I apologised to her again when I found her again and sent her an email in 2008.

I threw someone across the bar for having his feet on the table. His mate had accidentally knocked his tooth out and he was spitting frothy blood into a pint glass. Apparently he was brother to one of the barmaids. He was pretty much the very last one in there. Another barmaid asked him to leave. He was cocky. He told her to fuck off. I picked him up one handed by his coat collar and heaved. He was in the upstairs bit. His head hit the bar. A one handed throw of a fully grown man of about 15 feet. Even I was surprised. He hauled himself to his feet and hesitated for a few seconds. One of his mates was still milling around. "DON'T! This man will hurt you" his mate shouted. The guy looked at me and got the message. He ran for his life.

A regular – a nice, little chap with a bald head and thick black framed glasses who was part of a local band called the Swinging Laurels came up just as we were closing. I looked at him and wouldn't let him in. "Sorry we're closed" I grunted. It was as close to being the polite doorman that I could manage.

Then I left him at the door, expecting him to 'obey' my orders and went round to clear the bar. As I made my way around I found that not only had he walked in after I turned my back, he was standing there with his mates just starting a pint. I was very annoyed so took the trouble to be extremely sarcastic and rude. He was shocked. The next week I glared at him and warned him not to mess me around. He hadn't really done anything at all. He was very apologetic and probably very scared.

My mum and dad came to the door to say hello and see what I was up to. They later told that me I had ignored them at first, although I was so busy I really, truly didn't see them. My mum told me she pissed herself laughing but I doubt it. It was only when they came closer that I had no choice but to stop what I was doing and say hello in return. My doting dad couldn't understand my general behaviour. *'He used to be such a nice kid'* my mum told me he used to say. Within three months from the start of the year my behaviour had changed significantly. I was already in a trap, only ever up when I was training or working at night, I just hadn't realised it. I am not a hard man. I was not a hard man. The steroids were clearly having an effect on me other than great size and strength.

BTW: My parents also came to see what I was up to at the Centre Bar a year or so later. I had a girl I had met called Sharon at my side at the time and was far, far more receptive. Looking back it's clear that I was really getting out of control at Helsinkis though. I went back to Mel and Tony and demanded some back up. They put an ad in the paper. It had the wrong phone number. Mel tried to laugh it off. I growled at him in response. Another week by myself. They tried again and then Franklin turned up. Chrissie must've been getting desperate or getting some pressure from the gay guys.

Franklin never impressed me as a doorman. He was a lanky, scruffy looking West Indian, with ragged, long fingernails, which are a personal hate. He was also much older than me and one of at least two brothers. I got to know one of them as well. His name was Ernest who eventually worked on and off for me for a short while at the Centre Bar.

Like most West Indians in the mid 80's Franklin had a bit of an afro. Unlike the ones I knew he had a horrible habit of sucking on toothpicks. When the toothpick was sucked enough he used to put it in his hair. How hygienic. His theory was that if it came to a real battle he would pluck the thing out of his curls and shove it in someones neck. It would then 'walk' and be very difficult to remove without major surgery. I was shocked. He just liked trouble. Sigh – one of those guys. Despite my growing aggression it didn't sit well with me. He would turn his back to a women he fancied and tell me "watch me make her turn round and look at me." He'd then spend the next 5 minutes doing a series of head twitches and little jerks of his shoulders. It never worked.

In spite of Franklin and the changes to my persona I was still having fun even though I was **supposed** to be working. I didn't really view it as work a lot of the time. I remember that I'd started talking to a slim, good looking 17 year old girl with a pierced nose and blue tints in her hair. I soon learned her name was Louise. She just came through the door one night and beamed "hello" at me. I beamed back. Yep, she was underage and I knew. In my head some things were worth turning a blind eye to.

There were loads more underage that I didn't know about at the time mind you. I assume I'd given her the usual good evening. I'd been there about 2 ½ or 3 months but, amazingly, never really noticed her before. There were too many faces to assimilate and, in those days, I wasn't too good at it. I was still new to being a doorman and I fancied a barmaid there called Julie like mad. Julie had a sort of curly topped brown hairdo that was short around her ears and neck and a fantastic figure but she was always very aloof and never spoke to me. She would walk into the bar at the start of her shift, straight past me and Rob when he was there and we'd beam. She ignored us both. I started to call her the Snooty Fox to Rob and behind her back of course. I wasn't that brave. Later I changed that to the Snotty Fox, nothing like a man scorned. London Rob tried desperately hard to pick her up before he left and failed. I lived in hope. He told me that she did go out with him one night. I asked him what her name was (we didn't know at the time) and he claimed that he'd never got round to asking her. I thought that was very odd so cornered her a few hours later and asked her how the date went. "Him?" she scowled. "I never went out with HIM!" Oh dear Rob.

I was also trying to take everything in. Being on my third buddy already didn't help. I got much better as time went on. During the period of my professional career when I gave lectures or ran training courses, much to the amazement of my co-presenters, I was able to remember names and faces of the audience with ease.

Me and Louise got to be very good friends and would often chat briefly about her hair, the music, the weather, my choice of tie but not much else. I was still very shy. In return though I got to know her mates, the Sharon I mentioned before and yet another Julie and their mates and on and on. I learned these girls were all underage, unemployed and came from a local council estate. I was drawn in. So much so that I never made any attempt to turn them away and was always so glad when they appeared. In all the time I worked as a doorman, these 3 were the ONLY ones I learned the full names of.

As well as opening up to my little Goth girlfriends Chrissie got me to hand out flyers for the bar as the crowds walked in or to any reasonable looking passer by and I started to talk to more and more people. It helped calm me and my tight, almost reclusive Sugars Gym circle of friends and acquaintances started to expand and expand. I even plucked up the courage to have regular Sunday morning chats with a quiet, floppy haired guy called Eugene before I tootled off to Sugars. He was always in Helsinkis and I discovered sold newspapers on a makeshift stand just down the street to the gym. I saw him there one Sunday morning as I was waiting for my training partner to arrive and went over. After that I had a brief chat with him every Sunday and even gave him a lift home once or twice.

One spring night I was standing on the door when Franklin refused entry to some Rockabillies who were regulars telling them they were too young. He was looking for trouble. He knew they were regulars as much as me. A bit of a scuffle broke out as they rightly got annoyed. Some of their friends were already inside, others were in the doorway. We literally pushed everyone out into the street, but not before I'd fallen over Louise who was sitting more or less on the floor by the front windows. Well, to be honest, I used her to get some leverage to push everyone out. "You were fighting on top of me" she burbled. I was absolutely unaware that I'd stood on her. I'm glad I did, although she probably felt differently. It's not that much fun to have a 15 stone doormans foot in your lap but that was it. Our friendship was cemented. We started to say goodbye to each other with a kiss. I'm sure Louise initiated them. I clearly remember her mouthing kisses at me through Helsinkis windows with a frustrated looking Julie and a bored looking Sharon standing next to her. I would've been far too shy to start it.

Not long after the shoving match there was a revving of motorbike engines and fifty or so Hells Angels pulled up. Good job I was wearing brown undies! I recognised the first one in. He was a regular who would arrive in a check shirt and jeans and often wore a black leather cap on his head. That was typical attire for Helsinkis. I remember he had blond hair and a large scar down his cheek which is probably why I'd noticed him more than anything else. He wasn't dressed that way this time though. The biker look was more the style. He'd obviously been doing some scouting trips for where they could all go. I was taken aback. Franklin stood there. In a moment of sheer panic I made them leave their helmets in the doorway and then stood back and let them in. Wouldn't you have let them in? Mel was livid. His little face went all red. "All my regulars are leaving" he yelped at us. He looked like an angry puppy. Gay guys being angry when you were as big as I was. Not that scary. Far less scary than 50 Hells Angels anyway! Franklin paid him or them no attention at all.

There was a big pile of helmets in the doorway and bikes everywhere. The bar staff were amused. Far more amused than me. I looked over and could see and feel that Franklin was drooling for a battle. He sucked toothpicks like they were going out of fashion – okay – they never were in fashion, but you get the picture. Karen, one of the bar staff, a biggish girl with long fair hair came over and said "they're great." The bar ran out of Stella. It wasn't going at all well. Kevin, the ex-doorman, appeared from somewhere inside the bar and started to juggle with some of the helmets. He was no great act. I screamed at him in my girly voice to put them down. Mel minced around with steam coming out of his ears and then... the police arrived.

Apparently the staff from the hotel had looked out of the window, eyed up the scene and called them. It was my first ever dealings with the International Hotel. I was so short sighted I don't think I'd even realised the big building opposite was a hotel. I learned much later that if you sat in one of the rooms on the first floor you could see everything that was going on. One of the original managers there, Chloe, a curly haired lady once told me she'd looked out of the window and seen some guy having a wank in the Helsinki staff room. How very entertaining!

At the sight of the police one or two of the Hells Angels emerged. "Problem with bikes on the pavement?" one of them asked. "No idea" I said, trying to hide my relief. One by one they drank up. Picked up their helmets and rode off. No problem. Mel calmed down. I calmed down. It was near the end of the night anyway, but I'd been scared. That was almost certainly the biggest incident that I'd had up to that point. Thumpity-thump...   thumpity-thump...   thumpity-thump. Thumpity-thump...   thumpity-thump...   thumpity-thump. Thumpity-thump... thumpity-thump... thumpity-thump.

I checked my undies.

Later on I had much bigger and nastier scares but that night was bad for me. I went to Sugars Gym the next day and had a chat to a guy called Chris about it. He really was an ex-Para, with bread loaves for arms, a small port wine stain on his face and a hook nose. He'd left the army to work as a face worker in the Pits. Every time he blew his nose black snot used to come out. Why oh why did I look? Charming!

Chris told me Hells Angels usually carried guns in their saddlebags and how lucky I'd been. Good job I used to eat lots of eggs… how else would I have got so many good parps out? It was undie check time again.

I got hold of another doorman called North and acquired a rounders bat the next day for about £2 or £3. North told me to drill it out and fill it with lead. I didn't. For two or three weeks after, I stood there with it stuffed down my trousers. "It's too flimsy" said Franklin after swinging it around his head in a little alley that ran down the side of Helsinkis. I hope he held the warm end.

Eventually I came to my senses and got rid of it. I spent 20 minutes one sunny evening talking to a bored beat policeman whilst the bat was stuffed in my waistband panicking that he'd notice. Maybe he thought I was just well endowed. The bloody thing was big enough to go right up to my arm pit. I even bought a new jacket to hide the bulge. It covered the bat as well.

Good job there was no trouble. I wouldn't have had a clue what to do with it or how to hide it if I had ever tried to use it. I never actually carried a weapon ever again, although it wasn't the end of that damn bat. I also made sure that any doormen I worked with at Helsinkis never carried a weapon.

One thing I had at the time was incredibly sore nipples. This was an unwanted side effect of the gear. It got so bad that I couldn't stand a shirt touching them. One Thursday night in July 1984, as the Alternative Miss Universe played out in the bar, Franklin grabbed my bulging pec through a faded black sweatshirt and squeezed hard. It fucking hurt. I growled. I'd had enough of him.

There's a bloke I worked with during my 4 ½ year stay in Australia who conclusively proved to me he was there the night of the big pec squeeze by relating something we both witnessed and remembered. He didn't see the Franklin grab and grope but he did see an old Punk called Johnno parading up and down a catwalk in a black dress before falling off. I know. I've done some strange jobs.

Even then Johnno must've been in his 40's. He was a weird little bloke with a shaven pate and tattoos all over him and always looked like he needed a good wash. He seemed to be bullied a lot by some of the other Punks and I think at some point he'd been in an accident and had brain damage but I may be wrong. I used to nod hello to him as time went on in my door career but I have to say that even after 5 or more years he didn't have a clue who I was!

Apparently the guy in Australia reckoned his future wife was also there that night (before he even knew her) and he estimated that I was the fifth or sixth person he'd met who had been there. I don't how true this is. You've got to picture how remote the chances are. Pretty bizarre if it is true. I guess it was a busy night although I don't remember it being *that* busy. Maybe my nipples hurt too much.

In my last weeks in Australia I was invited to a barbie. There'll be other guests from the UK my host told me. When I got there I met a couple from Knighton which is the other side of Leicester to where I come from. We got chatting. Both of them used to go in Helsinkis and the Centre Bar from time to time. Go figure.

Time went on. Franklin was causing more trouble. He tried his head twitches and jerks again to pick up some women in there. They laughed at him. He was insulting to Louise either about her boobs or back or both as she left to go to Rock City with Julie. She turned round and looked at me and I could see the hurt in her eyes. I was really annoyed with what he'd said but to her was too shy to find the words to comfort her or to even find the words to give him a bollocking. It was all adding up though and I was getting more and more pissed off with him. So was Chrissie.

Mel and Tony were getting more and more pissed off with him, Chrissie and me. In the end it came to a head and Franklin was sacked shortly before Chrissie was. He came up to me "man... I quit" he grunted. I professed innocence and sorrow but I was glad but now I was back to being alone and I wasn't happy. What now? I asked at Sugars. Anyone interested? £10 a night.

I'm convinced that all West Indians have massive families. Sugars Gym was the only place in town. It was an ethnic hotpot. There were plenty of West Indians there amongst the crowd. One of them said yep, he'd do it. Enter Trevor. Middle brother of Stedroy, Robert and Esau. The 'F' clan. All of them trained at Sugars at one time or another. Sugar was married to their sister, Rowena. I'd been one of hundreds Sugar had casually invited to the wedding in Highfields a couple of years earlier. I think it was the event of the year. Sugar and his brother, another Robert, were dressed in gold 3 piece suits. All of the 'F' brothers had been around – I just didn't know it at the time. All of the them, with the possible exception of Stedroy, were big, aggressive, experienced doormen and up for a fight. In the end all of them eventually worked for me at some point or another. Most unlikely tale about them? Trevor and Esau were supposed to have been in a pub in the city centre when a massive fight had started. I don't know if they were supposed to have been working or just in there. During the melee both were throwing punches left, right and centre – so much so that Esau missed his opponent and his punch clocked Trevor heavily right on the chin. Trevor is supposed to have shaken his head like a dog and just carried on fighting. Is this story true? No idea but I'm sure they relished the image. I asked Esau once if it really happened and he just gave me a massive grin. He was always grinning.

Options? I was in a bind. With my nerves a jingle I got Trevor the job. Month 4. Doorman number 4.

Many, many years later I was told that other brother Robert moved into a new house where his neighbour constantly played loud, doof, doof music. Apparently Robert gave him a few warnings in the usual, charming 'F' clan way. His neighbour – amazingly enough – ignored Roberts charms. I'd have shit myself. According to what I was told Robert wasn't too amused and the story I got he went to get his ceremonial samurai sword, lined the guy up and hit him over the head with the flat of it. Dooiinngggg. Robert could be aggressive but that was a bit OTT. I like to think of it more as an attempt to get some more percussion into that doof, doof stuff.

Trevor worked as a printer at the local newspaper and was a big guy with a small afro, the inevitable goatee and big, big hands. He picked at the edge of his nose a lot. He's a couple of years older than me. The last time I saw him was when he came to my leaving the UK meal in 2004. Half way through he started picking his nose and farting loudly and without discretion. At the end the entire conversation was held with all of us holding our breath. He was still a big guy, although these days his head is shaved, he has little moobs and his belly and arse both stick out so much you'd think you were in an eclipse if you didn't know any better.

Anyway he turned up at Helsinkis as promised and, much to my eternal relief, he was okay. No trouble, no need to fight. In between picking at his nose he even went round having fun and once stopped a guy to ask if he was his PE teacher from school. He was. It took a few weeks but Trevor eventually got bored and went on to work all over town before coming back later to help at the Centre Bar. In his place stepped younger brother Esau. I'd known Trevor for about 6 years at this point but hardly knew Esau at that time, although I'd seen him around. Enter doorman number 5.

At 21ish and a former Rasta, Esau had big, bright brown eyes, an afro, a few thin straggly hairs on his chin and, of course, his grin. He once told me he'd never shaved in his life. He was also pretty big, but constantly denied taking any gear. He became a good friend of mine but he had a chequered past and there were many rumours about him. Funniest moment for me was when some young girl came to the door and asked for Winston. "Never heard of him" I said (true). Turned out Winston and Esau were one and the same depending on which girl he was seeing. He really was a Monday – Susan, Tuesday – Julie, Wednesday – Anne type of guy. He once went out with one of the Helsinki bar staff, a nice girl called Sarah.

Sarah was his Sunday girl and had weird orange and red short hair, a posh accent (why did all of the Helsinki bar staff have posh accents?) and wore long, flowing multi coloured dresses with thick black tights on underneath, topped off by a pair of bright coloured Doc Martins. The way she dressed was so weird he told me that he used to walk down the street trying to hide his face in case anyone he knew saw him with her. He also told me that he was in bed with her and she farted in excitement just at the critical moment. His words... as best as I can remember them were "man... me laggy just went errrhhh." He was always going on about his laggy. In the end I had to ask him what his laggy was.

Funnily enough I went for an interview in London a few years later. As I was standing there looking like the Equaliser, in my best suit, dads mac and wearing a smart tie up walked Sarah. Pure coincidence. She was as brightly dressed as ever.

Esau also had some daughters and a live in girlfriend or maybe she was his wife. I never found out. I caught him buying nappies in Boots once which just seemed bizarre to me for some inexplicable reason. He turned out to be alright too although I can recall him twirling his girlfriend / wifes thick, brown rounders bat around between his thumb and forefinger at the end of the night and me getting him to show me how to do it – so I must have told him about my smaller, slimmer version and the Hells Angels – but he could be unreliable.

As it got towards summer he often didn't turn up. When I asked him why either the next week or at the gym, he'd just say "well... it was a nice night... The dog needed a walk." To counteract that I'd often find myself at his house playing with his kids before giving him a lift, but he lived on the other side of town so it was costing me money just to make sure I had some back up and that didn't last. He got his own car, a pale blue Marina soon after. I walked down the street one night mindlessly putting flyers on all the cars as I went past. "You put one on mine" Esau grinned at me the next night.

He started off being pretty quiet despite the bat and just as I was breathing another sigh of relief and thinking the stories about these guys were just that when… **BANG!** It could only have been an hour into his second night of being there. Before I knew what was going on Esau had one punched a guy from the doorway into the road over nothing. Just whack. Crunch. The guy was a small ugly fella with a large nose and was trying to get in along with a small group of regulars. I don't even know for sure why Esau hit him. I think it had something to do with Esau knowing him from school and telling him he couldn't come in because he was underage, which was probably true. He went flying backwards and landed at just about the spot where London Rob had landed on top of the little skinhead but he wasn't down for long though and picked himself up and charged at Esau. I'd woken up by now and dived in between without even thinking about it. He ran straight into my arms with a thud. I held tight, waiting for the punch but everything just stopped. Then there was a kind of Mexican stand off. While I held the guy Esau jutted his chin out as if to say go on then try. Esau did that a lot when he was annoyed. The guy stepped back from my grip. I was happy to let him go. "One on one" screamed one of his mates. I ignored him. Next thing, he just turned round and walked off. His mates went with him. They came back the next week and I let them in. Esau was standing next to me. He never said a word. He just grinned.

In my entire career I only ever threw punches about three times and missed every time. Short sightedness or a different type of person to the 'F' brothers? Either way, not being able to see properly. Bane of my life.

12

Lotus Blossom and Co.

As I slowly emerged from my Marine Boy shell I got to know more and more of the Helsinki bar staff. Initially I'd just stood there, hid behind my shyness and not said much to them at all. They must've wondered what I was all about. Apart from Chrissie, who didn't give a shit, Sadie had been the first to really talk to me – and look what I'd done to her.

One Thursday night I'd appeared in the bar. I'd just finished training. I was bored and just went for a walk round in some little grey booties I owned at the time – they were cute. I'd also just had a mid week steroid jab in my bum from a nurse who used to hang around Sugars and was making a bit of money on the side. These jabs were on top of the ones I was getting from the Honey Monsters in their dorm. Unsurprisingly my bum ached from all the jabs. Not so cute.

Chrissie and Sadie were both working. It would've been around 7.30pm and the place was very quiet. I got a free orange juice and stood and nattered away to them. After about half an hour Chrissie smacked me playfully on the bum – just where I'd been jabbed. "Ouch… don't do that" I cried. "I've just had a steroid jab there." Oh dear. Secret out. I think I was a little bit proud of it. They both never forgot that comment and never let me forget that they'd never forgotten that comment. Phew. That's a lot of nevers and forgets.

With the exception of the Snotty Fox, a few of the other members of staff cautiously tried to engage me in conversation. We'd all sit there for a few minutes at the end of the night before making our various ways home. I always sat a bit apart. It was my shyness. Every time one of them spoke to me I'd answer with my trademark politeness but usually didn't say too much. I think that I also wanted to avoid getting into another glaring session with any of the staff. I was a bit ashamed of myself over Sadie really. In hindsight it probably made me look a bit aloof which has some downfalls but isn't necessarily a bad thing for a doorman – up to a point.

The staff were as eclectic as the customers. Sadly, apart from the ones I've already mentioned, I can't remember the names of a lot of them. Like most bars there was a massive turnover. Even owner Tony couldn't remember them all. I have a clear recollection of him referring to Sadie as Sophie. "It's Sadie" she said coldly in return. He shut up. Mel didn't have a clue either.

Tony clearly wanted to know me better. He had wandered up to the door as I stood there early one evening. A tiny oriental girl was with him. She was one of the bar staff. I'd noticed her fluttering around but had never spoken to her. She had a way of appearing to float when she walked. I fancied her. "This is Lotus Blossom" he said as an introduction. She frowned. "No it's not." "She's a lovely girl" he went on. "All dainty and twee." He twirled his arms around her head and body. She frowned again. "The other night she was in a hurry and I asked her where she was rushing off to." He paused for dramatic effect. He was so close I could smell his breath. He'd been eating the stew. "And do you know what she said to me?" he asked. I didn't have time to reply. "For a shit." Seemed that was a popular line at Helsinkis.

From that night on I always called her Lotus Blossom. She pretended to hate it but I think she loved it really. It gave her an identity in my head. I think it's how I remember some and not others. Those with a personality I can recall – those without. Well.

Lotus Blossom was a great girl. Full of fun and always smiling. The thing is I can't remember her real name. She was supposed to let me in the side entrance when Chrissie came dashing up to me and told me in her usual style that there were some lads pissing on the Welsh Dresser at the back. It would have been really hard to push through the crowded bar and it would have caused a bit of an unnecessary fuss anyway. The back entrance was the quickest way in. It was down the little alley where Franklin had twirled my bat around. I looked down it. It was pitch back down there. I wasn't that thrilled but short sightedly and slowly groped my way down. Franklin was there then. He stayed on duty at the front.

There was no sign of Lotus Blossom. I hung on for a few minutes. Still no sign. The thumpity-thumps started – badly. I waited another few minutes. Still no bloody sign. I was getting really worried. Suddenly a door flew open in the darkness and there she stood in the framed light. "Sorry" she said. "I forgot." Despite her looks she had a Leicester accent as thick as mine. I tutted and pushed past and made my way over to the dresser. The pissing lads had long gone. Left through the front door and straight past Franklin. There were dark stains up the side of the thing and a puddle on the floor. Beautiful. I left it to the bar staff. Saved me a job and some hassle but I don't think Chrissie was that impressed with any of us. I think Lotus Blossom left soon after although she still dropped in from time to time for a night out.

I do know there were a couple of blondes. One was Karen, the girl from the Hells Angels night. She was a big mate of Sadie's and went out with some black haired fellow called Scotty round about then. I often saw her in the street when I was walking to and from Sugars. Perhaps she worked nearby. She never recognised me out of my doorman outfit and would be constantly apologising for not saying hello. I didn't care.

In those days piercings like you see today weren't that common. Sure a lot of blokes had earrings (I didn't) and a few of the women had rings through their noses. Karen appeared at the door. She'd had her nose pierced too. Sadie was at the bar. She looked up as soon as Karen walked in. "You had it done then!" she cried, her face lighting up. Karen grinned back. Beamed really. Now days it's not only piercings through the nose, it's the cheek, the lower lip, the eyebrow. Every bloody where. It's tattoos as well. They weren't that common on women then but I do remember Louise's mate Sharon wailing on and on about getting one. I told her not to.

Just to reinforce how naïve I was at this point Karen had come bounding up to me asking if I had a spare Rizla. I had no clue what she was rabbiting on about.

The other blonde was Barbara who always had lots of teeth and gum on show in a broad smile. She also always had a pink or yellow ribbon in her hair. Perry went out with her for a while. She wasn't there when I started but came along about a couple of months later. She probably replaced Lotus Blossom and was one of the few who wasn't afraid of me. Some of them definitely were. I'd dragged her screaming across the bar when she'd been in there pissed out of her head. I'd been trying to empty the place. Like I've sort of hinted at, a tiresome job after a while. She grabbed on to my elbow and tried to heave me back, yelling "noooooooooo" as she did it. Funny thing is she didn't slow me down at all. I walked around with her dragging along behind me. We both laughed. To me, it was like tugging a feather along. When Perry came along I noticed he was always talking to her. I asked him if they were in a relationship. Polite, but nosy. All he said was "I've slept with her."

Then there were Ian and Jamieson. Ian was quite small, a caste of some sort with pitch black hair and never, ever wore socks. Winter, summer. No socks. He was very proud of that fact and always showed me to prove a point. How he managed is beyond me. He loved it in there and, like a lot of them, was often found drinking at the bar when he wasn't working. Jamieson was a tall geezer with a bit of a flattop. He was another gay and was the first one to spot me wearing my glasses. I'd been walking across town early on a Saturday morning before Sugars Gym opened and he was sitting on a wall outside a shoe shop. Apparently that was his day job. I'd stopped to say hello and the first thing he'd said to me in return was "I didn't know you wore glasses." I had these fuddy duddy gold rimmed things. For some reason I was annoyed with myself. I didn't want these people to know I couldn't see. I thought it may cause them to re-assess whether I could do the job or not. It's not that great having a doorman who was as blind as a bat. I also think I was beginning to realise how fuddy duddy I really was. Sigh. All that time in the gym.

These days I wear what I want but there was a time when I tried to become less fuddy duddy and fashion was important to me – even buying a stupid bright yellow T-Shirt with green trimmings from some trendy shop for about £50. A T-Shirt for £50 in the mid eighties. I must've been out of my mind!

The staff at the shop were some of the same guys who'd sold me that bloody brown jacket. They were amazed when I walked in. The rest were all Helsinki regulars as well. My mum had washed the damn thing once. I'd left a blue coloured ticket of some sort in a pocket that was on the front. After the wash there was a permanent green stain there. Green trimmings and green stain. I ended up using it to train in.

There was also two very gay looking mates. One was Richard, dark haired, paper thin and so quietly spoken I could never catch what he said. He let me stay overnight in his flat when I'd left my car at home. It was freezing. I was stunned and a bit relieved when he introduced me to his girlfriend. I was certain he was gay. Richard eventually left Helsinkis and joined the army. I couldn't think of a less likely candidate if I tried. The other was equally as thin as Richard but mousy blond. I never knew his name. According to a conversation I overheard between Sadie, the Snotty Fox and Barbara, he struggled and couldn't even mix the most basic of cocktails. I avoided him but he didn't avoid me and decided to have a go as I tried to clear the bar when he was doing something else. "We have a job to do too as well" he hissed at me. I don't think I smiled. He never spoke to me again. He was very camp, with big earrings in both of his ears. I overheard him asking Sadie if she thought he was gay and she told him yes. He wasn't happy. According to him he wasn't – but we knew matey, we knew.

At some point I used to give one of the bar staff a lift back to her house in the Samba. It was pretty much on my way home but I was still a reasonably nice guy for a lot of the time so didn't mind anyway. I'd wait until the street was empty and we'd dash up to my car. I often told her never to tell anyone it was mine. She must've got really fed up with me saying it but she never said anything. I suppose a lift was a lift. Better than waiting for a staff taxi. Her eyes opened W-I-D-E the time I slipped the rounders bat out from under my jacket and put it under the seat but she never said anything about that either. We used to chat about nothing in the twenty minute journey until she asked me what qualifications you needed to be a doorman. I just laughed. "A degree in thuggery and lots of bottle" was my reply. I was only half joking. I don't think she knew what to say. We spent the rest of the journey in silence. The Samba was so crap it didn't even have a radio.

The last of the staff to make a lasting impression on me over that period of my life was Tony's boyfriend, glass collector David. He was another stick thin thing and very quietly spoken. I think Tony treated him well but appeared to me to have a very strong and, probably, over riding influence over him. David would occasionally shyly talk to me but was always looking over his shoulder. He was a bit camp but, at first, I had no idea he was gay. I wasn't that good at reading the signs. I was astonished to find out him and Tony were boyfriend and boyfriend. Apart from anything else Tony would've been in his forties and David was about 18. I had always thought that Mel and Tony were the couple. Obviously not!

While I was working there Tony bought a new Escort convertible. A blue thing. All alloy wheels, chrome and back leather. He was very proud of it and would park it directly opposite the door for me to keep an eye on. Oh yeah. Short sighted Jeff. All I could see was a smudge. That summer him and David went to Paris and took the car. I wanted to hear all about it. They were gone for a couple of weeks. When they got back I asked Tony where he went, whether he'd enjoyed it. All the usual stuff you'd ask. The most he said to me was that it was okay but the car got broken into. David just gave me a look and shook his head. I guess it hadn't been a great break.

When I finally left Helsinkis Tony's influence on David came out. I had turned up just as the place was shutting to collect my last bit of pay. My replacement let me in. David was surprised as I walked through the door. Skinhead Mark had once told me he hadn't bothered to pick up his money when he left. "What do you want?" David asked me. "I've come to pick up last weeks pay" I replied. "It's not worth it" he said to me. I looked through him. Fuck you mate I thought. I've stood here for weekend after weekend and risked my face to protect people like you from life and all you can say is why bother to pick up my wages!

I walked in and sat down, silent and brooding. Tony gave me a stare then started to hand out the wage packets to some tired looking staff. He made sure I was the last to get mine. I didn't stand up. He passed it over without a word and I took it without a thank you, got up and walked out. Shame.

Jeff Shaw

13

A Change of Pace – A Change of Place

By now I'd discovered night life. I wasn't joking when I said I'd hardly ever been to nightclubs before. Marine Boy didn't really know life existed after 10pm.

I suppose it was inevitable really when you're doing that line of work. By about March, after I finished my Saturday night stint I'd hop in my car, drive across town and chat to the massive Jordie at Tipplers Wine bar, a long thin and smoky place away from the city centre in King Street. It didn't take too long before I had a regular slot there. I'd work at Helsinkis until 10.30pm, get everyone out, drive over to Tipplers and work there till 2.30am.

Even if there was no need for me to work, I'd drive over and chat to Jordie. I must've come across like Policeman Paul from Force 8 did to me. Two other guys from Sugars worked there. Rich, a dandruffy guy who was about my age and as short sighted as me and Robbo, an older, experienced doorman and former training partner of London Rob.

When Robbo couldn't make it, I worked and vice-versa. Later on the law changed and closing time at Helsinkis moved to 11pm, but I'd still get over to Tipplers and work from about 11.30pm or midnight to 2.30am. There was also an ex-policeman on the door there called Mick. I hardly knew him so he ain't worth mentioning too much, although I know he did once rescue a man being badly beaten in the street and was around when a policeman friend of mine called Ian, another one from Sugars Gym, was shot in the wrist on duty. Mick didn't have a great rep but probably deserved better press than he got at the time.

Some of the Helsinki customers went straight into Tipplers after I had spent 20 minutes getting them out. Invariably I would get there before them because they walked and I had the wonderful Samba. I was there one night when Tony walked in with Sadie and some of the other Helsinki bar staff. He was bog eyed when he saw me standing there. He'd had no idea. Why should I have told him anyway?

Soon I was standing in for Rich on a Tuesday night as well. More money. It began to flow in. My cash worries eased and my steroid usage increased. Hey, at least I thought I was spending it on something I wanted to do.

I ditched the nurse and began busily injecting myself in the locked bathroom at home. Sterile procedures? Ha... ha. I stood on the Helsinki door one night massaging my leg. I'd shakily injected a steroid in my thigh. I hadn't got a clue and had sat on the toilet seat to do it. Because I was sitting down my thigh was semi flexed so I hadn't put the needle in deeply enough and the oil leaked back out for hours, seeping a weird kind of smudge over my trouser leg. I had a bruise like a 50p piece.

After that I found that you're supposed to put needles in well away from any nerves. The outside of the thigh is much safer and your backside even better. I could've paralysed myself or given myself some sort of infection. What an idiot. Despite this, in my mind I was still a paragon of virtue. No smoking, no drinking.

One Tuesday in April I got to stand in for Rich at Tipplers. As usual I got there early. I parked the crappy Samba nearby and walked over to Helsinkis to chat to Chrissie. It was a very nice night. When I got there, there wasn't really anyone I knew around. The Snotty Fox was behind the bar. She served me a sour look and a frosty orange juice. I drank it miserably and alone and then, feeling a little displaced and unloved, crossed back over the town. I arrived in King Street just after nine. The police were there. A lot of police. Nothing seemed to be happening. I walked past a policewoman, she looked at me quizzically but didn't say anything. I went right up to the side window and looked into my car to check it was okay. It was. I moved off and took up position on Tipplers door and, apart from giving a drunk Scotsman 10p to phone home and asking one drunk guy to pull his trousers up nothing happened.

I stood there until 2.30am then hopped in the car and, after I finally kicked life into it, went home. By 8.30am the next day I was at my full time job. Knackered.

By now I was taking heaps of steroids, including a strong hormone replacement called testosterone and working 40 hours a week at my day job, plus 8 to 10 hours a week at Helsinki and up to 3 or 4 hours at Tipplers. On top of that there was heavy training for about 1 ½ hours 5 or 6 days a week. In total I was on the go for about 60 or more hours a week. I was building big muscles but my personality was changing for the worse faster than ever. Marine Boy with a bad attitude. A bit like Sooty telling Sweep to fuck off.

To give you some idea we used to take something called Methyl Testosterone. We called it lethal Methyl. You're supposed to take 1 or 2 tablets just before your heaviest workouts – e.g. legs. I was in a pissing contest with Ross and taking up to 15 lethal Methyl a day. A months supply every 2 days! Who knows what he took. If you ingest any form of synthetic testosterone your own production shuts down because it's not needed. I was so heavily overdosing on testosterone that it's no wonder I was becoming more and more aggressive. It's even worse when you stop taking the artificial stuff. At that point your own body isn't producing any. Then it's 'fun' until your natural production kicks in again.

I got a call at work at about 10am on the Wednesday morning. It was the police. Could I please go into Charles Street station? Carol, the secretary later told me my face was a picture. I was so tired. I was so aggressive. Driving into town wasn't really on the top of my wants list. I hadn't done anything wrong. Nothing had been stolen. What was up?

Turns out that I parked the crap mobile outside a fashionable hairdressers where the staff were all working late. One of the girls had looked out of the window, recognised me from Helsinki and seen me walk off. A few minutes later she'd seen some unknown guy come up to my car with a bunch of keys and try and break in. Good girl. She called the police and they literally caught him red handed. I never found out exactly who the girl was but she had my thanks. I reckon that even if the bloke had broken in he wouldn't have been able to get the bloody thing started anyway, not unless he was carrying jump leads, a spare battery, a hammer, a shotgun! The worst that could have happened was that I caught him and, in my exhausted, aggressive and distorted state kicked seven bells out of him. Not for the first or last time I was very lucky. Not only did I stay out of harms way, I was able to prove that my car was there at the precise time they caught the thief. The police told me I didn't have to go in after all. Relief all round.

One last thought: When I walked past the policewoman to check on my car, why the hell didn't she ask me if it was mine? I never did work that one out.

By August 1984 I'd been at Helsinkis nearly 8 months and Tipplers 5 or 6. It was all getting too much. The long hours, the 'gear'. I had to take a break and went to Paris for a holiday myself. I loved it there. It may have been a holiday and an immediate break from the gear, but it also had another purpose. Buy even more steroids! There was no way I was stopping using them for good.

A year earlier me and Ross had been there all the way on the train to see the Honey Monsters. This was just after I'd left Force 8. We got a special rate because we were so young. Leicester to London, London to the coast. Hop on a ferry. The French coast to Paris. It took us hours to get there. This was nearly two decades before the tunnel.

When we got off the train we were knackered and didn't have a clue where we were so just booked into the first hotel we could find. "C'mon" said Ross "let's go for a drink". To our utter amazement we were slap bang in the middle of one of the red light districts, Paris had three at the time. I spent the rest of the night sipping my drink and watching in wide-eyed wonderment and amusement. I wonder what was going through Ross' mind? Like me, he didn't have a regular girlfriend. That bloody gym! We ended up timing everyone.

One guy was in and out in less than 2 minutes. He gave me a big wink as he walked away.

When I got back in 1984 I brought loads of steroids with me. Perfectly legal. I wasn't dumb. I also knew I was out of sorts and reasoned that a short break from them wasn't going to be enough so decided to have a few months off everything and then have a real good go with the stuff I now had. Bodybuilders have a phrase when they lose weight quickly, "dropping like a sack of spanners." I dropped like a sack of spanners the size of my Samba. Boom. The truth of taking so many drugs hit home.

I think I was off for less than a month. I couldn't hack it. I was not in a good place. I do recall Roy of the drunken night at Mr. Kiesas, yelling at me "don't come here with your deca durabolin [2] blues" and me being extremely, and quite unnecessarily, rude to a nice lad called Gary when he asked me if I'd finished with a bit of equipment. I also had a major bust up with a chap called Herdle and another with a policeman called Stan.

Herdle was a nice bloke. In his forties, he was a presenter on Radio Leicester. Both Stan and Herdle were doing nothing more than using Sugars Gym to do their thing in. They had paid. They were entitled.

I used to call Stan, pissie, as in P.C. I'd heard the line in a film and thought it was great. Surprise. He didn't. He never stopped talking. In the end I vented my spleen at him and we ended up in reception where I was given a 'talking to' by Sugar for being rude. I didn't give a fuck, although I did grudgingly apologise a few weeks later. I think Stan got to a minimum of Inspector in the end.

In Herdle's case I asked him how many more sets he had. In my mind, twenty something years later, I am certain I growled it. He looked at me in return and sneered. He had a heavy Jamaican accent. "Youd guyzs think youd own dis place. Go and find anotha' exercise to do." Unless you listened

---

[2] Another steroid we used

carefully his name always sounded like "ordel" when he said it. His son was training with him that night. I think he responded the way he did not just because of my overt aggression towards him, but because his son was there. Whoops. I went berserk and I **DO** mean **BERSERK**.

I saw him on and off for the next 10 years. I tried to apologise but he wouldn't have it. I don't blame him really. We never uttered another word to each other. This time not only just sad, stupid as well.

I don't think I was too bad on Helsinkis door or around Louise, Sharon and Julie either but I was far from fine at any other time. Internally I ached, my nipples hurt, my size and strength were down the toilet. I lived for the weekends.

Even Carol at my daytime job told me I was a bastard. Apparently I'd glared at her dad who worked on the shop floor and had dropped into the offices for a brief chat. I wasn't even aware that I'd done it.

While all this was going on Roy had his own steroid blues to worry about. Apparently he just went up to another guy we both knew who was working a door somewhere and started abusing him for no reason. I have to say that Roy's nose was never the same again. I did see him a dozen or so years later and his physique had completely melted away. Odd things those steroids.

As I suffered, Esau left Helsinkis. I think he just stopped turning up. In his place Mel and Tony hired a tall, pencil thin Asian guy with jet black, collar length, shaggy hair as a replacement. Turns out his name was Kirpal. I never could pronounce it properly. They didn't bother to tell me or ask my opinion and he appeared out of the blue. In truth he was probably as experienced as I'd been in January but, right then, in my disorientated and unreasonable state I thought he was useless.

Chrissie came in for a drink with her boyfriend. She saw him and took the piss. "Ha... I wouldn't have hired that fucker to sweep out my yard" she told me with glee. He tried, but he just didn't have any authority or assertiveness. The only time I saw him do something was when we were standing there and there was an enormous crash. It was early and the place wasn't very busy. I looked around but couldn't see anything. Neither of us really knew what it was. I was now the experienced one. I took charge and told Kirpal to look upstairs while I checked the bar and he raced away. He came back a few minutes later shaking his shaggy mane of hair. That was his entire action.

I was puzzled by the noise. A dirty looking, tattooed Psychobilly was lounging near by, just about where I'd stood on Louise. I knew his face but not his name. He had a London accent and a big, blonded quiff. Turns out he was called Neil. He could see the confusion etched on my face and pointed. A big chalk board they used to put in the doorway advertising the place hadn't been stored properly and had fallen over. Phew.

Neil (complete with can of Red Stripe)
Picture Courtesy Amanda Edwards

Kirpal had a mate, another West Indian called Paul who was always hanging around. Paul was only a skinny teenager and seemed to love the place as much as the rest of us. He was desperate to fit in and work there as a doorman and even shaved off half his hair in some sort of look at me, I'm different gesture. Although I thought he was a nice guy, there was no way I would ever have offered him a door job. In my mind even the minimal trouble we had at Helsinkis would have eaten him and Kirpal alive. It almost did just a few short months later.

I remember that about that time some guy wearing a suit and tie with wavy, dark hair and a weird little upturned moustache that looked like a dead caterpillar came into Helsinkis one night and, without any hesitation what-so-ever, asked me if I wanted to work at the Centre Bar. I couldn't remember seeing him in there before but he seemed comfortable if a little out of place clothes wise. I later found out his name was Coulton and he was the bars manager at the International Hotel. I also came to learn that he was a gregarious, pretty heavy drinking (when he felt like it), non-smoking Sagittarian. I didn't know any of that then and, apart from the fun I was having most of the time, felt some sort of loyalty to Helsinkis and didn't know him so I said no thanks.

That all changed when I got a series of death threats in quick succession while Kirpal cowered in the corner, Tony refused to pay me the full rate for working one Saturday afternoon at the start of the soccer season because, in his sneering words "there's not been any trouble," someone threw a brick through Tipplers window and we all jumped, a girl had a fit and I didn't know what to do, Jordie got threatened and lost the hard man status he had held in my eyes for 10 years by running away and finally Rich had his hand slashed with a Stanley knife by the Baby Squad on a night when I was supposed to be working but he had stood in for me.

Thumpity-thump... thumpity-thump... thumpity-fucking-thump.

I needed a change. I quit Helsinkis and then Tipplers one Friday night in a fit of pique. Doorwork... over for me. Again. All my Force 8 fears and worries came back in a flood of hormones.

I have to be careful. Writing this is bringing back a lot of memories that I have purposely repressed. Today I look back and see some of it as a pretty dark period of my life. My mum has repeatedly told me I was a complete bastard then. I don't think I really ever understood what she meant until I sat back and started to write this stuff. This started as a light hearted account of my adventures but, when I remember, there were some very dark and dangerous moments amongst the fun and a lot of lucky ones. I learned a lot about myself and people – skills which I still use today. I have to reinforce what I said before. Working at Helsinkis changed me forever.

The next night I turned up on Helsinkis door in my jeans mainly to tell Louise and her mates that I'd had enough and had quit. It was late summer, it was still light. Lots of regulars walked by. "You're looking a bit cas" most of them said. "I quit" I replied blandly. Oh no was the general reaction. Had I made a mistake? Was my outward appearance nowhere near as bad as I thought it was?

I mooched off to the Centre Bar. I'd wondered how it compared to Helsinkis for a long time. It was the very first time I'd ever set foot in there. Romrig came up with the dead caterpillar bloke. I recognised his face. He told me his name. It was a name I got very used to. "Not working?" one of them asked. "I quit." "Fancy doing a one off next week?" asked Mr. Dead Caterpillar. "We've got a wedding that we need covering." "Okay" I said. I started there in September 1984, working with Romrig for what was meant to be one night. I finally left in April 1993.

I never did see my three little Goth girlfriends that night.

14

Two Bars. One World. Part Two.

There were so many ways to get into the Centre Bar that I lost count. You could go across the hotel reception and down a spiral staircase and enter by a single white painted door at the back, or through some revolving doors to the far left of reception as you walked in and down the same staircase.

There was a door by Strikes restaurant which was to the right of the revolving door. If you went in through there it took you two flights down to the Garden Room, a small cellar bar with big, wooden double doors, directly to the right of the Centre Bar. You could go through Strikes and in.

You could also go through the Garden Room, emerge through the back door, go down a little 10' long corridor that ran to the toilets and enter from the far left. You could come across reception, down past a flight of stairs to a big function room, through the toilets opposite and find yourself at the back of the Garden Room.

You could even get to the Garden Room through the kitchen and use the same doors. Dizzy yet? I was. Later on we all used the many entrances to our advantage in getting round the place fast and getting people out, but my first impression was sheesh.

Not long after I started to become a regular fixture I followed the assistant bar manager, Nigel, a tubby Welshman with curly, thinning hair and a droopy moustache to a door at the back of a tiny dance floor that was usually covered in tables. I thought it was another flight of stairs. He opened the door and – lo and behold – there were the light switches. I was shocked. I fiddled with them and got another shock. You should always dry your hands before touching electrics.

After that it became my job to dim the lights at the start of the night and turn them back up at last orders. See – all these things a doorman had to do and you all thought all I did was stand there.

Unlike Helsinkis the Centre Bar was only open to non-residents on Thursdays, Fridays and Saturdays and kept its doors locked until 7pm when the very first barmaid – Louisa – would go down there and set up the bar while I carried two big, black speakers out of the lights cupboard, put one either side of the bar and then open all the doors. The doors to the street had fiddly round switches at the top and bottom that you turned clockwise or counter clockwise to lock or unlock them. Very early on Louisa used to unlock the doors but I often found her stretching up, trying to undo the damn things at the top and would help. At least I was taller than her – well... slightly.

The doors leading to the bar were another set of doubles with drop down roof and floor bolts to keep them shut. Eventually they had a big, padlocked steel bar across them added that I used to have to take off and then put back on at the end of every night. Over the years many people tried to break in to steal the takings and the bars became warped and bent from the various kickings and bashings they must have received. The odd thing is that the tills were always emptied at night so there was no cash in the bar anyway!

The 'Alternative Patrol' Outside one of the Many Entrances
Picture Courtesy Suzy Sissons

Like Helsinkis, all the external doors opened outwards which, I came to learn, is handy for a doorman. Simply put, if someone pulled on the door to get in and I didn't like the look of them, I just let go of my side and they were left holding the full weight. That meant if there was any trouble I'd have both hands free whilst they would have one on the door and have to try and pull it back to get access to us. Cute trick.

It was smart inside and had been newly decorated with a mottled brown wallpaper and a few gold framed pictures on the wall. The tables were nice wooden ones, there were nice brown padded chairs, a few stools and bench seats with the same fabric and padding, potted plants and a one armed bandit in the corner by the door that led to the Garden Room.

With the tiny dance floor fully decked with tables and chairs the place had a capacity of 92.

All this was supported by 4 white shirted bar staff – also very likely Uni students trying to earn a few extra bob – who stood in front of a very small bar with mirrors at the back, a couple of tills, a few spirits on offer and lots and lots of Stella on tap and tins of Red Stripe for sale. The head barman was Nick, a short, mousy topped Yorkshireman with exactly the same birthday as me and who later became the Bars Manager. I thought Nick was a great chap.

By my first night I'd been off the gear for a few weeks and was in my own personal hell. Steroids make every organ of your body grow. Well, okay. Not *every* organ. Part of me will always be a bit of a tiddler.

In my best shape I had a 48" chest, 18" neck, 17" arms and a 34" waist. Even the biggest jackets I could find pulled tightly across my back. I couldn't get trousers my waist size over my legs easily so sort of had to salsa to get them on which was bizarre because I never could dance. It was a bit like a zombie doing the twist. I really must stop watching Strictly Come Dancing and get a lesson one day.

That night my clothes were floating on me. I met one of the managers. There seemed to be lots of them. He made me take off my jacket, scrawled JEFF in big red letters on a name badge and got me to pin it on my deflated chest. This was the same jacket I'd previously concealed the rounders bat under. I looked so small and skinny without it even Romrig, who claimed he trained at Khachik's Olympia Gym in High Street, looked well built in comparison. He was there when I arrived and wore a badge that said his Christian name in the same scrawly handwriting.

In those days it was very unusual for a doormen to let just anyone know their name. The nagging fear is that someone will take a dislike to you, find out where you live and do the Lee sparkplug thing or worse. I didn't like it. It's only a wedding I thought. I'm not doing 'proper' doorwork anymore. I still needed the cash. Remember, I had no intention of stopping taking any naughties. I was just having a rest. On top of that I still had quite a lot to pay on the car. It was only a wedding I kept repeating to myself. More accurately, it was the reception party. A party was taking place in the Garden Room.

Most people who went to the Centre Bar probably think I was the original doorman because I ended up being there so long. I wasn't. It was Romrig. That night the plan was that Romrig would be in charge and stand at the front of the Garden Room as people came down to the Centre Bar to stop them going into the wrong room by mistake. I assume we thought they were stupid and couldn't tell the difference between a load of Punks and Goths and a wedding.

I was supposed to stand outside the back door in the toilet corridor to stop the same happening at the other end. Fun. Watching people go for a piss and shit all night long isn't too pleasant.

Very early in the night I got bored and cold. I could hear music coming from the Centre Bar and the Garden Room but I didn't venture in either. I'd learned not to leave my post like I had so many months before. Hardly anyone went past. I didn't know the bar staff. I wanted to go home. Then nature began to take its course and people from both rooms started to use the same loos. The ones from the Centre Bar stopped and stared. "What are YOU doing here?" was the common theme. I began to realise I didn't know that so many people knew me. "So that's your name" said one pretty blonde poking my chest. I grinned. It began to go well. No one stopped and had a conversation but a lot of people said hi. Not so bad after all. Then, of course, it all started to go wrong.

These days I'm a very good facilitator and a reasonable lecturer. Facilitation is the act of identifying barriers and metaphorically kicking them down before anyone you're working with even notices they're coming up. Doorwork is really the same. It's about being there. About being ready. Stopping trouble before it starts and extinguishing it fast if it does happen. One of my old bosses once said to me he didn't know how I facilitated stuff, but I did it extremely well. Shit I thought. If only he knew.

That night, 25+ years ago, I might have worked at 3 different places but I was still basically a beginner. I got caught by surprise. The door of the Garden Room flew open. A big, fat scruffily bearded head came out and went "peek-a-boo" before the door slammed shut again. Wasn't it a wedding reception in there? The head did it again. It wasn't a Jack-in-the-box.

The veins in my forehead started to throb. Funny thing about testosterone. It's the predominant male hormone and it makes you bigger and stronger. Mine was low because of the steroids. When you're on them your body ceases it's own production because steroids are fundamentally based on testosterone esters. When you go off, there's a time lag before your body realises that there's a need to create your own stuff and then goes mad and produces it in overabundance. Bodybuilders have a phrase for this overabundance. They call it rebound. It's a time of great churn. I was in the no production stage. Small, weak, white faced.

I opened the Garden Room door. Some blokes turned round and laughed. I recognised one from Helsinkis. I'd refused him entry and he'd come over all tough. A lot of people used to do that. Maybe it was my sweet little face. A West Indian guy had been standing near me at the time and had got all upset. "I'll eat his face" he had growled at me. I tried to calm him down. The last thing I wanted was trouble in front and behind me. Somehow I managed to talk everything down. Now that REALLY was my sweet little face. A bloke I vaguely knew had seen me do it and told me the guy on the outside and who I was now facing again was trouble and that I'd done the right thing for not letting him in.

My face must've been a picture when I saw him at the hotel. Who knew if he recognised me? He probably did. This time I shut the door. And quickly. Fuck.

I walked through the Centre Bar as a working doormen there for the very first time and told Romrig. He was outside, leaning on the Garden Room wall, having a good time and a drink with his mate Mark, a half caste carpet fitter with a toothy grin and an afro. Romrig pushed past, ran across the bar into the toilet corridor. I trailed. Trouble wasn't really on my agenda. Mark followed me trying hard not to spill his precious Red Stripe. Nothing. Romrig gave me a look, spat out a venomous "bullshit" and went back to his little leaning post. I was left alone. I felt empty.

A few minutes later a very gay looking, small Goth with a heavily white powdered face, black spiky hair and wearing black leather and chains went to the loo. As usual, I knew his face. Seconds later the Garden Room door opened. Trouble and one of his mates walked past me, smirked and followed him in. Bad timing! I knew something was going to happen. It was obvious. I stood there, and stood there, and stood there. It's the only time in my entire life as a doorman that I could see chaos brewing and did absolutely nothing. Nothing.

Trouble and his mate re-emerged a few minutes later, gave me a triumphant smirk and went back into the Garden Room. Another 30 seconds went by. The gay looking Goth re-appeared. He was soaking wet, his face powder was all spotty and his spiky hair was flattened. Either he'd had an accident or... He looked me right in the eyes. "Bastards" he spat at me.

I was so upset. In my eyes I was being paid to do a job and I'd failed, miserably. I was a coward. In hindsight – I was out of sorts, I was small and weak, I had no testosterone in me and I didn't really want to be a doorman anymore. But then, that night, that instant I was ashamed. I didn't do a thing. I didn't even do the undie check.

Fortunately nothing else happened all night. The wedding reception finished, the bar emptied without me or Romrig even going round. To be fair, I didn't even try. I went home. I felt more hollow than ever. Romrig has since said that I was always hard to find and ran away from fights. Is that true? Well, I admit I did nothing and should have. As for hard to find? There was only the two of us and you could walk across the bar in 5 seconds. Make your own mind up.

The next week I went to pick up my pay. Everything was a week in hand then, and bumped straight into 1/3rd of my little Goth trio, Sharon. "Hello" she gave me a toothy smile. "Where have you been?" The truth is that I didn't really speak to Sharon that often at that point. I can't remember exactly what I said. I know I wanted to say where's Louise? I couldn't find her the other week. I'm sad. I'm lonely. I'm going through hell. I did nothing last week when I should have. My shyness kicked in. I probably said something along the lines of "ohhh, where are your 2 mates?"

I don't know if Sharon did it deliberately or not but she didn't seem to know. I think it was semi deliberate. I wasn't working. I spent all night with her. First in the Centre Bar, then Helsinkis and then back again.

I liked Sharon. A lot. She was skinny, especially her legs, but reasonably good looking with a heavily powdered face, black lipstick, spiky green hair and a pierced nose. She smiled a lot too. Maybe my mind is distorted, but after that we seemed to spend a lot of time together. I don't really know.

Unfortunately for me she was a heavy smoker. I soon found out that kissing her was like sticking my tongue in a dirty ashtray. Not that I ever licked a dirty ashtray, but you know what I mean. I've never, ever gone out with a girl who smoked since. Who knows what Louise thought. One minute I was constantly hanging around her, kissing and flirting like mad and the next I'd vanished from view, only to emerge a short time later with her mate. I live in hope she knew how short sighted I am and couldn't tell how skinny Sharon's legs really were.

The reality is I was still chronically shy under my muscles and steroid enhanced moods. I still am. I have just learned to hide it well. I hid it reasonably well in those days too but maybe not too well. I guess when Sharon started to pay me so much close attention I was flattered and didn't really know how to handle it all.

By the end of September 1984 I was standing outside the toilet door at the Centre Bar reasonably frequently – maybe once or twice every couple of weeks – and knew who had a weak bladder and who didn't. Slowly, what had started off as a one nighter then became every week or so. Invariably Sharon was with me. On the nights I didn't work I used to go in there As usual Sharon was soon by my side.

Romrig was there every week and was supposed to be the liaison between Coulton and me. If Coulton needed anyone extra the message would go from him to Romrig and then to me. I would then appear, like magic, at the appointed date. Sadly organisational skills weren't one of Romrig's strengths.

More than once Coulton rang me at home and asked me where I was. I'd always apologise for the confusion, get changed, put on my JEFF badge and turn up. Once Romrig's sister, a full on Hells Angel, rang me on his behalf because he'd forgotten to ask me to be there and she was embarrassed for him. He was amused when I saw him the next weekend. "You spoke to my sister" he gushed. "She's part of the Ratae[3]." "Ohhhh" I said, wondering if she'd been there that night at Stinkis. I found out later she had. "Yep" he carried on. "She's always got her colours on... they're filthy." "Doesn't she wash them?" I asked innocently. "You NEVER wash your colours man!" he screamed in return "...and they HONK!"

Soon Mr. C gave up going through him. The entire hotel was already getting busy for Christmas and he needed reliability. The bar was extremely busy. By the third or fourth week of October I donned my jacket and was working there with Romrig every Friday and every Saturday.

More so than Romrig, I soon found myself getting a call to work there the odd Thursday night as well. Whenever there was a promotion, such as a Malibu night, or need for any sort of door cover. I even did one night working the door for an 'Emigrate to America Night' of all things.

What can I say? I found I missed doorwork. I was already back on steroids. I had the car to pay off.

---

[3] Leicester Hells Angels

15

To Honey Bun from Lou Lou xx

I began to get bigger again. My jacket filled out and my confidence grew. I wrote a poem. Yeah. I know. Me… poetry. I can't remember it all. There was a top bodybuilder around at the time called Ron Koontz. He had a tattoo of Thee Animal[4] in a fancy scroll on his shoulder.

My poem started: "Thee Animal is within me, Ready at my call." Make no mistake, this wasn't a poem that went Thee Animal… tra-la-la-la. It was a Haka like Thee **ANIMAL** is **WITHIN ME**… **READY** at **MY** call. It reflected my steroidal mood at the time. I'd been through a lot with my withdrawal from the gear and never wanted to go there again. Consequently I decided to only take a fraction that I'd been taking before. It's a truism that, no matter how hard I tried and I tried very, very hard and I still try hard, I never, ever got in as good shape as I was in April / May 1984 again. Much to the relief of my nipples I never took lethal Methyl again either.

In the very early days at the Centre Bar we didn't care which door people used to enter. The doors by the Garden Room led to the outside. It was getting chilly so, ever the one for comfort, I took up position at the door at the bottom of the spiral staircase. Much warmer. Romrig followed suit.

There were little alcoves either side of the door. I put my orange juice there, Romrig put his beer and we lent on our elbows. Mark the carpet fitter came over. So did Sharon. Romrig spent all night talking to Mark while I spent all night talking to Sharon. Now that's what I call work!

I ditched the disliked name badge. Occasionally Claire, a short curly haired lady who, I believe, was the HR manager would walk through. She was always telling us off for slouching and trying to make us stand up straight. The instant

---

[4] Nope… not a typo

she turned her back we'd slouch again. One time I did it too quickly and she turned back round and caught me. I just grinned and stood up again – until she was out of sight –- naturally. Louise used to go in there as much as anyone else so she soon found out where I'd gone. Maybe Sharon told her. Not surprisingly really, she was a bit cool towards me. I was too dumb, innocent, shy, arrogant to understand. Big body, small brain.

Romrig turned out to be so hit and miss. He was a nice enough guy but, never mind organising me, he was useless at organising himself. A few weeks went by. He was always late or failed to show. He did nothing for the minor bits of trouble there were and he was unnecessarily sarcastic to some pretty townie girls that used to get there early every week before the place filled up. Typical me, I used to shyly flirt with them. Turns out one of them had posed for Escort or some other adult mag which he'd read and he made some comment about not recognising her with her clothes on as they left. The girl literally cringed as he said it. They never came down again.

I even recall the DJ, a half caste, dread locked chap named Simon who went out with the same Sadie that I'd given the glare to, asking us to chuck someone out for complaining about the music. This must have been early in my career there. Me and Romrig went over and listened to Simon complain. I was still a bit uncertain of everything so hovered in the background. Next thing Romrig sneered *"tough shit"* and walked off. I just shrugged, gave a wan smile to Simon and started to follow him. Simon was disgusted and gave us a lot of abuse. I did my best to ignore it. So did Romrig, but secretly we both scowled.

The guy doing the moaning was a skinny, grey faced teen I knew as Gavin. He used to wear a big RAF greatcoat and soap his hair into a flattop. This was way before the days of gel. If you looked closely enough you could see lumps of the stuff stuck in there.

Simon's frustration at our lack of action didn't seem to bother him for too long though and on the nights I'd wander in when I wasn't working, with Sharon at my side and sipping drinks I'd buy for her, I would chat to him while he enthusiastically told me the names of the bands I'd been listening to for nearly a year. He even let me go round the back and put on the odd record. In those days the DJays used to come in with cases and cases of 12" discs – often staggering under their sheer weight and number. I thumbed through Simon's when he wasn't looking. There were records by groups and individuals that I did recognise like the Thompson Twins and Prince, but there was the other stuff by Nina Simone and Jackie Wilson (Reet Petite) that I didn't recognise until I played or heard Simon play. It was only then that I began to connect the dots.

There was also a plethora of stuff by real unknowns to me such as the Sisters of Mercy, the Cure, the Cramps, King Kurt, Theatre of Hate, Siouxsie and the Banshees and one of Sharon's favourites, Killing Joke. I asked another apprentice at my day job if he'd heard of the Sisters of Mercy. He looked me up and down with piercing blue eyes. "Of course" was his two word response. I felt a bit left out. Shit. Too much time at the gym after all!

Coulton asked me if I'd heard of the group Orange Juice. I didn't have the foggiest. He prattled on and on about how you could control a joint by the music you played. Suppose so.

I was all at sea with the music so I made it a mission in life to understand it better and happily stood behind the bar one night playing at being the DJ while Simon wandered off somewhere. I put on some Ramones. Two half caste twin sisters Monique and Nicole gave me the thumbs up. I tried another record. By this time Sharon and Louise had wandered round and were on the other side of the tiny DJ box. "You're crap" Sharon told me bluntly. "Put some Siouxsie on and leave it to Simon." I laughed. Louise filled the gap. "Er... that is Siouxsie" she said. Sounded a bit condescending to me but what do I know? Sharon looked pissed off but shut up. She never criticised my choice of music again. Mind you other

107

people must've had the same view. They never let me play at being DJ too often after that.

The truth is, because I'd never heard of most of the stuff I played or that Simon played, I was discovering it for myself by messing around. Nick the barman liked to have a play as well. I liked the music so much that one Saturday morning I crept into a record shop near the clock tower and blindly bought my first Sisters of Mercy record – "Temple of Love." When I played it I realised that it wasn't my favourite. The next week I blindly bought "No Time to Cry." That was better. I've still got them both.

A short time later Simon had just started his set one Friday when some townie came up to the bar. It was one of my nights working and I had only just got there as well, otherwise I wouldn't have let him in and, true to form, there was no sign of Romrig. First the townie went up to Simon and had a go about the music. Then he went to the bar staff and started complaining it was the worst pint of beer he'd ever had and wanted a free replacement. I hovered in the background. I wasn't sure. Thumpity-thump. He'd drunk about 95% of his pint. Funny that. It had taken him nearly the whole pint before he decided it was undrinkable and he wanted a fresh one. The poor barman. He looked at me and I eventually gave a brief shake of my head. I didn't fancy trouble.

The townie hadn't even realised I was there. He turned round and looked at me standing there and had a sudden change of heart. He just grabbed his coat and walked out without another word. I felt my heart rate decrease. Phew. Now, what the townie didn't know was that I knew him. The Sugars Gym boys – often with me in the lead – used to wander around town on Saturday mornings after our workouts.

By now I suppose I was pretty much the leader, or one of the leaders, of the pack. One of our favourite haunts was St. Martins Square which was a 15 minute walk away. In those days it was brand new and full of trendy designer clothes shops. We'd strut around in a big group, anywhere from 5 to 15 of us or more and look at all the gear in the shops, very occasionally buying some of it if it struck a chord. This particular guy was the manager of one of those shops. The day after the crap beer episode I decided that he needed to know a bit about manners so, early in the morning I wandered up to his shop and stood at the window and stared. It was very quiet, just about 9am. He was only just opening up. He looked up and his jaw dropped when he saw me standing there. Result!

As I was deciding what to do next, Helsinkis Perry came up. He was wandering around too. I hadn't noticed him behind me. He saw me staring at the townie. His blue eyes went wide. "What have you done to him?" he asked. I smiled. It was probably a cold smile. "He looks scared to death" Perry continued. "Good" I grunted. "Maybe he'll be more careful when he upsets our bar staff in the future" and with that I flounced off leaving an open mouthed Perry in my wake. Would I have done anything? I doubt it but it did feel rewarding to give this guy just a little stress in return. He never ventured into the Centre Bar again.

Poor Romrig. At the end of the night he preferred to stand there talking to Mark. I did all the work. For the most part I didn't care. Despite odd moans about music and the odd arrogant townie, even more so than Helsinkis, there was hardly any trouble. I'd been doing this for nearly a year with virtually the same crowd. I knew lots of people. I delighted in putting on my suit and tie and getting 'dressed up' to stand on the door. I was back to being fastidious about my appearance. I flirted with the ladies – by now most of them knew my name because of the bloody name badge and I was universally known as 'Big' Jeff. No one calls me that these days!

I spent my nights there walking round, using my shyness to my advantage, having fun. Romrig felt it necessary to criticise my short back and sides while Sharon was there. He told me I had furry ears. I had no idea what he meant. "Hairy" he told me with glee. I was strangely irritated. Another time he didn't show until gone 10pm. "Don't start" he whined at me. He wasn't like Franklin, but I'd had enough. I started to whinge. Another characteristic that sadly became a bad habit of mine.

Coulton stopped him pay if he was late. "Oh… we've had a pay rise" he said to me once. Seems that less hours on his payslip had meant less income tax and he'd come out with more money than me for not being there. I told the boss man. He laughed in response but he must have been getting fed up too. Romrig was sacked soon after. According to him, he then went on to work at some very well known places with some "very serious people." Good luck to him. Personally, I never saw him again and everything I've learned since is what he's written in response to the earlier versions of this book.

Romrig came in the night he was sacked and told me he'd quit. I knew he was lying, just like Franklin. Oh well I thought, back to being by myself. I was wrong. Coulton had a bit more sense than the Helsinki mob and knew just how tough and dangerous doorwork could be. He phoned around and got an ex-boxer he knew with a wavy perm to cover one week. Wavy perms name was Mark, but he didn't like it there and got his cousin to cover in his place the next. I didn't like either of them.

I wanted people I knew with me so volunteered to get some extra heads. I went back to Sugars and asked around again. First stop – without any hesitation on my part – the 'F' brothers. The money was more than Helsinkis. £12.50 a night. Esau's face lit up. He came down and met the boss. Coulton took us to one side and out of the side of his mouth told us that if we had criminal records – we hadn't!! I still haven't. I didn't and still don't want to know about Esau.

Wavy perm Mark ended up losing his hair very shortly after. I knew those perms weren't good for you! A few more years down the line someone stamped on his leg one Christmas as he worked some club in town. Apparently it snapped like a twig. He came limping back into the bar nearly 10 years later. He may have lost all his hair but I recognised him instantly. He maintained he didn't know me. Oh well. He did only work there the one night.

This time around Esau was a bit more reliable. His kids were growing up. He needed the cash. If he wasn't able to make it he generally let me know. He grinned with my flirting and, in between telling me how massive my arse was told me "you're good looking... innit" for every girl I flirted with and THAT would have added up to a **LOT** of times. He disliked Sharon and would often whisper to me "her sisters a prostitute." I eventually found out this was true. How he knew, I have no clue. All I can say is that in 1984 I didn't know and didn't care. I ignored him.

Esau still had his moments though and a lot of nights I stood and waited for his inevitable displays of jutting chin and aggression but for the most part, and to my continued relief, they never came.

Another half caste guy, from the inevitable Sugars, by the name of Ronnie sometimes stood in for him. He was a very light skinned teenager, thin with a little goatee. Ronnie was Leicester born and bred and worked in the local knitwear industry with his training partner Dean but liked to talk in a Jamaican accent. While I stood there all night and flirted he came out with classic let me fuck you lines often uttering "blaadddclat" when he was turned down. My growing list of lady friends hated it. They complained to me so I asked Trevor to stand in when Esau couldn't make it rather than Ronnie. He did. Ronnie was pissed off and told me in no uncertain terms. Once again I didn't care. Coulton really didn't have a say in it. I was naturally taking the lead. It was getting busier and busier in the hotel. There were so many doors to cover. At my suggestion, and Coulton's recognition of keeping the place in control, Trevor started there full time and the two became the three of us.

At the end of the night we'd all be in the bar herding everyone out, me going round quietly asking everyone to drink up, Esau grinning away and Trevor bellowing "can you finish your drinks now and leave." He made a mistake once and, much to my amusement, yelled out "last orders at the bar" instead. Everyone laughed. And then, when the place was virtually empty, the 'F' brothers stopping what they were doing, stood together and started singing a sort of rap that went "… hear me now, hear me now…". They had a little dance that went with it. Trevor would regularly grab my shoulder and try and get me to join in. Singing? No chance. Dancing? Bloody hell! Even Simon saw us and was busy shouting to anyone who would listen "look at the dancing doormen!".

Now there were 3 it was my bright idea to stop standing at the spiral staircase door all night. One of us stood there. One stood in reception and one stood outside the Garden Room door. Every so often, on my command, we'd all move one place forward. Trevor even started referring to me as being the boss. It was the first time anyone identified me as the being the Head Doorman.

Having Fun
Picture Courtesy Jeff Shaw

Jeff Shaw

I slouched at the spiral staircase door early one evening. The bar was virtually empty. Trevor was upstairs. Esau was at the Garden Room door. There was Louise standing by herself at the bar. Julie must've been in the loo. She was wearing black lycra tights with red stripes in them. Thumpity-thump... thumpity-thump... thumpity-thump. In my mind the tights looked great. Eventually I got to her face and smiled. She ignored me. I beckoned her over to come and sit next to me on one of the bench seats. She was very reluctant but eventually did. I sat next to her and chatted and flirted away. She looked at me with distrust and disdain. I didn't get it. Speed is not my middle name. Finally Julie re-appeared and they both left for Rock City. I was frustrated. I looked at Esau and shrugged. He gave me his best grin. "She was pissed" I lied. He nodded his head sagely. It went well with the grin.

It was Julie who broke the ice that had formed between us really. The steroids were working their magic. I was feeling so much more like my old self and had put a lot of size back on. I decided to enter what would become my last serious bodybuilding competition in mid November that year[5]. The contest was at the YMCA in Leicester. I tried to engage Louise in conversation – excited about the contest. She wasn't the least bit interested. Bodybuilding doesn't have too many exciting aspects to it. Julie genuinely was. The conversation between me and Julie went on. Louise softened and at the end of the night she kissed me on the cheek. I'd missed her kisses. I was stunned and pleased, very pleased. I went home a happy man that night.

[5] I did enter one final one in 1986 but my heart wasn't in it and I didn't even bother to turn up after the half way stage

Me at my steroidal / contest best (1984)
Picture Courtesy Jeff Shaw

Usually preparation for a bodybuilding contest is very hard. There's dieting, shaving off your body hair. Then there's tanning, practising posing. I didn't do any of it. Sure I shaved off the few wispy hairs I had on my chest and legs and slapped on some fake tan. I looked orange. That was the full extent of my prep.

In those days contests took place on a Sunday. Pre-judging was in the morning and the finals at night. On the Saturday night I parked the Samba on the other side of town, near Sugars, and walked across the city to the hotel. I used to park it there often. I thought it was out of the way and less likely to be bashed by some drunken tosser. I'd taken the night off and was dressed in a brown checked lumberjack shirt. Even to my own eyes I looked massive.

I loved that shirt. The Army and Navy shop I'd bought it from in Silver Arcade hadn't been able to find one big enough. They'd sold me one too small and in a steroid rage I'd gone mad at them. My poor old mum had to sort it out in the end. I was too scared to go myself in case I lost it again. That night I saw Louise and she kissed me on the cheek before she left for

Rock City and I hung round in the bar for the rest of the night. I was in a steroid / Louise enhanced happy mood. When the bar shut I stood there in my shirt with the sleeves rolled up and gave a little posing display. Romrig was in there. He'd been having a drink. So were Coulton and Esau. Trevor was also off. He was entering as well. I guess Ronnie covered for me and Trevor but I can't be sure.

Mr. C just caught the end of the display "what's going on?" he asked, looking somewhat bewildered. I grinned. "You look fucking huge" said Romrig. Esau grunted approval. It was a week or so after my 24th birthday. When it was all over I walked airily back to the car. Happy birthday I thought.

As I entered the street it was parked in I saw that the cars in front of mine all had their wing mirrors torn off. I walked up to mine. I didn't look at the car. I looked on the pavement. I always was perceptive. Sure enough – there was the wing mirror. It fitted on with a ball and socket type affair. I banged it back in place as best I could, got in and took off. Let me tell you, roid rage hardly covers it. Happy mood eh?

I had changed training partners earlier in the year. Ross had gone – joining Khachik's gym because he "wanted to be in the clique." There seemed to be a lot of unhealthy competition and in fighting between the two gyms. Me and Ross had grown apart anyway but I was pissed off that he thought that much of our friendship that he'd just gone. I'd stayed at Sugars to avoid Khachik and was now training with an tall fellow called Lew who lived somewhere off Narborough Road.

Because of my mood those workouts were extremely aggressive and hard beyond belief. Good old Lew. He had long, dark hair and a walrusy moustache. What was it with moustaches in the mid 80's? Lew stuck with it as I pushed him harder than he had ever been pushed in the gym in his life just so I could get him to push me further still. It worked.

It wasn't all bad behaviour though and we had some good laughs including a massive snowball fight with Roy and Nev, his training partner, as we walked back to our cars after a typical session. It ended with me and Lew driving off in the

Jeff Shaw

Samba with the drivers side window down and snowballs at the ready. By that time I didn't really care what happened to that stupid car. As I drove slowly past a partially hidden Roy he struck first and, I swear, a snowball came whizzing in through the window, brushed my nose and brushed Lew's nose before smashing into the closed window on his side. Amazing.

Lew had a girlfriend, Denny who was often in Helsinkis and the Centre Bar and was another one I regularly spoke to by now but she was never in there with Lew or – if she was – I never noticed. I had no idea of the connection between the three of us until I started to chat with the newspaper guy, Eugene. As I saw Lew approaching in the distance and started to move off to meet him Eugene simply said "oh… so that's Lew… Denny's boyfriend." It was only then that the penny dropped.

To this day I have no idea why Lew was never with Denny when she was in the bar. I tried very hard to get him to join me at Helsinkis during the periods I was working alone. He wouldn't. I asked why. Eventually he reluctantly told me he'd had problems earlier in his life and there was no way he was going to risk having to face that sort of thing again. Remember, I was still new to bouncing at this point. I was still pretty innocent and I had a poor grasp of the potential consequences to myself, despite what I was doing and where I was in my own life.

I was openly shocked that my quietly spoken mate could have gotten himself into any sort of trouble. Apparently my mouth hung open. Lew told me to shut it because I was catching flies. This was about the same time as the rounders bat. Lew saw me buy it. "I don't want to see any notches on that" had been his warning. Good job my brain eventually saw through the steroid fuzz before the Fuzz saw through the bulge in my jacket!

Anyway, by the time of the contest Lew had just broken up with Denny. Consequently he'd moved into a new bedsit round the corner from where he'd been living. He was having a flat warming, I had told him I couldn't go because of the contest the next day. I had to do *some* prep!

That night, after I slammed the wing mirror back on, I threw my car in gear and raced round to the party. Lew was already pissed and was gob smacked when I walked in. I asked him for a soft drink. He didn't have any and offered me a tin in return. I had a tiny sip of the beer. It was horrid. Now I know why I don't drink. I left it on the edge of a table and stormed back to my car. Some guys in the street, outside his house started to give me some abuse. I guess they recognised me. I gritted my teeth and ignored them. The mood I was in I'd probably have kicked the shit out of them. Lucky me, lucky them.

The next day I entered the contest clean plucked like a turkey, orange, stressed, water logged and pissed off. I came a distant third. There were only 4 people in my entire class. I've still got the trophy. Trevor won. A guy called Alfredo came second.

Alfredo was a 40 year old Italian with a terrible comb over who used to spend six months in England and six months in Germany with his wife, Trudy, every year. When he was in England he trained at Sugars. Before that he'd been at Bradallens. Amazingly he also worked at the hotel as a general porter, waiter, barman come all sorts. Sugars Gym: 1st, 2nd and 3rd. The International Hotel – same positions. Bizarre.

Alfredo and Trudy invited me to their room one night. Some Asian guy who was a well known local strongman had videoed the contest. Video cameras were very new and expensive then. Only a few people had one. Esau told me he used to make porn movies with it. Another exaggeration? This guy had once come to me in Sugars and asked if it was okay to drink an injectable steroid. I told him it was. Now there's a whopper.

Me, Alfredo and Trudy sat in their tiny room and watched the footage of us posing. Apparently a lot of the hotel staff had already seen it. It was odd to see myself. I didn't buy a copy because I didn't own a video player. They were still relatively new too. I wish I'd had more foresight. I never did manage to get hold of a copy.

The night of the contest the Leicester Mercury had sent a photographer there. At the end he got the 3 of us to stand in a line and hit some poses backstage and snapped away. I was still pissed off over the car. Trevor stood in the middle. I was on his left, Alfredo on his right. I put my arms in front of Trevors head and body as many times as possible. The story ran the following Monday. There was a picture of Trevors grinning face from the neck up. They couldn't show any more. My arms were in front of his chest.

Because of his job at the Mercury Trevor was able to get copies of the photos at a really cheap rate. I ordered the lot from him and was supposed to meet him at Sugars one Saturday to pick them up. We were both late. I was on the other side of town when I realised I should've been at the gym. I ran all the way across the city. At 15 stone of muscle, hardly poetry in motion. It was nearly December and freezing cold. I bumped into Trevor just round the corner from the gym and collapsed on the ground in a gasping heap. He had a girl I didn't know with him. They both looked at me lying at their feet, a smile playing at Trevors lips and he just passed the photos down to me. The girl looked at me as though I was crazy.

I dragged myself to my knees and gave him the money and he toddled off into the city with the girl while I staggered back to my car. Does weight training keep you fit? It took an hour for my heart rate to drop back to something like normality.

The results from the contest were listed in the paper. I've still got the cutting. The following Friday I stood in the Centre Bar. Julie came up with Louise in tow. "You came third" Julie said. I looked through her at Louise and smiled. She smiled back. Thumpity-thump… thumpity-thump… thumpity-thump. We re-established our friendship.

I lived for the weekends, for my flirting, my time with Sharon, my quick peck on the cheek from Louise. In the end I said to her "you must be short sighted." She looked puzzled. "You keep missing my mouth."

It was getting closer and closer to Christmas. Me, Esau and Trevor started to work all sorts of hours and week nights covering the bar, functions, weddings, parties. You name it. We were exhausted. I came off the gear again and stopped training. It was too much. I lost a stone but this time round I was too knackered to care or worry about any changes in my personality.

The General Manager of the hotel at that time was a skinny bloke with glasses and a goatee beard. I can't remember his name. He clearly wasn't too sure about us and liked us to be known as "Client Supervisors" or "Crowd Control Technicians." He really wasn't too keen on his hotel having employees known as Doormen or worse, Bouncers!

One night Trevor let one of the Goths in through and across reception to go to the bar while the function rooms were in full swing. It was a common practise. We didn't care. The GM saw it and went nuts, although I have to say he was careful at going nuts to Coulton and Nigel and not us. Nigel came over and told me off. He was clearly a bit wary as well. I had no idea why he was being so timid. I had no intention of giving him any grief but when I look back, my appearance, my behaviour as I came off the gear. All questionable.

From that night on we locked the revolving doors and made everyone use the doors by Strikes that led down to the Garden Room. We didn't tell anyone so a few didn't realise at first and still tried to use the doors they'd used before. The GM moaned at us and we asked more than one to leave because of it. As you might imagine, lots of the clientele complained that we wanted their money but made them feel like second class citizens because of the way they looked. I was sympathetic but there wasn't a lot we could do.

I do think the GMs mind changed about us that Christmas when there was a lad being mildly rude and aggressive in the toilets. He was pissed. The GM discovered him and asked him to leave. I knew this lad from my Helsinkis days and had never had an issue with him. Anyway, at the command of the GM I followed into the toilets to help. I was hulking about in the background. The lad laughed in response to some skinny guy asking him to go so I stepped forward. He took one look at me, said "hi Jeff. I'll leave for you but not that twat" and then went without another murmur. I didn't have to do a thing.

After that the GM was always asking for me if he suspected there may be some trouble although he did lay out a set of rules which said we had to give people at least 3 verbal warnings if we were going to use any level of force to evict them from the premises. A rule which we all duly totally ignored. When someone is about to punch you, throw something at you or is just verbally abusing you there really isn't much time to say "I do have to warn you", let alone say it 3 times!

I had another bright idea. My second that year. I was doing well. Now no one was allowed to come across reception there wasn't much need to stand by the spiral staircase door so I changed where we stood. Two of us on the Garden Room door, one in reception. Swop every 30 minutes. If anyone made to leave by the spiral staircase door we leapt across the bar like Batman and called them back. I was in charge and called the shots. I couldn't be in the bar all the time but I **ALWAYS** made sure I was at the Garden Room door when Louise left. I never missed a kiss. Come to think of it never did Louise. Mind you, by now I hardly ever stopped and chatted to her. It was all about Sharon.

Sharon was now standing with me from time to time when I was upstairs. I kept her hidden from the GM. Coulton caught us once. "Look at her skinny legs" he said with a grin that beamed out from under his dead caterpillar as she tottered off. I smiled back. A knowing smile.

As Christmas arrived Louise took a photo of me and Nick in front of the bar. She gave me a card. It read "To Honey Bun, from Lou Lou xx." I was pretty pleased but it was about the only card I got. It took pride of place at home. I gave her one back. I had one written for Sharon that I kept in my jacket in anticipation. She never gave me one. I was frustrated so I never gave her mine.

The last time the hotel was open that year was Christmas Eve night. I had taken the night off because I wanted to go out with the Sugars Gym boys again. A year since my slurred conversation with Lee at Mr. Kiesas. In the afternoon we'd opened the bar at dinner time. Sharon came in. No Louise. I was disappointed. That Christmas afternoon, Mr. Showman (i.e. Coulton), had forgotten to get a DJ so there was no Simon to play any music and no records for me to mess about with and play in his place. The place was still packed though. Don't tell him, but I pretty much ignored the door. Apart from watching a flattop guy called Colin cry his eyes out because his dad upset him, all I did was talk to Sharon.

Coulton had hired some thin, dark haired guy I didn't know called Mark to work that afternoon without telling me. We stood in the middle of the smoke filled bar and wolfed down ham sandwiches I'd scrounged from the kitchens. Sharon looked at me in disgust. "Meat… yuck" she proclaimed. I tried chatting to Mark but his entire conversation was about the fights he'd had. I thought he was a dickhead and told Coulton never to employ him again. Fortunately he agreed. Not long after I heard that the Baby Squad got hold of him at some other place and slashed his buttocks to pieces. He couldn't sit down for weeks. I didn't like him but I felt for him. Poor sod.

We closed the bar at about 3pm, I kissed Sharon goodbye and then went home by myself. That night I dragged the reluctant Sugars boys down there. They walked into a sea of mohicans, black spiky hair and weird music. There were real howls of "what the fuck is this?" We didn't stay long. I'd had my two pints and was legless. I ended up lying on the floor in Tipplers.

Chris the ex-Para, face worker was with us. A few days later he told me that Sharon had been in the Centre Bar when I was staggering around. I didn't have the foggiest. "Look after him" Chris told me she'd said. Some hopes. He didn't give a shit. He'd left me alone and pissed at the train station while he got a taxi home. And they call these things a good night!

We had a week off. I needed it to sober up. Then we were all there again for New Years Eve. We didn't open the bar. Me, Esau and Trevor covered the function rooms until 2.00am New Years day. By now my experience at handling all sorts of different crowds was expanding dramatically. First Force 8, then Helsinkis and Tipplers followed by the Centre Bar and every type of function and crowd in the hotel you could think of.

I have to say, the young Doctors were by far the worst. Noisy and trouble. We once caught a line of guys queuing up to shag one very drunk young lady in a part of the hotel we nicknamed the rabbit run. It housed a few crappy offices, including the Bars Managers and was very dark and dank. Most weekends no one used it and you only knew it was there if you cautiously tried one of the very many doors that were all over the place. We got a tip-off from one of the staff that something was going on and burst through the doors. There she was just lying there in the semi darkness – blue party frock up, knickers down – with a stupid grin on her face. What a sight! To the disappointment of many we broke the queue up. To think, these people are probably surgeons now.

Company Christmas parties and even weddings could be bad as well. About a year or so later one company party gave me a real battle but, that night, nothing memorable happened. Helsinkis was packed but only a few stragglers came across. I guess a lot of people had gone to Rock City. We were bored. Being a self centered prick I missed flirting and being kissed. I was off the gear. I went home, alone, eyes stinging and throat as sore as normal, went to bed and felt deflated.

I woke up the next morning feeling even worse. That happened too many times after that. Not my favourite time of year New Years Eve.

16

Fun in Reception and Beyond

It hadn't even crossed our minds to cover reception when Romrig had been there. We just ignored it and stood in the bar. This time I have no idea who made the suggestion that we needed to keep an eye on it. I was probably the GM, although it could've been Coulton. I think he was quite proud of the fact that the hotel had doormen on show. I know he'd discussed it with his counterpart at the Grand, a luxurious establishment on Granby Street in the city, a 30 second walk from Sugars. He even ran across the road to a pub on the opposite corner of Humberstone Road called the Three Cranes with me and Esau in tow. It was to sort of show us off to the doorman there.

The Three Cranes was supposed to be a bit rough. I didn't know the guy on the door but Coulton did. He smiled. "Oh… look at Coulton with his musclemen" he said as got closer. All of us smiled in return. It's always good to be friendly with the other doormen around the city. You never know when you may need each others help.

What most people didn't realise about the International hotel was its size. It was undoubtedly a huge establishment. A bit like the TARDIS. Apart from the bars and function rooms there were 6 floors and about 250 rooms. Most of the 6th floor was devoted to staff quarters and was by far the shabbiest with dirty paintwork, worn carpets and peeling wall paper but the rest of the rooms, apart from a small number on the first floor which were used as offices, were for guests. Adjoined to the hotel was the International Conference Centre. I've been in there when it was empty. I used to think you could house an entire army in there and no one would ever know.

The hotel reception was vast, brightly lit and on 2 levels with comfy leather sofas and chairs and tables all over the place. By my reckoning it was at least 5 or 6 times or more the size of the bar and, of course, was the gateway to all the function rooms, the lifts, the rooms, the phones, the toilets, the conference centre – everything. The black framed main doors where we stood were in Rutland Street but the actual address of the place was Humberstone Road.

Humberstone Road runs at a 90° angle to Rutland Street and is where the external entrance to Strikes was, the revolving doors were and where the alternative entrance to the Centre Bar lay. Once inside, directly in front of the Rutland Street doors was reception itself. Pretty much the first thing you saw was a pair of dirty brown lift doors and the massive Charnwood function room. To the left of reception was some telephones set on the wall and a flight of stairs which led down to the even bigger Albermarle function room.

Standing alone up there could be extremely boring. Yet again we were instructed to stand up straight. No slouching and absolutely no sitting down in case any residents saw us. Half an hour away from the fun of the bar was more than enough for me. We couldn't even sip orange juice and just used to hover in the doorway making sure that no one other than people staying the night or partygoers, if there were functions on, tried to get in. For the most part I found it was hardly a thumpity-thump zone. If someone I knew went past I'd leap out into the street to say hello because I was so bored. Usually this was Sharon. Sometimes she would stay the whole half an hour but usually it was only a short chat because she wanted to get down to the bar and enjoy herself. If I did catch sight of her, and she was in a hurry, I would cut short my stint up there to meet her back down in the bar. Oh, such is the life of the Head Doorman.

Esau and Trevor never complained but occasionally they would cut short their stays up there too – presumably out of sheer boredom. The main problem in working up there was that there were still so many entrances available that the odd undesirable got in no matter what we did. It's not like they had a badge on that said I'm not a resident – I'm a troublemaker. I used to lock the revolving door to try and limit the ways in but the staff would often unlock them again as they went home for the night and that would mean I would occasionally have to chase after someone who had wandered in by a door I thought was locked so I could find out what they wanted. Usually it was all quite innocent stuff – like using the loos or looking for a public phone or one of the regular crowd trying to take a short cut but there was the odd guy who wanted to make trouble and we threw more than one person out of Strikes for harassing the waitresses or being rude to other customers in there. I always found it weird that people would cause trouble in a restaurant, but they did.

One night me and Esau had to go crashing in there after we got a message down in the bar that there was a group of lads who'd had a meal but were refusing to pay. When we arrived they soon changed their minds but then one of the waitresses claimed her coat had gone missing. I'm sure it had nothing to do with the lads – how could it? They started to leave, claiming complete innocence and already annoyed that we had stopped them doing a runner. Esau tried to get them to stay until we got it sorted out but they just took the piss out of him and I could see his big eyes getting harder and harder, his mouth tightening into a thin line and his jaw beginning to jutt out. I was less concerned about keeping them there. There was NO WAY the coat could've had anything to do with them. When I saw Esau's eyes my head said shit. I felt the thumpity-thumps starting. Suddenly the waitress found her coat. It had fallen down on the floor. A let out an audible sigh of relief and the group left without any further hassle. I could see Esau was seething but this time he managed to keep himself in control. I breathed another big sigh of relief.

Another time I was staying overnight in a staff room. Halfway through having a shave the phone rang. There was trouble in Strikes – could I go and sort it out? I picked up a face towel, quickly wiped off my shaving foam and headed down there in my shirtsleeves. When I got there I found that another doorman had already arrived. A few guys were being pests but our presence was enough to shut them up and off they went without any bother. I smiled and toddled back to my room. When I got there I went to finish my shave and realised that not only had I gone down with a half shaven face, in my haste I hadn't wiped my face properly and the stuff was up my nose and in my ears. Funny that – being scared of a doorman with a foamy nose and ears.

On Coultons instructions I once ejected a hunchback with a thick blue jumper, long greasy hair and glasses who was milling around. He was carrying a black leather shopping bag that looked empty to me. "Get him out" was the order. "He's always hanging around." I chased after him and he tried to do a runner. I had no idea what the issue was with him but it wasn't really my place to argue in those circumstances. He ran straight into the locked revolving doors and bounced off them right into my arms. "This way" I instructed. I was gentle. I didn't touch him, just pointed towards the main door. He started to protest – not physically – just started to ask me why he had to leave. I just reverted back to a just doing my job role. "I'm not interested" I replied and off he went, grumbling incoherently under his breath. A few of the reception staff and managers were standing around watching. "You've got some patience" one of them said. I gave her a bland smile. Not really I thought. I really was not interested! It wasn't like he wanted to fight me.

I'd use a lot of discretion as well. Probably more so than any of the others who just used to stand there and let their presence stop any undesirables from coming in. When a mute guy dived in and starting patting himself on the head and indicating he was desperate for the loo I just showed him the way. When an arrogant Asian tried to waltz past me I stopped him and demanded he showed me his key card. He didn't have one. He didn't get through the door.

A lot of times I'd keep looking over my shoulder at the door but would pretty much wander away to chat to the receptionists to fill in the 30 minutes. Even messing about with little magic tricks which I bought when I was about 10! A lot of them were pretty. Why do you think I took the time to do it? I was soon able to carry on flirting and having as much fun as I

126

could but I used to get mildly scolded every time a manager wandered past. Mind you, I'd flirt with the female ones too ☺. I don't think that Trevor or Esau tried this same trick but I guess I got away with it because of the way I could thrust my shyness forward as a tool back then. Never-the-less I learned a lot of names over the years – everything from Sharon, to Teresa, to Donna, to Claire and more. I didn't get too far with most of them but let's just say I got to kiss and hug a whole lot more girls!

The saddest part about constantly looking over my shoulder at the door is that I still do it! One sunny night in late 2008 I sat outside the main door of a pub in Melbourne called the Espy. It vaguely reminded me of both Helsinkis and the Centre Bar. Helsinkis because it's fairly grungy and the Centre Bar because it had a live band playing, but it's really a shabby dive. There was me and a few friends. It was very odd for me to be at a pub. Only the second or third time in my whole stay in Australia. I sat there sipping my usual orange juice while I felt my eyes flicking to the door and back all night long. D'oh! I guess it's embedded now.

We weren't supposed to go behind reception but I often did just because I was nosy and wanted to see what was going on in there. I used to get mildly scolded for that too but it didn't really stop me. It wasn't anything interesting anyway. Just a small room with patchy, yellowing wall paint, a couple of old, grotty desks and chairs and maps, bulletins and yellowing memos sellotaped up everywhere. There was also a flickering black and white video image of the hotel car park which was below the whole place and had space for about 30 or so awkwardly parked cars, but I never saw anyone take too much notice of it. After a few years we all used it to hide our own cars down there, taking up spaces that were meant for the residents. No one said a word.

At about 10pm or so the Night Porters would arrive and take over from the receptionists. There would usually be two of them. Jim, the head porter, a portly, bespectacled guy in his late fifties / early sixties and an ever revolving list of others –

usually young guys just making a living. Most didn't work there for too long. I doubt it was a great job. My dad got offered it once while he was going through one of his breakdown periods but even he said no thanks. I always found Jim to be a nice guy but for some reason he didn't get on with Trevor who once leant over the reception desk, grabbed Jim by the collar of his coat and demanded that he get him a taxi home.

Poor Jim. The hotel used to provide staff transport home in those days, so it wasn't unusual for any of us to have a staff taxi but we always had to wait until everyone else had left. I guess Trevor was in a hurry that night. Jim must have pooped himself. Maybe it was the steroids. I don't know. I guess I'm assuming Trevor took them. I never knew for sure.

Many years after he left Trevor popped into reception for a chat. Jim was on duty and asked me to get Trevor to leave. That was fun. I was extremely embarrassed and a little worried about how Trevor would react but he took one look at Jim, tutted under his breath and departed in his own good time. I didn't rush him. I'm not stupid. I don't think guys like Trevor saw the odd barny with a Night Porter in anywhere near the same light.

By Christmas 1984 we'd all end up standing up there once the bar closed. That made it more bearable – at least there would be someone other than the receptionists to flirt with or the Night Porters to talk to. The place would be heaving as function rooms filled up in the early evening and even worse as they all closed at the end of the night. I'd spend time still trying to be nice and direct people to all the various rooms but they often ignored me or didn't listen and headed off in the wrong direction so I gave up a lot of the time. I think the others were the same.

When it got to around 2am, we would spend our time quietly wandering from function room to function room, trying to get the DJays to stop playing music and get people to leave. It was pretty hard work because it was warm in there and it was cold outside. Jim worked his balls off getting taxis for those that asked while me, Esau and Trevor worked ours off in somewhat vain efforts to keep people moving and sometimes we could be there until 3am or even later. We were often criticised by the clientele at functions as being intimidating which I found unnecessary, although it must have been odd for people flocking into a hotel to see burly and tough looking doormen standing around. There was one time we even had a genuine policeman's ball in there. A former colleague from the steel industry was in that night. He'd joined up and had got to sergeant. His surname was Hall but in the usual Leicester vernacular he used to pronounce it 'All. I called him Fuck. Work it out. He saw me standing there and came over with some of his mates to show off. "I know him" he bragged. "He's soft as shit." "Soft as shit" he repeated for my benefit. "Well… I wouldn't want to bump into him in a dark alley" one of his mates said. "Soft as shit" Fuck said again looking right at me. I just laughed. It's true – I think I could still be Marine Boy on the outside, but when I needed to be I had a job to do.

Not everyone criticised us. A few times we got compliments for our quiet and friendly approach. There was even a little Pakistani called Raj who DJ'd at a lot of functions. He'd get the guests to play party games. One of his favourites was to get the women running out of the rooms to find us and grab our ties. After a while most of us got wary and went and hid. Some of the others loved it.

Looking back I guess I had less respect for the hundreds and hundreds that flocked to the functions than those who filled the bar. Of the two, I'm sure it wasn't the bar that was keeping the place afloat. We'd look at them as they left – often staggering from too much drink or giving us verbal abuse – and quietly and privately amuse ourselves over any that had trousers that were too short and showed their socks. There were plenty of them. I have to admit we all spent a fair bit of time eyeing up the attractive girls too. I did it so much so that I eventually got a good bollocking for doing it.

Trevors favourite trick was to spot a girl he fancied and quietly utter *"yo… pssssstttt" as* she walked past. You'd be amazed at how many heard him, turned round and came over.

I tried it as well. No surprise there then, but had nowhere near the same level of success. Okay. I had NO success. I never did understand why. Then again, when we went out to nightclubs I kept my dick in my trousers and Trevor usually didn't.

Most nights functions had run we'd all just go home at the end of the night. Every nightclub was shut by the time we'd finish, we were knackered and, personally, I was always glad to breathe fresh air, get in the Samba and drive off. My suit, skin and hair would stink of cigarettes and stale booze for days, my throat would be sore and my eyes would be red for hours. It can't have been healthy.

There were a few times that I was hired just as additional hotel security. In early 1985 there were a lot of rooms being broken into by a gang of professional thieves. It cost a fortune in replaced door locks and insurance. I spent a Wednesday and Thursday night just hulking around the place. Up the floors, down the floors... just to try and catch them. Nothing. Remember, this place had 6 floors. I went straight from the gym. Not a good idea! In the end I was aching from head to toe and would walk slowly up and around each floor, get to the top, sit there for 15 minutes and then walk slowly down and around before hiding for another 15 minute break at the bottom. The break-ins stopped. Nothing to do with me – the gang just moved on. I have to say – I learned my way around every inch of the place doing that.

We also had a night when an anti-abortionist mob had a rally there. Me and Esau turned up and stood there bleary eyed and bored just in case. There was a huge crowd chanting away outside. A couple of policemen were there as dull eyed and bored as us. Half way through the night me and Esau started to make eyes at a pretty girl standing in front of the windows before Coulton saw us and told us off. In the end the hotel received a threat of a bomb and we evacuated the place. Poor us, we were the last ones in there. God knows what we'd have done if it was real. Fortunately it was a hoax.

Over the years I received a lot of directions, the odd shout for Mr. Peters, which was the secret scramble call, threats and warnings in that bloody reception. Charlie Kray was in town – watch out, three Dutch gangsters were on the loose – let the police know if I saw them. When I wouldn't let some big, fat Egyptian looking guy in one Christmas – I was dead. When someone tried to run away without paying for his bottle of wine – could I go after him? What did I mean he hadn't paid? I was a liar. I was insistent. He put out his hand. I thought he wanted to shake so I stupidly put out mine. It's like an instinctive reaction in most of us. He grabbed it and squeezed. I just looked at him. He squeezed harder. I looked right into his eyes. He went red in the face with effort. Finally he let go. I carried on looking at him. He'd lost. He went redder still, got out his wallet and tried to give me the cash. I told him to see the girls behind reception and off he trundled, moaning every step of the way. The receptionists happily took his cash. Blah... blah... blah from him. Wanker.

We also had a lot of functions and guests that I found very interesting and stuck my, often unwanted, nose in. In 1984 there was a Star Trek convention. Guess which nerd is a fan! The World War 2 Spitfire Aces had a couple of reunions there in the mid 80's. Guess who was completely drawn in and in awe! I should've got some autographs. They were all in there, Sir Douglas Bader had just died, but his mates were alive and kicking. Never thought of it at the time. Now that **is** a shame and is something I will always regret.

In later years some swimming championships were on at St. Margarets baths in the long run up to the Olympics. Swimming superstars Sharon Davies and Nick Gillingham were in the hotel. They were both regulars on TV then. Could I make sure they were okay and not bothered? The group with them were a pest though, dropping glasses from their hotel bedrooms on to passers by in the street below. The night manager was a chubby bloke with glasses by the name of Fairey. He was only young and it was his first weekend as the night manager. He started to panic. In the end me and Esau went up to the rooms knocking on doors and had to get them to pack it in at the risk of chucking them out. Most of them were only 14 or 15 ish. They were having great fun. We just thought it was stupid. Fortunately no one in the street got hurt. I never did get to see Sharon Davies.

Another time there was an international karate championship held over a weekend. A man who was to become a big pal, Lloyd, was working there by then. He knew all the names of the guys who stood in the foyer by the revolving door at night and warmed up. Master this. Grand Master that. He was fascinated. I found it all very amusing as I wandered past – arms out to my sides, trying to make myself look even bigger still to show them I wasn't intimidated. None of them paid me any attention at all. They were ALL far tougher than me. Got to say though – most of them were limping or sporting black eyes by the second night which did give me a bit of smug satisfaction. Selfish git!

We had a load of professional boxers in as well some time later. Same story. I amused myself with the number of black eyes I saw the next night.

A language school had a convention of sorts there. Some language teachers are really good looking! I claimed I could speak the odd phrase of French, German, Arabic, and Japanese. Er... No I can't. Not unless you consider being able to count to ten and say hello or goodbye is 'speaking.' I have tried to learn all these languages but I'm crap.

Also in later years SAGA, the old peoples group, used to turn up and take over the place every Christmas. I joined in the guess the number of jelly beans in the jar. We asked what SAGA meant once. Sex And Games for the Aged was the twinkling reply.

Townies would pass by in the street and look at us standing there. I suppose we were still a deterrent. One group of exuberant ladies went by. They took one look at me and one screeched "loverly." "We int gonna git in thur er wi" screeched her friend. Oh the lovely Leicester accent.

Many residents would sit there as well, chatting between themselves, watching us in action. Questioning between themselves what we were doing there. I'd often wander over and have a natter, always keeping one eye on the door, sometimes having to say excuse me and dashing off to stop some lost soul wandering in. They would ask me what my job was and I would variously answer using the words the GM wanted us to say. Crowd Control Technician, Client Supervisor. Bouncer? They'd ask.

One guy at a Jewish convention asked me what I did if anyone trying to get in started to get rough. "Oh...I just speak quietly to them" I told him. "What if they won't listen?" he asked, a dubious look on his face. I grinned. I grinned almost as much as Esau when I first started. "Oh... I just speak a little louder" was my response. I'm sure he thought I was serious. He gave me a startled look, eyed up his watch and said "excuse me, I have to go and pray now." I hope he wasn't praying for me!

Oddest moment up there? Standing just in front of the lift doors as they opened to see Coulton pulling up his flies and his then girlfriend pulling down her dress. They both seemed quite... er... happy... um... and breathless. I don't think they ever knew I'd seen them – until now!

Overall, it all kept me busy. And employed. On second thoughts – it probably wasn't too bad up there after all.

Me and Esau Clowning Around in Reception
Picture Courtesy Jeff Shaw

17

Get out of the Way... We're the Wreckin' Crew

One of the reasons for moving from the odd night at the Centre Bar to full time was that Coulton used to organise bands to play in the Garden Room in between other parties. Entry to the Centre Bar was always free but we charged an entrance fee into the Garden Room in those days. The place was so newly opened to them that most people hadn't realises you could use the back door by the toilets and get in free. The majority of the bands were upcoming Punk or Rock groups. Over the years some people played and drank in there that made it pretty big in their little scene including the Meteors, UK Subs, Crazyhead, the Hunters Club, the Great Red Shark, who evolved into Gaye Bikers on Acid, Into a Circle and the Filberts, who became Diesel Park West. It's one of my few claims to fame. Okay, it's my only claim to fame.

When I wasn't leaning in the spiral staircase alcove or standing alone in reception I was leaning against the Garden Room wall, leaving an International Hotel ink smudge on peoples hands, shoulders, chests and foreheads, wherever they asked me to stamp them. Later on I got a bollocking from HR manager Claire for doing that and was forced to stamp people on the back of their right hands. Boring.

Even I have to admit I did take the leaning thing too far though. Bored, I'd collapsed back against the wall in my little alcove to the sound and feel of a crunch. Oh oh. I turned around and, sure enough, I'd hit the fire alarm button hard enough to set it off. Red lights started to flash in the roof but the place was so busy, noisy and dimly lit only me and Nick in the bar noticed. We swopped anxious glances – me because I was guilty and him because he didn't know what was going on and was ready to grab the tills and herd everyone out. I didn't bother to explain but flew upstairs in a valiant but failed attempt to stop the fire brigade coming out. Whoops. They charge a fortune for false call outs. I wasn't flavour of the month that night.

I got the bands thing wrong occasionally as well. A Psychobilly called Geoff had agreed with Coulton that his band could play in the Garden Room. No one had bothered to tell me and when a load of skinheads started to appear to watch I turned them away. In general they were a bit of a no, no. There was a group going round at the time called the Clockwork Soldiers, led by Wilson and Timmo who were both 17 or 18 or so with self inflicted and ugly looking tattoos of crosses and teardrops on their foreheads and cheeks. Millionaire winner Ryan was part of this gang.

We occasionally let them in and Wilson used to spend all night going round asking people for money. It wasn't a school playground. We all got a bit pissed off with it so they were on the not very welcome list. Much, MUCH later I found out your average skinhead was a peace loving guy – more into reggae and ska music than anything. The shaven headed image and the BNP gave them a really bad name and tainted them forever.

There had been a load of skinheads in there when we saw tables and chairs going everywhere. Me and Esau dashed over yelling "move... move... move..." to the stunned crowd around them. It was the Soldiers. We chucked them out and I have to say they ran as we approached. That was the night the girl kicked the glass pane in that nearly severed her leg. When Trevor escorted one of them off the premises the method of choice was to poke a large black finger deep into the guys cheek and push him out with it. He went without a fuss as well and never came back.

Another time I was doing the reception stint. I decided it was time to swop over and made my way down to the bar. Esau and Trevor were nowhere to be seen. I walked across the bar, by the Garden Room and up the 2 flights of stairs to the street. There they were. Trevor was all flushed and looked huge. Steroids have that effect when you're in fight or flight mode. You just blow up like a balloon. Once, my neighbour across the road used his car to purposely block me from reversing down my drive. He hated me. I'd never done a thing to him. He just hated me. I got out of my car and, with his wife screaming "leave him alone... he's an old man" in my ear, pulled him out of his driving seat. I was incandescent with steroid fuelled rage. My dad was there. He told me I just looked enormous.

It seems the Soldiers had upset Trevor in some way, he'd thrown them out and they'd all run off only to come back carrying a railroad sleeper. I never saw any of this. Trevor told me it was so big they couldn't carry it between them. He'd gone out into the street by Strikes. They'd been staggering under the weight of this thing, looked up, seen the size of him, remembered the finger in the cheek technique and run off. When I got there the police had just arrived. There were 2 of them. "Here we go" said one as I arrived. "What happened?" 'Nothing' I replied. "We heard a noise, came up to have a look and found everything quiet." He gave me a quizzical look, looked at his mate who shook his head and they buggered off. Not something you want, having the police there all the time. It causes problems when it comes to renewing your drinks licence.

The night of Geoffs band was one of the rare nights we charged. I let loads of Psychobillies in but took the skinhead thing so far that I even turned his girlfriend away. All the time coolly standing there and stamping anyone else who decided to venture in. I also took the time to chat and flirt away to the teeny, dark haired, receptionist Nikki, who sat on a stool outside the door and collected the money. Oddly enough Geoff was annoyed with me and gave me lots of abuse.

As the night went on, so did Geoff. My stress levels started to rise. The Garden Room filled up and the music started. I peeked in. There was a mass brawl going on! Already stressed from the abuse and with my lack of brain power I dived in and then noticed that everyone was smiling. I backed off, confused. I saw 2 pretty flattop girls I knew from Helsinkis.

"It's wreckin' " one of them screamed at me over the row. Fuck me. The mass brawl was a dance.

If you've never seen it, it's not something I would recommend. Basically all the shirts come off. One poor sucker stands in the middle and everyone else around him starts flapping their arms more and more violently. As the music builds they all rush in and clobber the hell out of the guy in the middle. When he's had enough someone else takes his place. The longer they last, the greater the kudos. The alternative name for all this is the Chicken Dance. Nope. Nothing to do with Spitting Image. For the most part Geoff never spoke to me again.

When we went back to work in January 1985 Coulton had booked the Meteors to come and play for the first Saturday in the month. It was a big score but they attracted a rough crowd – the Wreckin Crew. I reckon you had to be insane to 'dance' like that. Not one to be fooled easily I went straight back on to steroids.

The night of the Meteors I stood outside the Garden Room door with Esau and stamped peoples hands. I'd been a 'proper' doorman for a year. There were tons of Psychobillies. Everyone expected a big fight. My thumpity-thump thing was going all night long. They had their own security guy with them – a big fucker from "up north." He had a bag. He opened it and showed me. It was full of truncheons and clubs. Fantastic… Fenech, the founder of the group came to say hello. The Meteors then disappeared. To me they seemed to spend a lot of time getting ready in the kitchen behind the Garden Room. I found out later that their prep involved straws and a lot of sniffing.

They came out and played. The Wreckin Crew went into a frenzy. It was nuts. There wasn't an iota of trouble. It was so shockingly quiet after all the expectations that me and Esau got bored and wandered up to Trevor who was standing in reception. As we walked up there were a number of female staff hanging about. Course, I'd flirted with all of them! One by one they all said "hello Jeff." I was surprised. "Good looking…

innit" said Esau and Trevor in unison. I guess my reputation was moving in a different direction by now.

I was there at the encore. Fenech asked what song the Crew wanted them to play. "Joe 90" someone shouted. The chant went out... "Joe 90... Joe 90... Joe 90." What the hell is that? I thought. Fenech hummed and hawed for a bit. "We don't usually play that one live" he said "but..." and then they started... Joe 90... da dada dum de de dada. I went and secretly bought that one as well.

Fenech (1985)
Picture Courtesy of the Internet

The very next day (Sunday) was the hotel New Year come Christmas staff party. The place was a thriving business then and there were a lot of staff. I only knew the four from the Centre Bar. Coulton asked me to cover it. Esau and Trevor couldn't make it so he asked Romrig. I wasn't surprised when he didn't turn up. I stood there alone. A guy I knew as John BB, came up to me. He was a chunky, bespectacled geezer. "By yourself?" he asked. "Don't worry – any trouble and I'll help you." Where had I heard that before? One of the barman, who I vaguely recognised came in fancy dress. Someone had played a trick on him. He was the only one who had dressed up. His name was Mohammed, commonly known as Slim.

It was the first time I'd ever really spoken to him. He had a large, round Moroccan face – replete with hook nose, thick black hair and was yet another one with a silly moustache. I grinned at his costume and said hello. He grinned back. "Hello" he said. He had a thick Moroccan accent. Everything he said ended on a high note so hello actually came out as hell…ooohh.

All went well. I could hear music from the function room but I kept out of the way, standing in reception. It was a Sunday night and I had my full time job the next day. I was bored. Then some chunky geezer with long mousy hair and a small entourage appeared. "Oh… sorry" I said in my squeaky voice. "We're closed. It's a private party." He wasn't impressed – maybe it was the voice. He gave me a dark look. "We've been invited" he growled. I didn't recognise any of them. Not him. Not the girl with him. No one. He moved into reception. His entourage followed.

I'd made a mistake. I was still relatively inexperienced. I could have stopped them in the doorway. John BB and the duty manager, who turned out to be his wife and was called Frances, came and stood behind me. Coulton hovered in the background and then all hell broke loose. The guy went berserk screaming "Steve… Steve… Steve." I leapt at him and shoved him through the door. I felt someone trying to pull me down from behind. I was off balance and fell over and got a heel on my temple for my efforts. I still have the mark. You can see it when I get hot. I remember scrambling back to my feet, turning round and grabbing whoever was behind me and throwing them head first into the doorjamb. It was the girl. I genuinely hadn't realised.

I looked round. Frances BB was lying on the floor with her hand over her eye. John BB was groping around on the floor. So much for back up. The guy was in the doorway still yelling "Steve." The girl was on the floor. The man in the doorway suddenly went apeshit. He started smashing his hand into the reinforced glass of the doorway. Bang... bang... bang... My eye hurt. My temple throbbed. At some point I'd also been punched in the face but was so scared I hadn't even noticed it. It was the first time I'd ever received a blow.

It seemed like only seconds to me. The next thing the police had arrived. Flashing blue billies, the lot. Door basher and his mates were arrested straight away and off they all went. I didn't know what to do. The police came in and asked us for statements. Most of the hotel staff had filled reception. Slim was standing there trying to look tough in his fancy dress. "Don't give them one" hissed the boss. I had no idea why.

Turns out that our Mr. Coulton had actually invited this guy. He just hadn't bothered to tell me – and you thought he was reliable. Door bashers name turned out to be Steve and he was the son of one of Leicesters own Crazy Gang – a notorious group of hard men. The girl I'd pushed to the floor turned out to be his sister. Not only that, but their younger brother Craig had was a regular at the Centre Bar and had worked as a barman at Helsinkis until they discovered he was under age and given him the boot.

In 2009 Craig told me he quit the Helsinki after one of the male bosses pinched his arse, apparently quite a traumatic experience. I don't know the real truth. Never-the-less. Talk about close knit world in those days. BTW: Even I had sussed he was very young and tried to stop him from going in to work one night. I relented when he told me he was a barman there. Amazing that no one at Helsinkis realised at first.

By not giving a statement I made it hard for the police to act. I understand these things a lot better now. We were later told that the sister got charged with carrying a knife. The police were supposed to have found it in her bag. Remember – I had my back to her. The sister has her own version of events and has expressed her unhappiness at what I've written here, but I can only write what I remember and what I was told. The bit about the knife may well be some of the bullshit we were fed at the time.

The police claimed that Steve door basher and his crew were pressing charges against me but I simply didn't believe them so to avoid any more hassle for any of us I came up with a garbled tale and told the police that the confusion was because door bashers name was Steve and so was our managers. As far as I know Steve door basher got off scot free.

I went back to the Centre Bar to work the following Friday. The steroids had worked their magic. My black eye had virtually completely healed. Frances BB also sported a black eye. She'd been knocked flat by Craigs sister. Allegedly John BB had rushed in to save his wife and his glasses had been knocked off in the melee so he'd felt lost. Frances couldn't believe I mended so fast.

Louise came in with Julie that weekend. She was all excited because her parents had put an announcement about her 18th birthday in the Mercury. I was excited because Louise had come in. No one noticed my eye – not even me. I saw Craig that night as I stood on the door. He was a bit wary around me. I had no idea it had been his family involved in the punch up and didn't know what was up so asked him. He told me. He was pencil thin then with dyed, jet black hair, although he sometimes had a Mohawk, and had a voice that was higher pitched and squeakier than mine. He also told me that his sister had found John BB's glasses and held on to them for safekeeping. She'd returned them the following day. According to her the whole night had been 'fun'. I laughed. More relief than anything.

I was worried about retribution. Then, when nothing happened for a week and my nerves were just about getting back to normal, the head barman at Helsinkis came running down to us as we were getting the last of our regulars out. He was another Steve. A nice guy, early 20's with had a small lisp. He was all of a lather.

"Can thu helfp quick!!??" he pleaded with us. "What's up?" I asked. "We'fve got big trovble." Now, bear in mind that all of us had worked at Helsinkis. We all knew him. We all liked it there. We'd all had fun. On top of that both Esau and Trevor, but not

142

me, liked a fight now and then. "Okay" I said unhurriedly. "Let us just finish up here."

At 10 past eleven the three of us walked out of the reception door and, in a line, headed the 10 seconds across the road towards Helsinkis. Our blood was up. We looked massive. Sadie was there that night. She had been down to the Centre Bar with the Snotty Fox in tow but had hardly ever spoken to me after the glare. Even she came up later and told me we looked like 3 of the hardest, meanest, scariest life savers she had ever seen.

I led the way through Helsinkis door. The coat stand was empty. Kirpal and Paul, my replacements, looked small and scared. The place had about 20 townies in there. They were refusing to leave. The bar staff were all crowded at the end of the bar as far away from the group as possible. Tony was there as well. I saw his eyes. He looked panic stricken.

The three of us walked straight up to them. "Time to leave" I said in my toughest, girly voiced tome. "Time to leave" echoed Esau with his rather deeper West Indian twang. They all looked at each other. "We're waiting for our mates in the loo" one of them said. We didn't budge. Trevor turned round and, by himself, went up the stairs to the toilets where we'd caught the guys trying to shoot up and marched in. Two minutes later he was using the finger in the cheek technique again and two or three lads came tumbling down. Trevor shoved them straight out. Incredibly brave or stupid – depending on how you look at it.

Me and Esau crowded in on the group. They looked at each other nervously and simply walked out. Later that night someone put a brick or two through Helsinkis windows. I've got a good idea who it was. Tony continued his practise of not speaking to me and never said thank you. Oh well.

I don't think Kirpal or Paul ever worked a door again. The next time I looked Mel and Tony had hired some agency guys. Two of them were hanging around the door. One of them turned out to be a guy called Victor who was one of Cefus' many brothers and the other was some huge, hulking guy I didn't know. I later found out his name was Phil.

That weekend we decided we needed to go from 3 to 4 doormen. Not because of the trouble at the staff party or fear because of retributions from the events at Helsinkis. The place was just so busy that we felt we couldn't cope properly.

18

Lots of Bottle

Even though it's clear that events were causing me to toughen up, it's more than fair to say that I was still quite easily intimidated. I kept remembering Big Johns words at Sugars Gym. Bottle. Lots of bottle.

The trick as a doorman is to not let your fear show. **ANY** doorman who says he isn't feeling it at some point in his career is **ABSOLUTELY LYING!** You just have keep it all under wraps and make any 'opponent' that you may come across think he's under more stress than you. Although I don't particularly like the way a lot of writers, such as Geoff Thompson, portray their adventures Thompson did write a small, 10 minute screenplay called Bouncers which starred Ray Winstone.

There's one small part of it that really captured how I felt a lot during my early years. Winstone's character has just ejected some idiot who then pulls a knife. Winstone then just calmly lights a cigarette – which would never have happened – and asks the knife wielding tosser to "step into the arena." The guy with the knife doesn't know how to react and eventually runs away screaming about how all doormen are cowards and he'll kill them all later etc, etc. A lot of people used to do that to all of us. I suppose it made them feel 'big'.

Many years into the role I had asked one ginger haired guy with a London accent to leave a downstairs function for some forgotten reason. He just wandered up a flight of stairs and out with me and Slim, who had moved from barman to doorman by then, idly trailing 10 or more feet behind, chatting away and taking no notice. As he got to the door in reception he turned round and, quite out of the blue, screamed "it took two of you to chuck ME out." I was startled but also a little goaded so instead of saying nothing I told him "don't flatter yourself mate." He asked me what I'd just said so I took the opportunity to repeat it. Twice. He looked stumped, shut his mouth, turned back round and walked out into the street. I knew I'd probably made a mistake but at least he was outside and that was the only goal. The trouble was that once the cold air hit him I think the booze in his system got into full flow because he spent the next 10 minutes screaming "come on then bouncer boys" and kicking at the windows before he staggered away. We just looked at him, rolling our eyes in amusement. I think he eventually realised that we didn't give a shit and staggered off, presumably to upset someone else.

The subtext of Thompsons screenplay has Winstone talking about how his part in the little knife dance included a lot of self-bravado, about how his were legs shaking with fear and the fear clawing its way up to his stomach. For me, that part of the storyline is so very true. I would hate it if I could sense trouble brewing. The nerves would claw at me, making my hair stand on end and my teeth jangle. The thumpity-thumps would start. In many ways it was always much better if we were just standing there, an argument broke out and we dived in to sort it. No time to think and no time to get nervous. This was the Centre Bar and it didn't happen very often but it did happen.

I'd only just gone from the occasional night to being a regular at the bar when Coulton came running up. I was by myself. I can't remember but I assume Romrig hadn't turned up. Coulton screwed up his face. "These two" he shouted, pointing at two townies who had crept in unnoticed "out now." I was surprised and still a bit of a novice then so was a bit slower to react than I should have been. If you believe everything he said, Coulton had been a bit of a hell raiser himself on the quiet in his younger days. He was always going on about the size of his hands and getting you to touch the scar under his hair. I'm sure he loved it.

As I stood there transfixed Coulton leant forward and grabbed one of them by the collar and heaved. I don't know who was more surprised, me or the lad. His arm went up and his beer went flying all over me. By the time I got my nerves under control and my feet working and moved to grab the other one Coulton was already through the doors and pulling his captive up the stairs by the Garden Room. The other guy looked at me with wet beer stains all over my jacket, raised his eyebrows, gave a half shrug and just left. I didn't have to do a thing. The boss shoved his guy out into the street while the other one lamely followed. Not a word or cry from either of them. Worked for me.

Once he was sure they were wandering off Coulton turned on his heels and marched back down to the bar. I shuffled down behind him. Who knows what Coulton was thinking but I was pissed off by getting soaked, mainly because of the stench of stale beer which made me heave. The boss was fuming for an eternity. Boiling with rage.

As I tried to towel myself dry, I asked him who they were and what had happened. "They were being rude to some friends of mine" was all he said. If they really were – I didn't notice – and I had been standing right next to them. Maybe it was something else because the next week Coulton told me that these same two lads had been caught breaking into his barely functional pale blue Escort from where he used to illegally park it on the pavement right outside the revolving doors. I guess it was prime nicking area.

Not long after I was trying to clear the bar by myself just as a lad decided he wanted to start playing on the one armed bandit. He had a crowd of about 8 or 10 or more around him all watching. My heart rate increased – the notorious Baby Squad! I had no idea how they had got in or how long they'd been in there. I asked them again and again as politely as I could to make it their last go so that we could close. The lad playing the damn thing just sneered at me. Some of his mates wandered off but the rest were just hanging about. I was getting ready for world war 3. I remembered Daz and the mess they made of him and the slash on Rich's hand at Tipplers and then, just as I felt it was about to start, they just got fed up with my witterings and left.

Thank god for that. I didn't mess about. I quickly shut all the doors to the bar and me and Louisa, the barmaid started to lock up, then I realised that I hadn't locked the outside doors so went up the stairs by the Garden Room and straight into the entire mob of the Squad still lingering about in the street. I nearly died.

One of them peeped through the open doorway and asked me if I'd got a light and I mumbled a "no." Then he laughed. He must've seen the fear in my eyes and taken pity. "No need to be so scared mate" he chuckled and they all wandered off towards town, having a good giggle at my expense.

Louisa was right behind me but she obviously had no idea what was going on. She wanted to go home as much as anyone so she just shut the doors on my back and started to lock them. I was trapped outside right in the middle of a group of the worst gang in the city. Oh... my... god.

I pushed through the group and dived back inside through the revolving doors and locked them behind me as fast as I could. Good job they'd been open but those things could be bloody difficult to lock at the best of times and were especially difficult when your hands were shaking. I'm sure I touched cloth. The Squaddies were all looking at me but I did it and was soon behind some cover. Lucky, lucky man.

Because of incidents like that, at that time I still thought that peoples appearance and their behaviour were related. From Force 8 onwards it was being drummed into me that townies mean trouble, skinheads are pains in the arse and that Goths and the like are no problem at all. Of course, I came to understand that's absolute crap. There's a normal sort of distribution amongst all these groups. I just think the townies had or have much more of a bad reputation because their numbers are so much bigger than any of the other groups and, consequently, stories of trouble coming from them were much more available to be passed, and exaggerated, from doorman to doorman, usually in the doormans favour of course.

After we ejected the two townies and the incident with the Squad I made it my business to do what I should always have done. Weigh up every person I ever saw approach a door. I probably had little else to fill my mind. On Sunday nights I used to drive round to my grandmas house to pick her up and take her to my mums place for a few hours. I'd look at everyone as I drove past and decide. Were they a townie? Would they cause me a problem if I met them on the door? How would I handle them? What would I say? How would I grab them if I had to? Now, this might seem bizarre behaviour now but I pictured myself struggling with these people and always winning – never losing.

Years later I discovered Neuro Linguistic Programming (NLP) and the power of positive thinking and realised that I'd built into my head a pattern of success. Always winning battles never, ever being defeated. I never did really lose a real battle, although I did come close and ultimately did get pretty badly injured.

My fixation on peoples appearances was a bit much at times and did end up giving me some unnecessarily anxious moments. That ended the night I was leaning in the alcove at the bottom of the spiral staircase in the Centre Bar when a skinhead and his mates came in. I'd already had a scare when the Mr. Peters signal had gone out right at the start of the night and I couldn't find the guy causing the problem because of my eyesight. Coulton virtually had to lead me by the hand!

I couldn't have been working there for very long. I know it was after the townies and the Squad and that there was no Romrig and no Sharon to talk to. The skinhead came in when the bar was pretty busy, but still not packed and was in a small group of 4 or 5. They were standing so close to me I could have stretched out my arm and touched them. This guy in particular got my attention. He was only a young guy, thin and was wearing all the standard skinhead regalia. They all were. My thumpity-thumps started.

I think the worst bit about his appearance in my mind was that he had a tattoo on the back of his neck of all the four aces from a deck of cards. Despite his appearance he was quiet and just drinking merrily. I couldn't help it. I felt the thumpity-thumps getting worse. I looked at my feet and wiped imaginary smudges off my glass. Remember – Lots and lots of bottle and **MOST** important – give them absolutely no clue what-so-ever. After about 10 minutes he turned round and looked at me. I raised my head and looked him in the eyes as best as I could. My heart had frozen. I was sure he had felt my eyes on his back and trouble was coming. He smiled. "Cheer up mate" he grinned. "I know it's a boring job but someone's got to do it. Anyway... someone the size of you is going to have no problem with the people you get in here." I couldn't help it. I smiled back. Relief oozed through me from my head down. In one fell swoop my views of how people looked and any associated behaviour they carried with them changed. He'd been as anxious about me as I had about him. What a relief! I was truly, truly shocked. I'd like to thank him. I don't ever remember seeing him down there again.

Maybe my appearance did scare him away forever but it was always busy in those days so who knows. Shortly after Trevor's girlfriend of the time came down and said something almost identical about my size and coping with the people in the bar. I have to say, words like that always made me very happy more because I hated to be thought of as small than absolutely anything else. It's no wonder I liked taking steroids.

After that I was only really, really scared by appearances of dogs, and I do mean the canine variety. Me and dogs have an understanding. You can't fake your bottle with dogs. Bloody things. I keep out of their way and they keep out of mine. I'm not as bad as I was, having been given some training by a dog handler in the late 90's but until then the appearance of a dog... any dog used to scare the hell out of me. I think terrify is more appropriate.

To put it into perspective, Kingy from Sugars, had a dog he used to take into the gym from time to time. It was one of those Rhodesian Ridgebacks, a hairless African jobbie that I've been told are used to chase any stray lions away, although maybe the guy who told me that did it on purpose to scare me even more. Even the mighty Kingy had trouble controlling it and I have a vivid memory of him roaring at it and straining to hold it back as he stood in Sugars reception. I'm sure everyone was a little scared. Make no mistake – I did a runner back to the changing rooms and never went remotely close to it. Everyone around pissed themselves laughing at me, even the fucking dog laughed.

I'm positive this fear stems from the time one chased me up the street when I was a very young kid after I went to pick up my football. Why? Simply because I remember it so well. My dad was scared of dogs too. Just for your info I'm also scared of heights. Good job I'm not very tall.

Esau had a big brown Rottweiler of all things which made an appearance a few times over the years. The first time was when I used to pick him up to go to Helsinkis. It was a young pup then and bounded into the living room as I sat there playing with his kids. Esau followed it in, took one look at my white face and big eyes, grinned the grin and dragged it out by the head. I let out a loud and stinky parp. His kids looked at me. They didn't get it. I know one of them asked me what I was so scared about. I probably almost managed a smile.

As for the parping, luckily I was, allegedly, the adult so I just blamed the kids for the smell when Esau came back in. I don't think he believed me though. The next time I saw it was about 3 or so years later. We'd heard that one of the many football crews were in town spoiling for a fight so Esau brought it down to the bar for additional protection while I stayed on the other side of the room all night and let the damn thing bare its teeth at everyone. In reality I think it was as soft as shit.

BTW: If the football mob were around they certainly didn't make it down to us.

The final time was when Esau pulled up in his car. He had gone from the hotel by then. We had just finished our shift and were probably off to the Studio nightclub for a bit. He stopped and got out followed too bloody quickly by this salivating, huge monster. I was already in the street when he arrived so had nowhere to go. I was terrified and started backing off – really, really quickly. The dog looked at me and started to follow. I was trapped. I didn't know what to do so started to walk back towards it which, I've learned since is a real no, no. It stopped and stared. I stared back. I tried to smile. My eyes were as wide as they could get. It growled and I'm sure it licked its lips. I think it was looking for an additional meal. Oh shiiitttt. Esau let it glare at me for an eternity. Okay then, a few seconds before calling it back and it went off with a sullen glare and foam drooling from its mouth. I looked at Esau. Guess what he did. Yep. I got the grin. The others were all watching and laughed. I let out a few parps. I don't know how I was breathing. I dived for the Studio. It's amazing what the safety of the big closed doors does for your ego. On reflection – I *may* be exaggerating about the dog a *teeny* bit here.

19

A Numba Wan or a Numba Two?

We went through a lot of different doormen going from 3 to 4 at the Centre Bar. I can't remember them all. Trevor had got bored and left. I would guess it was due to not enough action – either in the love department or the fisticuffs department. It's no wonder doormen have a terrible reputation.

In February 1985 there had stood Lloyd. I think it was his first door job. Trevor that got him in there. They were best mates. I turned up and there he was. A Trevor doppelganger. About my height, welder by day, couple of kids, red belt in Taekwondo, a few years older, big eyes, liked to drink the odd short, moustache, curly permed hair and fancy shoes. Boy, did Lloyd have a lot of different shoes.

I wasn't at all bothered that Trevor had seen Coulton without telling me and that he had gone ahead and hired him, mainly because Lloyd and me hit it off straight away. Being Trevor's younger brother, Esau already knew him and would often take the piss and call Lloyd goggle eyed. Lloyd would just smile and tell Esau to fuck off. We had a great laugh.

The fourth man kept changing. There was Pete from Sugars who was the guy who had adjusted Roys nose. He turned up in a shabby shirt, jeans and no socks. He spent all night telling me I was too aggressive... Me!! Coulton paid him less than I'd said the money would be. I remembered what he'd done to Roy. There was no way I was getting into strife with him. Guess where the additional money came from.

Then there was Martin another West Indian, quietly spoken and with a scruffy beard, Abdul, a shaven headed Iranian and Ernest who was Franklins brother. After them came Robert and Stedroy of the 'F' clan, a guy with a beard who used to be the head doorman at the Palais, a curly haired mate of Coultons who was a motor mechanic, a half caste martial arts expert called Paul and his best mate, an ex military Red Cap called Kevin who was a Stinki / Centre Bar regular that I'd got to know and then there was Tam – a big, burly Scottish geezer the boss had met on holiday.

Tam was a very interesting guy. He was quiet, polite, kind, sometimes worked as a waiter as well as a doorman and… er… turned out to be a very tough and well known Glaswegian hard man. At first I'd had no idea. Coulton just said to me "I've got a guy to help. He's Scottish and his name's Tam." I shook his hand and asked him a little about his experience as a doorman – really expecting him to say not a lot. I was wrong. He told me a lot about his history, including the fact that his real name was Thomas – something he rarely revealed, especially to a wee, pasty faced Sassenach like me.

Tam had a wispy Scottish accent that didn't fit him at all. His favourite story was about shiny shoes. Black patent leather pairs were all the rage then. I had some. Unsurprisingly, so did Lloyd.

In Tam's version of events he'd been working the door at some place in Glasgow when things had got out of hand. It had ended in a mass brawl with all the doormen taking a kick at some guy they'd wrestled to the floor. The bloke had escaped and run to get the police. Problem was he was so drunk and in such a state that he didn't really know what had happened so all he kept shouting was "shiny shoes! … shiny shoes!" in reference to the feet he seen around his head. Apparently the police thought he was crazy. Make up your own mind time again.

Tam lasted about 2 months before going back to Scotland. He was one of the few ever revolving fourth man that I really respected. I even managed to accidentally stand on his foot one night. "Mai corns" he shouted. Shit. I looked up, full of apology and then I noticed he was smiling as he said it. I missed him when he left. During that time I never did find out his surname or what became of him.

When we couldn't get a doorman we'd use anyone. We got a bloke called David to cover one night. He had a massive arse. Much bigger than mine and was the brother of Coulton's girlfriend at the time. He was just an extra head, not a doorman at all. I made it my duty that night to scare the shit out of him with tales of doorman horror just like Bespectacled Dave had done to me at Force 8. It worked. He never did it again.

In the end we even had fun dressing up Neil from the chalk board incident in Helsinkis in Nigels jacket, my tie, some black plimsoles and a little woolly hat and had him standing at the bottom of the spiral staircase.

Neil used to make me laugh. He was gap-toothed, from somewhere in the rough arse part of London with a massive bat tattooed on the side of his noggin and at the time worked as a scrap burner at Frank Berry's scrap yard near Filbert Street. It's not there now. It's a mixture of a housing estate and the new Leicester City football stadium. I think him and Red Cap Kevin were mates but I'm a little cloudy. I do know that a guy called Austin used to hang around with Kevin. I liked Austin but he sadly succumbed to cancer and died of a related illness at a very young age. At the time I'd heard he was ill but had no idea he'd died until much, much later when I casually asked one of the Psychobilly's how he was doing.

They all dressed in the same vein but Neil particularly liked to wear a big military great coat in winter, studded belts, military boots and was covered in tattoos. To top it all off he had a completely shaven pate except for his extremely long, blonded quiff that stuck out about 4 or more inches in front of his nose. He told me that when it wasn't all lacquered up it came down below his chin. He didn't have the bat on his head when I first met him. The first time he turned up with it done me and Esau looked on in astonishment. I asked him why and he shrugged. In the end he told us it wasn't quite what he wanted but it would do. It would have been bloody hard to get rid of!

One clear recollection is the sight of him drinking from the slops bucket one Christmas and loving it – ugh!! A second is of him having a fight in the street, taking off his studded belt and wrapping it around his hand to use as a weapon only for it to break and his opponent then using it on him. He refused to get his head fixed and had a visible dent for months afterwards. I even remember he drank some red coloured snake bite stuff. So toxic you shat your liver out the next day.

Neil was generally not too bad but he had his moments in there. I do have a vision of him causing trouble when friends of his were playing a gig in the Garden Room. A very inexperienced group called The Tools had played first. They'd played at the bar a few times and I'd often chatted to them but they'd never played to such a big crowd before and were having so much fun that they over ran their set. Neil got all upset that he was kept waiting for his mates to play and climbed up onto the stage to... um... offer some encouragement. The poor lads playing were scared shitless. I calmed it all down with a laugh and a joke. Poor old Neil had to go and apologise.

Neil's girlfriend was Shaz. Someone else once described her to me as a big, tall blonde, scary looking woman. I remember seeing her in town one Saturday morning just after I left Helsinkis and she said hi. I was still very shy then and didn't know whether to run and hide or smile. I think I did both!

In the end, after a medical where Neil told me his piss sample came out just like a badly poured pint, he joined the Paras and came down a couple of times in his combats. He was much quieter. I guess the army did him a fair bit of good. I wonder if he's still there. Doubt it. He'd be in his 40's now. I wonder if he regrets the bat on his head.

Sometime doorman Red Cap Kevin had been around since I was at Helsinkis so I'm not quite sure when or for how long he actually was a Red Cap. He was about my age, maybe a little younger, stocky, flattop. I found him a really friendly guy. Prior to him working for me he'd come up to me one night in the toilet corridor. The bar had been packed. Knee deep to get a drink. The staff used a door in that corridor to get to the bar and usually left it wide open. Kevin stood there with his girlfriend as I walked by. "Do you think they'll serve me from here?" he asked with a grin. "Give it a try" I replied and, yep, sure enough, he called them over, ordered his drinks and they served him. One way round queueing I suppose.

Neil, Kevin and the incredibly quiet Richard from Helsinkis weren't the only ones that were in the army at some point. A little chap called Keith, who also dressed as a Psychobilly joined up as well. Unfortunately he hated it, went AWOL and did a runner back to Leicester where he hid for about 2 years before the army finally caught up with him. As far as I know he took his punishment and spent some time in a military prison. Red Cap Kevin told me how hard those places were.

Prior to joining up Keith was always in there from about the age of 16. I'd first met him at Helsinkis where he came up one night and I wouldn't let him in because he was obviously too young. He showed me his older brothers ID which was pretty stupid because his brother went in there as well and I knew his face but I relented and let him in anyway.

Keith managed to piss Esau off at the Centre Bar by saying something stupid. I have no idea what he said. Esau spent the next few minutes tossing the guy into the wall, punching him in the ribs as he fell down and then throwing him into the wall again. I cringed and told him to pack it in but Keith was pretending to be tough and trying to make out he was enjoying the 'fun'. It only stopped when Esau finally got bored and Keith made a very fast – and painful – exit. He came back the next week but very warily stepped round Esau.

At the end of January '85 it had snowed horribly. That weekend we had an influx of ex-Paras in there under the guise of a sky diving club. I thought they were all nutters. They used to come every year. Having completed my own tandem skydive in 2003 – I'm sure they were all nutters. I remember one who was well over 6' tall hanging off the bar while he stood next to Sharons legs. I was worried he'd lose it and do something stupid. He didn't. I rescued her and made sure she spent the rest of the night talking to me. She seemed more than happy to come over. I guess it was the free drink she got in return.

At the end of the night she asked me to drive her to her sisters house in the snow. Apparently she got more dole if she claimed she lived there. I refused. Hey, the snow was BAD. The more time I spent with Sharon, the more she opened up. Some of it was funny, like the time she went on and on about not being able to put anything but silver through her nose and how you could get high by snorting the fumes from an empty hairspray can but some of it was pretty unsavoury to me. She was always going on about having 666 – the mark of the devil on her head. Weird.

Later she started to tell me about her adventures with a couple of guys and the time she was caught in a car they had stolen. Then she went on about the time she thought one of them had got her pregnant. I didn't really want to know.

Another time I found Sharon wandering aimlessly around the bar. She was stoned out of her box. I took time and energy to drip feed her orange juice to bring her round. I think I even missed my kiss from Louise that night. After I got her functional, and it took a lot of orange juice, she called Louise a "fucking c*nt" for not looking after her stuff, said "ta" to me and then got me to run her home in the Samba. As soon as she could she leapt out of my car, so fast one of her high heeled shoes came off, and buggered off down the street shoe in hand – leaving me alone.

Around then she was sharing a platonic relationship, living in a flat with a tall, very thin guy called Richard who eventually played with Crazyhead. That night I assume she ran back to the safety of her room. I started to feel a bit used. I always was a bit dopey.

The bar was getting busier than ever and the clientele more and more outrageous in their dress sense and more open in their conversations with us. We loved it.

A girl called Helen, a nurse, who was Richard Crazyheads girlfriend at the time came in. I remember she usually wore glasses but this night she was holding a hand over one eye. "I've lost a contact lens" she screamed at me above the music.

We all spent the next 5 minutes searching around on our hands and knees in the half light for it.

For kicks we'd stop people at the doorway and tell them they had to wipe their feet before they could come in. Some told us to get stuffed, some laughed and – bizarrely – some actually did it, telling us how fussy we were in the process.

I was so taken in by it all I even dyed my hair jet black in the August. My hair was far too curly to try and coax into a flattop. I had asked Romrig once and he'd told me there was no chance. My mum, never one to hold back was horrified at my appearance. "You look like a prostitute!" she screamed at me.

I went on another trip to Paris for the usuals this time with ex-Para Chris the next week. We got plenty of stares. A couple of big, tough looking guys. One with short, jet black hair. I had it all cut off at some place in Coventry couple of weeks later. Right down to the bone to get rid of the black. The barber made some sarcastic comment.

When I got back to the bar a girl who sang for a band called Corpus Christie came in with white face, big back hair, black lipstick and full on whip on her hip and Neil begged her to use it on him. I'd caught her once at Helsinki spraying the name of her band in gold all over the walls. Chrissie had tried to get me to throw her out but, as usual, I fancied her so I hadn't really tried too hard and pretended I didn't know who was leaving all the graffiti. When Neil fell to his knees in front of her there was nothing she could do but laugh. We all laughed with her. I think that the fact we never laughed at them was a great source of comfort and a sense of feeling at home. It really worked well.

I also recall a girl who always dressed like Cruella Di Ville, including the hair, the flowing black tails and, probably, the monocle, although I can't remember. Then there was an extremely pretty girl called Suzy who came in one October 31st with full on Goth white faced war paint, crimped red hair with a big bow in it while wearing a white wedding dress. I asked her why she was wearing the dress and she told me "well... it is Halloween."

Suzy was in there most weekends and spent a lot of time with a tall, thin geezer dressed in combats or black (weren't they all?) mostly with long black, spiky hair but sometimes with a shaven pate and a long pony tale, who went by the name of Ayesha. His real name was Carl.

Ayesha (Carl)
Picture Courtesy Suzy Sissons

A year or so before the Halloween dress I had seen her follow Carl into the loos one night and was suspicious so I quietly trailed. The toilets. Everything from sex and drugs to rock and roll went on in there. For all I knew Carl and Suzy were going for a crafty shag. Even in my mind that was a step too far. I know for sure that it had happened with other couples before. Oh no. It was all perfectly innocent between these two.

Suzy was just standing and chatting away while Carl stood half turned to face her while he was at one of the urinals one hand on percy. In the end I stammered to her "I think you'd better wait outside." They both grinned at me. I think I was the most embarrassed of the three of us. I later found out Suzy was 15 at the time. Did I stop either of them coming in? What do you think?

I understand that Carl got hit by a passing vehicle while he was busy moving house or crossing the road or something like that about 15 or so years ago. These stories vary depending on who tells them. Anyway, he died as a result of his injuries.

The Wedding Dress
Picture Courtesy Suzy Sissons

Apart from the rather voyeuristic peeing one of the oddest things I ever witnessed in those damn toilets was a flat topped, leather jacketed guy standing at the urinals with a pint in one hand and his willie in the other. He supped and peed in unison. It was a kind of in one end – out the other scenario. I also did a quick check in the gents one night and found the floor flooded. Everybody was standing in pee to have a pee, so to speak. The ladies had nice orange seats in them but really weren't that much better and we often rushed in there on rumours of drugs, sex or both. Despite the mess these loos could get in, truly, not one word of complaint from anybody. This crowd were mostly lovely people.

Because the bar was situated in a hotel there were other toilets spread all over the place. Anyone could use them. The toilets upstairs sprung a leak one winter and black water started to cascade down into the bar right on top of one of the tables. The room was full again and the girls sitting round the table directly under the downpour always sat there. Because it was winter they had a brolly so they just put it up and stayed put. I didn't have the heart to tell them the water wasn't quite pure. It stunk. How on earth they couldn't tell.

During all of this I continued to manipulate the changeovers so that I could get my kiss from Louise. "We know what you're up to" Esau said to me. Now, for all of those that have sussed it... yep... I desperately wanted to take my relationship with her further. For those that didn't – d'oh. I think she *may* have wanted to as well for a very short while.

I was so jealous of any other boyfriends she had. I remember one night she was running round the bar organising a group summer holiday to somewhere exotic. She never came near or by me. I was upset and told her. "Oh... sorry" she smiled. In the end I heard a lot about what went on in that holiday from Sharon.

For a time I know Louise went out with Gavin, the same one that moaned about Simons DJaying. I can remember them getting to the top of the stairs when she realised that she'd left her mittens on one of the bench seats. I was busy closing up but she asked me if I could nip downstairs and find them. Course, I knew exactly where they'd be sitting. At that time anyone else, absolutely anyone, I'd have told to get lost, but she smiled at me and that was it. What a softie there really was under that steroidal physique with the jacket and tie.

Despite my feelings I never took it any further. Chronic shyness. Infatuation with the attention from Sharon. The story of the holiday or the toilets. Who knows? It was entirely my fault.

I talked to my training partner Lew about Sharon but kept my feelings for Louise from him. He told me "you're in lust." Maybe I liked legs like toothpicks. Louise was *just* 17 when I first met her. I was *just* 23. Very, very young. In the end we both moved on and Louise eventually met and married the late Darren, a lovely lad with bright eyes and a blond flattop and they had four kids together.

A few years later she had come into the bar by herself. I have no idea where Darren was. I scurried over, pleased to see her and tried to spark up a conversation. She gave me a glare and frostily told me "the problem with you is that you think we're the same people... and we're not." To be honest it cut me in half. I turned away, tail between my legs. I hardened my heart and head as was my practise by then if anything hurt me and, on purpose, never spoke to her again. I think I only ever saw her once after that when I vaguely waved to her as she sat in Helsinkis by herself.

As 1985 progressed a strange thing happened. I was outside the Garden Room. I was by myself for some reason. Two teenagers made their way out. Joy and Maria. One Thursday night, in the very early days, we'd been covering some promotion when it had been really quiet in the bar. Joy and her boyfriend had been pretty much the only ones in there dancing on the tiny dance floor when Coulton let off some dry ice for his own amusement. Joy then spent the next two minutes or so coughing and harmlessly trying to flap it away before they both retreated to the toilets for... er... respite!

Romrig was still there at this point and had found them getting a bit, how can I put this, intimate in there. He'd tried to throw them out. Joy claimed she was only cutting her boyfriends hair and, with Romrig seething in the background, I dismissed it. Joy always spoke to me after that and I even went out with her one night.

Maria was one of her mates, short and very pretty with an angular chin and nose. I'm sure anyone reading this will soon realise I thought MOST of them were very pretty. Ho hum.

That night as Joy and Maria left I stepped back to let them pass. They walked towards me. I backed off. They forced me backwards to a corner. I didn't know what was up. I must've looked scared. "It's alright" beamed Joy. "We just want to kiss you." Hey... who am I to deny such wishes? After that I used to look round and there would be a queue of girls, mostly Goths, lining up for a kiss. "Good looking... innit" said Esau and Lloyd.

I may have spent a lot of time kissing Louise and hanging round with Sharon but secretly I was becoming Jeff the "Goth magnet". I wonder what they thought. They probably didn't care. I have to say that none of this was ever intended or planned. It just happened.

Joy (and Peter)
Picture Courtesy Haley Wiggins

We moved through the whole of 1985 that way. A new word had emerged. Alternative. I lived for the weekends, took steroids, was a bastard any other time, trained at Sugars Gym, kissed Louise, chatted to Sharon, hugged and kissed plenty of Goths and even some of the hotel staff, listened to bands that played in the Garden Room, secretly crept in and bought more records from the shop near the clock tower, constantly wiped black lipstick from my cheek and mouth...

For the most part there was still no trouble. The doormen would stand there all night and talk about nothing. I do remember asking Esau once if he was carrying a weapon. Following my own earlier stupidity I wanted to make sure the guys I was working with were all clean. He balled up his big brown fists and gave me the inevitable grin. "Only these." I asked him what had happened to his own bat. The one he had twirled in front of me a year or so earlier. He gave me another grin. Apparently it had been used as part of Scotsman Kevin's kidnapping exercise and was now police property! I'd never known.

I still got the thumpity-thumps from time to time but became more and more immune to the bits of trouble there were. The place was constantly packed. I even turned away a load of Hells Angels that tried to get in from the spiral staircase entrance. "Do you know who I am?" asked one of them. "No" I lied. Of course I knew him. He was a well know troublemaker around the town – fresh out of prison. He looked at me. His pals looked at me. I just stood there and smiled. They looked at each other and left. No entry, no hassle, no problems. It was a LONG way from that terrifying night at Helsinkis.

One of the Angels tried to come in by himself a few weeks later. He'd often stood chatting to Rich on Tipplers door. He was slack jawed when he saw me standing there and thought I'd let him in because we knew each other by sight. He was wrong. He even borrowed someone else's jacket and tried to sneak by a few weeks later. He was wrong again. How do I know it was someone else's jacket? Because he smiled at me, took it off and gave it back right in front of me. I just laughed.

Dread locked Simon got told off by Coulton for loudly swearing at the customers when he was playing records. He was forced to apologise over the microphone. I think it really pissed him off and he left very soon after. Shame, he was by far the best. Consequently we went through a few DJ's trying to find a good replacement and, although it was still mostly the same, the quality of the music played varied all over the place. These included Mary Byker who went on to play with Gaye Bikers on Acid and Kev Reverb, a tall thin guy with black framed glasses, who also later played alongside Richard with Crazyhead.

We went through a lot of bar staff as well staff. Slim moved from being a general barman and started working in the bar on a regular basis. A couple of Rockabilly girls, sisters, nicknamed me "Nana". We had fun. We were invited to, and went to, the odd house party. We danced on the door in the bar. Okay in my case it was more like a zombie doing the squirm.

Me and Esau used to clown around walking around in each others footsteps. Him in the lead and me less than a foot behind him. It was a bit like me and my shadow in reverse. I got one of the many bands playing down there to get the entire crowd singing happy birthday to me.

The fourth man kept changing. Lloyd wore a different pair of shoes every week. I tried to keep up but gave up in the end. He went to a flattop from the curly perm, grew and shaved off a moustache, kept telling me he was going for his black belt. He never did.

All good things have to come to an end. In my minds eye I can see the time Nigel came in with another manager, Sally. Shit. There really were a lot of managers in those days. Stand Up Straight Claire had left ages before and Sally seemed to have taken her place. They both looked a bit flushed. Nigel went round his stubby finger going up and down as he counted. He came over. "There's at least 400 people in here" he said. No shit. Four times the legal limit. "You guys have got to stop letting so many people in!!" We obliged. I see it as the beginning of the end. It was weird to turn people away.

In November that year I took my trusty SLR camera down to the bar. I liked photography and even did my own developing. Esau took a photo of me in the Garden Room. I've still got it, now faded and brown. By this time the steroids had changed my personality, the job was changing my behaviour and I was really losing my innocent looks and, even though I was having lots of fun, I was starting to look like a very tough character. That photo in particular makes me look like one of the Kray brothers henchmen. I'm wearing my jacket, a thin black leather tie and a scowl. I showed it to two of the regulars, Ken and his girlfriend Steph. They grimaced.

There's a date I stamped on the back, the November 1985, just before my 25th birthday.

And here it is
Picture Courtesy Jeff Shaw

I had tried to get ready for what I decided would be my final contest, also in November. I felt I wasn't really responding to the drugs at all physique wise but decided to give it one last go. I was training like an animal but it was all too much for my training partner Lew. He never re-appeared after a holiday abroad. One day he was always there supporting me, encouraging me, driving me and the next. Maybe it was me.

I was really, really upset. For a long time I thought he'd disappeared to the Bermuda Triangle. Recently I found that he'd just returned to his home town near the coast. Not as exotic, but equally as far away. Frustrated I abandoned my contest plans. I finally, finally realised that I'd never be Mr. Olympia. It took me years to come to terms with that. It really hurt. A double whammy. Loss of a great training partner and the ultimate, sinking, heart rendering realisation that a dream will never be. I once heard the Steve Davis talking about the night he missed the final black and lost the World Snooker Championships to that Irish bloke with the big glasses. He said that it took him 10 years to get over it. Believe me. I do know how he feels.

By Christmas the bar had really calmed down. A new Alternative nightclub called Reflections had opened just around the corner. It was just a small room with a bar that was down a side street but in the same building as the Studio. A lot of our clientele left at about 10.30pm to go there because it was cheaper to get in before 11pm. I think a few of them went early to avoid hassle from the townies queuing outside the Studio main doors. They called them Trevs or Trevors. Nothing to do with my own nose picking mate. Sometimes I had followed Sharon in there after I had finished in the Centre Bar. The trips to Rock City must've suffered because of Reflections as well. Over time two other places, the Fan Club and Sector Five cashed in on the Alternative scene and the Centre Bar suffered even more.

During that Christmas period the rest of the hotel was as mega busy as ever, with functions going on all over the place. I soon found out that there was enough trouble in those functions to keep us busy. Down in the bar we were polite and I spoke quietly, trying very hard to keep my trademark approach. It's fair to say that I tried the same upstairs but townies aren't generally as nice as the Alternative crowd. In the end we all threw out enough people to convince the management that our jobs were more than warranted but it meant we were all there, covering the whole place, until 1am or 2am. Sometimes even later.

I remember the worst was when the others had gone home but I was still there at about 5am because we'd had so much trouble. Coulton asked me to stay in the hotel and start at 8am the next day to make sure nothing happened. I just couldn't. I was knackered and quickly getting more and more exhausted with each passing night. In the end I decided that I was going to take December off from training like I had the year before, and give my body a rest from the rigours of the drugs and the gym after working so many hours. Maybe I'd respond better after a good break.

We didn't open the bar on Christmas Eve. Only because I was free and felt lost without doorwork or something to do I agreed to work that night with the guy that would eventually become my new training partner, Big M, at some trendy place called the Swinging Sporran. It was heaving. Denny was in there. She said hello and asked after my health. I was back to being deflated, white faced. Small, cold, tired. Afraid. Health wasn't too good actually.

Cefus was supposed to be there but he didn't turn up. We worked with two other guys that neither of us knew. They were more hopeless than I'd been at Force 8, and that's pretty bad. For a while we had a laugh, taking cans of people who tried to smuggle them in, with Big M shaking them as hard as he could when no one was looking so the owners would get a bit of a surprise when they popped them open. Then there was some trouble and me and M got threatened by the Baby Squad.

M always was a lot tougher than me and laughed his head off. He was still having fun. I was scared shitless. I really must buy more pairs of brown undies. The two other guys looked at each other and pooped their pants as well. They had brown ones on by this time even if they didn't start off brown. The threats were empty, meaningless and we survived. We always did. Maybe I was a bit charmed.

At the end of the night they gave me Cefus' wage packet. I was surprised. Then I found out the job had been organised through the Unit. I'd just spent the night working for Khachik! Now that was a BIG no, no so I never went back. All hell broke loose there on New Years Eve. The two other guys took a bad beating and ended up in hospital. M laughed. I fretted on their behalf.

I worked at the Centre Bar that particular New Years. We only opened the bar our normal hours. Louise came in with Julie. She was dressed as Danger Mouse and having a great time but my roving eye didn't dwell too long so I still did nothing about it and then had to stand upstairs with the others, still feeling small, weak, moody and frustrated with myself until the wee hours. Like I said, not my favourite time of the year.

We moved into early 1986. The hotel was still packed solid. Bands came and went, the Meteors came back for a second time. The big fucker from up north remembered me. I remembered his bag of tools. He still had it.

Our fourth man still rotated. I wanted to try something different from bodybuilding. Big M was very good at any sport he turned his hand to. Of course, bearing in mind my lack of any natural athletic prowess, that meant he was a much better bodybuilder than me. He started to play American Football for the Leicester Panthers and made the first team straight away. I was pretty jealous so convinced him to go with me and play for the Leicester Huntsmen on Sundays. Who you ask? And well you may.

I don't think they lasted more than one season. They were crap. I was in the right place! Then, out of the blue, I started to get torrential nosebleeds. In the gym, on the door, on the loo, driving my car. I was working when Esaus Sunday Sarah came dashing in. She'd left Helsinkis and was working down in the bar. "Someone's bleeding!" she yelled. It was me. My nose was pouring. I couldn't stop it. I stood all night on the door with blood running out in a torrent. Julie saw me and was aghast.

She had a skinny, pale faced boyfriend at the time by the name of John. She used to insist he wasn't her boyfriend. Funny that. I'd caught him once jumping across the bonnet of the Samba as he was showing off to his mates and given him the scare of his life. He rarely came near me after that. He saw me trying to mop up my blood in the loos. I was literally awash with blood. "Christ" was his only comment.

I looked in the mirror. My face was as ashen as his. By February my nose bleeds were becoming extreme. On the first Sunday we played American Football I was driving Big M and his girlfriend Carol back home when one started. He didn't drive in those days. It poured. I had to stop the car and get out. I was swallowing so much blood I was choking. A gang of Asian lads walked past and tried to help but I was so wound up and in so much distress rather than accept help I was aggressive and rude. They quickly strolled on. Poor buggers.

I jumped back in the car and drove on. Psychobilly Geoff and his skinhead girlfriend later told me they been out looking for furniture and saw us drive past. He had almost got over the night of the band and was occasionally talking to me by then. I didn't see them. I was in a bit of a hurry.

I got back to M's place and dropped him and Carol off. The bleeding wouldn't stop. I was feeling sick from swallowing so much blood and very weak. On top of that I hadn't changed out of my playing kit and both of us were pretty cold, wet and dirty. Carol and M had to wait while I went to their bathroom and stuffed toilet paper up my nose to stem the flow. Their kids just looked at me as I ran by them. Good job they didn't need to use the loo. I don't know how long it took – 5 minutes, 10? – but I managed to stem the tide for a short while, cleaned up the bathroom as best as I could and made a dash for it.

By the time I got home – another twenty or so minutes drive – my favourite brown jacket with the busted zip had turned red at the front. I had to chuck it. Gruesome. The bleeding eventually stopped about 3 or 4 hours later.

I played American Football for 2 weeks. On the second week I went to pick Big M up from his flat but neither he nor

Carol were anywhere to be seen. I was annoyed. I thought about going home but decided I'd gone half way there so made the rest of the trip by myself. What a mistake that turned out to be. We were undisciplined, badly trained. They do this thing where you stand in the middle of a circle of guys and one by one they headbutt you. It's called Bull in a Ring. It's supposed to toughen you up, get you used to being hit.

I stood there in a nylon blue shirt, with the number 65 emblazoned in yellow across the front and back, that was jammed over some borrowed defensive linesman shoulder pads, the biggest pads available. I'd bought the top from failed Helsinki doorman Renton for £15 with my first Helsinki wage packet. He told me it was an American Football shirt. Turns out it wasn't – it was a Canadian hockey shirt. Similar but smaller across the area the shoulder pads fit. Consequently it was VERY tight and hard to get on and off. This ensemble was topped off with some one else's black helmet pumped up with air to fit snugly on my head, proper blue coloured American Football trousers bought from a magazine, long white LCFC soccer socks and cheap UK soccer boots bought from Leicester market.

Soccer boots are significantly different to American Football boots. The number of studs is different and their layout is different. American ones have a toe stud which gives you good grip for all the pushing and shoving that goes on. UK soccer ones don't. I wasn't wearing any other pads. No neck roll, no rib protectors, no thigh protectors. Nothing. **ABSOLUTELY CRAZY**. By the time it came to my turn the circle had become very loose. Instead of being hit from a foot or two away I saw one guy in a green shirt take a run and fly at me horizontally. I took it full on the face mask. It broke my neck.

All I remember is a load of snot shooting out and the pumped up helmet nearly coming off. The chin strap ended up under my nose. It was a massive hit. The bloke who did it was laughing. I can't remember if it was February 4th and minus 8 or February 8th and minus four. I was on the floor. Stunned. A few guys came running up, concern all over their faces but it was so cold I didn't even feel it, told them I was okay and then carried on playing for another 4 hours. They shrugged and let me. They should have put me in a neck brace and called an ambulance.

In essence I walked away from what could have left me in a wheelchair. I was almost certainly saved by the thickness of my neck at the time, which was about 19" and the fact I had the wrong boots on so partially slipped back as I was hit.

At the end of the session I had to have help getting the shirt off to retrieve the pads. It was so tight every little move of my neck was agony. It was the first time I thought I may have been seriously hurt. My team mates wanted to cut the thing off but I wouldn't let them. I liked it. Once it was off I skipped a shower, jumped in the Samba which – eventually – warmed up and by the time I got to my home which was right on the other side of Leicester I couldn't move my head at all. I ended up having remedial therapy but refused to accept my neck was broken and was back in the gym in less than a week. On the doors the following weekend. I didn't tell a soul outside my family. I know. Didn't I say I had a thick head?

Ross came into Sugars shortly after. I'd not seen him for a while. I could hardly walk properly and I couldn't turn my head fully. I still can't. "What have you done to your legs?" he screamed at me. They were like Franklins sucked toothpicks. Nearly as bad as Sharons.

Despite the nose bleeds I took even more gear to recover. It had no effect. One day a guy called Ian walked into the gym. I was still trying to recover from my injuries. He looked huge. I'd known him since he sat shyly in Sugars Gym reception when he was a schoolboy.

He'd been studying teaching in London and I hadn't seen him for months. He had his hair all cropped off. With my usual care and consideration I reasoned that it was the short hair that made him look bigger. I thought it looked cool. I went to Vitos on London Road, by the train station that same day. Vito looked at me. He was a balding little Italian with a curly, oiled up perm and an inch long fingernail on the little finger of his left hand. I thought he was gay. "You wanna numba wan or numba two?" he asked. "How did you know?" I asked him back. He smiled. "Es my job to know." I had a number two.

I used to have it cut every 10 days. It cost me a fortune. In the end, at the suggestion of one of the flattops in the bar, I bought my own clippers. The haircut made me look tougher still. Mind you, when I next saw Ian he'd let his hair grow and it was down to his shoulders.

I realised I had to get off the drugs but by now I was well and truly hooked and couldn't train or really function properly unless I was crammed full of gear. It got to the point that I didn't think I'd live to see 35. It became a great milestone in my life. It was almost a relief when I got to 36, then 37. Now I'm trying to count backwards!! A lot of the guys I looked up to have since died. Heat attacks, suicides as a result of addiction to hard drugs, alcoholism, rare liver diseases. You name it. Too many from a relatively small pool for it to be sheer coincidence.

20

Night of the Chinese Defence

I play a lot of chess these days. Twenty or more years to get from Marine Boy to Love Train and then to nerd. I don't know. Maybe I was a nerd the entire time. I'm pretty good at chess. Probably well above average. It helps me think. I enjoy it. I'm a great believer in strategy and planning. I especially like the openings. There's Queens Gambit, Kings Gambit and many more. I'm pretty good at defence too, although one move I never play is the little known Chinese Defence series of moves.

I think Coulton was, in some way, trying to wrest control back from me. He'd been promoted to Entertainments Manager. Tubby Nigel had left. The goatee bearded GM had offered me a job as the bar manager, working at the weekends. I wasn't sure. He told me that Mr. C didn't know. Reading this may be the first time he finds out. I looked at the bar staff, Slim, Nick. All very experienced. How could I be in charge of them? I said no. He was a bit surprised but didn't say much.

In the end they gave the job to Nick. Soon after Coulton caught up with me early in the evening as I was milling about in reception. We were still going through the fourth man like nothing on earth. He told me that he'd hired some guy called Rick, an American Chinese living in Leicester. "He's ex-US army" Coulton gabbled. God, he can talk fast. "He's pretty big and chunky." I wasn't bothered – at first. I'm not racist. I trained at Sugars for years. In those days I worked with and trained with West Indians, Asians, Moroccans, people with weird little upturned moustaches and regularly used to chide Esau that the odd Guinness he had gave him such a healthy colour. We even had a Nigerian guy in Sugars whose surname was White. He always wore green shorts, so we called him Mr. Green. It was all in good fun and he never took offence. I hope.

These days I still do meet and have worked with a variety of people and nationalities and appearance, well, all except those with funny moustaches. I just didn't like Rick. He had long fingernails. I reckon he used them to pick his nose. He turned up the next week.

Coulton sure must've had a distorted view of 'chunky'. He was like a matchstick with the wood shaved off. He's the only person I know who had thinner legs than guess who. Not only that, I knew him from my all too brief stint at American Football, although he claimed he didn't remember me. There was no two ways about it. He was the worst of the worst. He had no experience, no clue and no place being a doorman. Because I could be a nice guy by this time when I wanted to, ha ha. I soon got around to renaming him. Wan Qwik Fuk was the order of the day.

I also used to tell him the best way to stand was to cross his hands in front of his groin (remember the very silly protecting your dick look) and then make him stand upstairs in reception out of the way. After I let him fry up there for about an hour I'd go up and make him stand at the spiral staircase door. I couldn't put him on the front door. Even the softest of the Centre Bar clientele, and there were plenty of them, would've eaten him alive. We were loving it down in the bar anyway. Who wanted to stand upstairs and be bored shitless?

Every time he stood in the bar I used to keep a wary eye on him and moved whenever he did in case he couldn't cope. Unsurprisingly really it didn't take too long before he moaned about being stuck in reception for so long compared to the rest of us. I was with Lloyd. Esau was late. "Fuck off upstairs you chinkie bastard" was my response. Lloyd nearly gagged on his OJ. He went without a murmur. About 5 minutes later a still goggle eyed Lloyd said to me "did you just tell him to fuck off upstairs?" I gave him my biggest grin and he nodded more in disbelief at this side of Jeff than anything else.

There were times when I relented and let him stand on the front door, but not that many. He would just stand there, hands clasped in front of his dick, not saying anything to any clientele and making no effort to stop anyone from coming in. The most he did was make comments about a beard I was growing, the number of girls I kissed and try and make American Football tackles on me. The tackles all took place in the tiny corridor between the Garden Room and the door to the bar where Romrig used to stand a couple of years before. Despite his light weight – especially compared to me – there was no way he was going to win. I was pretty motivated to make him feel stupid anyway and managed to constantly grab his jacket and make sure I pretty much squished him every time he tried it on. In my mind it kept me agile and I just saw him as target practise. Lloyd would sometimes watch us and my level of violence towards Rick and roll his eyes. The people who walked past us must have thought we were crazy men. I wonder why Rick stuck it? Perhaps he needed the cash.

A few weeks after me telling him to fuck off upstairs Rick was standing miserably on spiral staircase duty. Me and Lloyd were chatting away outside, leaning against the Garden Room wall. One of the Psychobillys came dashing out. He looked petrified. "I think you'd better get in here" he yelled. There was a mass brawl going on between bat headed Neil, Red Cap Kevin and some other guys. Rick was harmlessly flapping around shouting "enough guys… stop it… purlease." I walked up and shouted "oi… stop it." The fight broke up instantly. I know. Sheer magic. The power of my nasal twang.

The boss appeared looking all panic stricken. I assume one of the bar staff had let him know, probably before they realised they ought to let me and Lloyd know. "Where were you guys?" cried Rick. "You usually jump every time I move." Bless. I just looked at him part in disgust and part in humour and he skulked off back to his little standing post where he remained sulky and tearful for the rest of the night.

I was still hovering about in the bar. The fighting parties were still eyeing each other up and we hadn't really ejected anyone. Lloyd got bored with the indecision and went back outside. Suddenly Neil took the opportunity to run into the loos. Apparently Red Cap Kevin was already in there nursing a split lip. I dashed after Neil, followed by Coulton. We thought the fight was sparking up again. We flew in. Kevin looked up in surprise. The trap door was shutting. Neil must've been in a hurry. We heard the lock go and kicked at the door. Who knows what we were thinking? A fight in a locked toilet? Surely not. "Fuck off... I'm having a shit" came this gargled London accent. We let him finish. When we walked back into the bar everyone had gone. Bit of a storm in a teacup really. I went back to chatting with Lloyd.

Considering how useless he was and how I treated him, Rick lasted a pretty long time. Depending on how busy it had been the Christmas scene would start around September and go on to March or even April. One company held off and had their end of year bash around April or May of '86. I was upstairs with Rick. There was some drunken guy causing the waitresses hassle, the bar staff hassle. A real pain. In the end I went up to his table and, with Rick at my elbow, politely and quietly (ummm...) asked him to leave. He was a teeny little fellow with straw coloured hair and the inevitable moustache. As soon as I asked him to go he started to scream and shout. He was pissed out of his brains. I wasn't having any of that so grabbed him and started to escort him out. There's an understatement!

The reaction I got wasn't one I'd been expecting. The whole table of people, and then some, jumped on me. One of them was screaming "let him go... let him go!" in my face. My blood started to pound and then, out of the corner of my eye, I saw Rick do what I came to call the Chinese Defence.

Basically it consists of opening your eyes as wide as possible, looking horrified and then running backwards whilst still facing the action. I couldn't believe it. Well, maybe I could.

I put my head down and heaved. I drove this guy and every single person hanging on me towards reception. I was wearing an expensive jacket. I remember it cost me £70. I still don't know how I remember this stuff. The sleeve tore off at the shoulder. I kept going. Apparently we all fell over. I must've got up again really quickly, grabbed the guy and continued to shove. I do know people were still screaming at me and my blood was pounding and pounding. I drove him straight across reception and shoved him through the main doors and out into the street. Then I looked round. There was a pile of bodies strewn behind me like flotsam and jetsam.

Susan, one of the other managers looked like she was about to die. I checked all my bodyparts, especially my favourite one. Yep. Still intact. The whole place was eerily quiet. I watched as the human debris slowly picked themselves off the floor and skulked back to their tables. No one said a word. Where was Wan Qwik Fuk during all this? He'd completed the Chinese Defence and by now was hiding behind the bar. What a manoeuvre. He stayed there the rest of the night while I marched round with my sleeve hanging off. I never did take the jacket off for some strange reason.

Susan has since reminded me she asked me if I was okay and I just smiled back and said something about it's what I'm here for. Oh… such bravado! I do recall Nikki, the girl who used to take the money outside the Garden Room, offered to get me a drink. I said no and then spent the rest of the night with a throbbing head. My head throbbed for about 3 days. I was absolutely fuming.

Rick didn't come near or by me. His pale Asian features looked even paler. I think he was terrified. I think he was right to have been terrified. With my urging Coulton sacked him the next week. I think he was a bit reluctant. We'd been through so many guys.

The final act of the Chinese Defence was Rick's excuse. In his final conversation he came up with the line that he'd "acted with restraint." Perhaps he was right. By now I was no angel but he SHOULD have backed me up one way or another.

When Gladiators started up on TV I was an avid fan. Fit women, well, any women in tight lycra. To my surprise Rick was one of the very early contestants. I was stunned when I saw him there. The bad, old boy Wolf knocked him off some sort of pommel horse thing. Rick cried.

The guy I chucked out from the party came back 10 or 20 minutes later. It was the first time I'd got a good look at him. He really was tiny. It was no wonder I'd been able to shove him all the way out. "I'm so... so sorry" he bleated. "I'm ex-Army. I was amazed that you got me out so easily. Can I come back in?" Idiot. My head was pounding and my sleeve was hanging off. What do you think I said?

The last part of this tale is the repair to my jacket. The hotel offered to pay and I was about to take them up on it when Judy, one of the bar staff said "I'll do it for you." Trusting soul that I was. I happily handed her my jacket and she gave it back to me the next week. It was intact for sure, but there were visible stiches and knots everywhere. What a mess! I was very pissed off. I showed it to the night manager, Andrea. She was yet another one I'd, at one time, been relatively close to and we'd spent a lot of time together. Er, thinking about it... how the hell did I find time for all these women? "Get it done properly" she told me and we'll pay. So I did. It was a perfect job. I never let Judy know.

A chap called Valentine turned up in Ricks place. He was an old friend of Coultons and used to work at the Centre Bar even before it was the Centre Bar. A time of townies and heaps of violence, led by him, a local thug named Thomas and another black guy called Alfie. In the end I got to know all of them. Thomas, in particular was a surprising character. He had just turned up one week and started to train at Sugars with his big mate Elliott.

Stick thin, quiet and covered in tattoos, I liked him and he was always fine with me. I was amazed when I found out he was the same Thomas that was renowned for causing mayhem in the pre-Centre Bar days. Yet another of those 'you would never know moments'. Coulton told me that Thomas had once chucked a guy out and in doing so had stamped on his head on every step of the stair well. You've been reading this story, you figure out if that was more doorman bravado or whether it really happened. I don't know.

Elliott had been around for years. He also had a bad rep and has a scar on his face similar to mine from a similar incident, but I'd trained with him for a couple of sets at Sugars, been to his house when he serviced my overheating car, met his wife and kids. No problems at all. He'd even shown me some photos of him shirtless, holding a rose when he was trying to become a Sun Page 7 fella.

Khachik used to call him Billy Fury because of his almost white fair hair. I have no idea if it was dyed. I do remember him and Thomas turning up in the Centre Bar when it was in full swing and them being as quiet and as nice as pie while my heart did its usual flip-flops in my chest. After they'd gone Richard Crazyhead gave me a look. They'd been standing next to him and his buddy, Crazyhead's lead singer Anderson all night and I'd given them the odd worried glance. Richard had seen me breathe a huge sigh of relief as they'd left. "All doorman are paranoid" he told me. No they're not mate.

When Alfie appeared out of the blue one evening I had no idea who he was. He came with full entourage of girlfriend, friends and hangers on. Coulton was there and introduced us. I didn't really take too much notice. He was a small West Indian and seemed fine to me. At the end of the night I went round and asked him and his buddies if "they could start to drink up and make their way out now please." My favourite line and a long way from the whispering at Force 8. Two of his buddies, long thin West Indian geezers sneered and laughed and made no attempt to move. I ignored them. Alfie was as nice as pie – drank up and left. The sneerers went with him. Good job really. I wouldn't have hesitated but once again I didn't have to do a thing.

I will never know if the stories about guys like that are true or massive exaggerations. In my entire time I never came across anything that came close to what they were *supposed* to have done.

Jeff Shaw

21

Too Many Faces

The ever revolving faces of Helsinkis bar staff was nothing compared to the Centre Bar. It wasn't just the bar really it was the whole place. Staff would come and go with such amazing speed that I'd only just get to recognise them and then, vamoose. I talk about a lot of them as I make my meandering way through this story but in this chapter I've tried to group some of them together to give you some idea.

Louisa and Nick were there when I started. Louisa would've been a teenager and was heavily into the Sisters of Mercy. I think she was the first person I ever heard mention the group by name – even before DJ Simon. She always wore as much black as the job would allow – but it didn't go well with those white shirts they had to wear. She didn't stay too long. The others who were there when I started were two young lads. All I can remember is one had red hair and freckles and his mate was tall with blondish hair. By the time I was full time they'd gone and the carousel had begun.

First on the ever revolving list were two women. One had dark permed hair and terrible breath and the other was a blonde. I don't know any of their names. From memory Curly perm lasted about a month. In my generosity I'd offered her a lift home, just like the girl at Helsinkis. By the reaction I got I don't know what she thought I was offering. Doormen did have a terrible reputation at the time but mine was only just starting at the hotel. More than a lift? Er bad breath and bad perm? Not for me thanks.

Blondie managed to stay behind the bar for quite a while. Slim probably remembers her name. She worked all over the hotel as a barmaid and spent some time talking to me but I thought she was very cocky. In the early days they used to put little beer mats on the wooden tables. Around the time the GM asked me to be the bars manager a decision had been made that they were a waste of money. They'd told me because everyone thought I was going to take the job but they hadn't told the bar staff. Great. I saw blondie putting out the mats so said to her "better not do that." She gave me a dark look. "Who are you?" she sneered and carried on. I was annoyed but let it go. It wasn't worth the effort. I thought about saying the same to Slim who was behind the bar as well by now but thought better of it. Course, in hindsight she was absolutely right. I wasn't the manager. She didn't know what they'd asked me to do and they hadn't bothered to tell her not to put the stupid mats down. I must've come across as a know-it-all. I suppose it went with the bastard that I could be.

Soon after that a couple of female hotel guests came down, bravely pushed through all the Goths and Punks and asked for white wines. One medium and one sweet. I was messing about in the DJ box so heard it all. Blondie went round the back, got a bottle of white and filled two glasses. I looked round. Nosy again. My eyes must've opened wide. She looked at me and shrugged. "Funny how they both come out of the same bottle" she said and walked round to the bar. As she handed them over the lady doing the ordering asked which was which. I'm sure there was a *slight* hesitation, but not much. "This is the medium and this is the sweet" blondie said as she handed them over and she then went off in the direction of the next customer. That's one way to do it I suppose. Blondie left soon after. I don't think it was anything to do with me but who knows.

Then there was a lass from Liverpool. She was a big, good looking girl, with long, dark wavy hair, big hands and a chunky gold bracelet. She sticks in my memory for two reasons. The first is that I was messing around with a knife. I was bored and standing behind the bar. All that weight training had left thick calluses all over my palms. I could stick forks and knives in them and not even notice – and I often did. It was one of my party tricks. I was busy showing off to her with the fork. She didn't say much, then I tried the knife. A horrified expression

Jeff Shaw

came over her face and she tried to snatch it away. Stick a blade in there – no problem. Try and pull it out when it was there – slice my hand open. I dropped the thing and gave a grunt. "Sorry" she pouted. "A friend of mine just got stabbed and I was worried for you." D'oh. She very nearly gave me a nasty cut.

The second reason had to do with soda. She spilled some all down my front. My lovely jacket. I looked down. She grabbed a damp cloth and started to wipe. Let's just say she went a little low. I don't think that's where my jacket was. After a few seconds, maybe sixty ☺, I said to her "I think you'd better stop." I wish I could remember her name.

My other party trick was to form my hand into a karate shape I'd read about in a book and whack a table or the bar or anything really with the edge of it. I'd go faster and faster thumping down harder and harder. If you get it right it doesn't hurt one iota. Anyone can do it. If you get it wrong it breaks your little finger. Next time I see you I'll show you my hand. Make your own mind up on what damage I did to mine.

One name I do remember is Claire. She was there for a while too, probably about the same time as blondie and the Liverpool lass. Claire's boyfriend at the time was Adie and she'd even gone out with later training partner Big M – they'd both worked at Mr. Kiesas. Him on the doors and her behind the bars. Adie was another doorman. Nice guy but, seriously, deaf as a post. I'd met him at some point, but I'm pretty sure it wasn't at Sugars. Everything you said you had to repeat twice. It was funny.

Claire was another large lady with a blonded flattop. I tried to lift her up once and even she said to me "I wouldn't do that if I were you." Like I said, she used to serve at Mr. Kiesas before the Centre Bar but ended up being one of the longest serving ones down there before even she eventually left. The last time I saw her, the blonded hair had gone back to mousy brown. The flattop had gone. Her hair and was over her ears. She'd lost a lot of weight too. I didn't recognise her at first.

Claire worked behind the bar with a guy who whinged more than me. His real name was Wayne but he was so bad I soon renamed him Whine. Esau used to call him the mongoose because of the way he stood and cast his eyes fervently around in the hope of finding something to moan about. Everything was wrong for him – from the customers we served to the music we played to the prices we charged and on and on. In the end he moved from bars to room service. Everyone breathed a sigh of relief but I used to bump into him around the place from time to time and listen to him whinge about the toilets, the chemicals they used to clean the place, the number of rooms he had to do. I think he got the push in the end. He probably whinged.

Claire also worked with a totally flat chested Goth with a mohican that liked to be called Fin. Who knows what her real name was. Her flat chest was made up for with big, big eyes. I fancied her but she never said much to me. I left that to a bad boy from Psychobilly band the Meteors. He chased after her like mad. Like many she just vanished overnight.

There was one who had huge hips and breasts that constantly flirted with me. Her hips were so wide that in my head she looked like a pregnant hippo. As usual the others were egging me on. I have to say my main attention in that bar was towards the Goths. She was another with a keyboard for a mouth: One black tooth… one white. I did think about it because it would have been easy but left her for someone else after I made it clear that I wasn't interested. See. I may have thought about it but I didn't chase them all.

We also had more than a couple that I'd rather forget. There were two girls that started the same night. One was a tall girl with long dark hair and her mate, a wee Scottish lass. The Scottish lass was pretty pleasant, pretty really, but – I swear – she had never brushed her teeth in her life. Every time she spoke you could see this thick brown gunge on her gums. It looked like she'd been eating shit. Her mate had a big oval face and long brownish hair and – for a reason that I never understood – started to call me onion head. It may have been the haircut. I can't think that my hair smelled or that any part of me smelled really.

Coulton came up with the idea of a beach party night. He tried very hard to get the doorman to come dressed in beach wear but we absolutely refused. My excuse was that it wouldn't have looked good to stand in reception wearing a sweatshirt and shorts. I don't think he was very pleased. In the end he managed to convince the bar staff though. Oval face served behind the bar wearing nothing but a pale blue bikini nearly all night long. She loved it but seeing her bits everywhere quite turned my stomach. It wasn't that she was fat or anything – just saggy. Very. From top to toe and in that bikini we all got to see it. Yuck. In the end someone lent her a shirt so at least the top bits were mostly covered up. Mostly, because she left it open leaving everything for us all to see.

Both of them worked the bars all over the hotel before also disappearing into the ether. I know that Fairey from the night of the swimmers chased after the Scottish lass really hard. I wondered he noticed the shit in her mouth or just didn't care.

Two others that stick in my mind were former clients turned bar staff. Coulton had the bright idea of letting them dress as if they were coming to the bar as customers and suddenly we had two very alternative ladies serving the crowd. One was a tall skinny thing who went by the name of Haley. She was a heavy smoker and had that aroma of stale cigarettes about her. She also had no idea about the safety of the doormen. We never served people bottles in there. They can make nasty weapons. Probably worse than the glass I got hit with. Haley was constantly handing out bottles of some sort out. Potentially very hazardous to my health. I got more than a little pissed off with it and asked her to stop. She asked me why, so I told her. I probably wasn't too gentle. She then spent the rest of her time sarcastically asking me if it was okay to have ashtrays on the tables or hand out slivers of orange and if they could hurt me.

Her mate, whose name escapes me, was a much better barmaid but she turned up one night looking like The Penguin from Batman and Robin, with long tails, a white face and black lipstick. After she'd finished in the Centre Bar they moved her to one of the functions for the rest of the night. I think Coulton was nicely asked to revise his ideas after that and neither of them worked there again.

Tina and Sarah also ring a bell. I constantly called them by the wrong name. They hated me for it. I wasn't doing it on purpose. I just couldn't get it right. They looked and sounded completely different to each other, it just wouldn't sink into my over excited – and quite small – brain. I'm pretty sure they were students who shared accommodation and had managed to get a job at the hotel together. One always had a bell shaped hair cut and wore bright red lipstick and the other was taller and had longer, wavy brown hair.

They'd been working in one of the functions when the Mr. Peters signal went out. Me and yet another stand in doorman – a lad called Terry – ran in. Terry changed his surname and his history on a daily basis. First he was Dutch and had a tattoo on his shoulder like a famous Dutch bodybuilder of the day called Berry DeMay, then he was from the north and had slept with a Miss Universe... blah... blah... blah. You get the picture by now.

The Mr. Peters call could occasionally be a false alarm, the result of a twitchy DJ or over zealous dancing and – sure enough – nothing happened this time. It was all quiet but Tina or Sarah, whichever one it was, was not amused. "You guys love it" she told me. "You love it" she repeated. Not true. As far as I was concerned I was paid to do a job and that's what I did. I just loved the music, the flirting and the kisses.

I once took Terry to train with me. He claimed he was as heavily into bodybuilding as me. I'd moved from Sugars by this time. I drove all the way into town to pick him up but he seemed unsure. In the end I persuaded him to give it a go – just the once. As soon as we went into the gym I could see he had no idea. On the way back I saw my mum walking back from the village as we zoomed past and stopped the car to give her a lift. Terry jumped out and fawned over her and her bags. "Who was THAT?" she said to me later.

There were plenty more bar staff. Russ, younger brother of manager Susan was there for a while. He was a lanky geezer and I had a lot of laughs with him but he had an argument with the GM in front of me and walked. Nick was there that night and was pretty pissed off when Russ went. He didn't see the argument but I've got to say the GM didn't do much apart from ask Russ to tidy the place up a bit. He must've wanted to go and was looking for any excuse. Russ was there around the time as a young lass called April because I'm sure he always referred to her as Apes. If there was ever a nickname that didn't fit the person Apes was it. Mind you, I was always calling him rustle. He just used to grin and bare it. It amused me anyway.

One guy who dropped out of med school was also around. Obviously dead clever but he came across as lazy to me. I'm pretty sure his name was Richard. He spent all night walking around as slowly as he could and serving as few people as possible. He managed about one Christmas before he gave up the ghost and left. It was during my worst period as a bastard. I took the piss about his work rate. Let's just say he didn't find it funny.

There was also a gay looking and sounding Goth. He would arrive in the dead of winter with a grey scarf, grey mittens, black hair and pink nails. He was always okay with me but Coulton had taken an instant dislike and told me he was only going to let him work there the once. He stayed for about a year in the end. When I asked the boss why he'd let him stay he just shrugged. I think the answer was that we were going through as many bar staff as door staff.

The final one that gets a mention here is Judy of my torn sleeve fame. Her regular role was as barmaid in the residents lounge but she also served in the Centre Bar more than once. A lot more than once! She'd be in her fifties then so was, by far, the oldest person in the entire room. I think she'd been a barmaid for years. Her favourite trick was to pour a short without using the measures. Slim caught her doing it once when he was standing next to me and quietly pointed it out. I was clueless. It's no wonder the short drinkers always went to her to get served. In the end Coulton had to deliver some very bad news to her while she was serving away down there one Christmas. Her son had fallen in the river and drowned. I can't remember if she ever made it back down there.

At the beginning, once the doors were shut we'd all sit in a big heap and have a free drink – on the ullage. I'd still keep my distance, but not as much as when I was at Helsinkis. Coulton hated it when I had my orange juice. It's pretty hard to put that down to pipe cleaning and wastage. Er... With that sort of thing going on it's no wonder the place eventually went out of business. Umm. I wonder if the senior management ever knew. Probably. We were all at it.

After a while the doormen didn't hang around at the end. There were places to go, people to see.

22

The Four Horsemen

Even my brain comes to a point when it realises something needs to happen. The nosebleeds that I had been getting had been an important clue. In 1986 I stopped taking steroids. Cold. That **REALLY** is the hard way.

I went through everything. No testosterone, rebound, the lot. It was incredibly hard. The roller coaster ride from hell but I was determined to stay off. Training became very, very infrequent. I carried on working at the Centre Bar. Good job there wasn't much trouble. My mood swings were incredible. My moaning was out of control. One of the many revolving managers Tony, and one of the receptionists, Emma both told me I was a moaning tosser. Lovely. I didn't see it. I probably moaned that they moaned about me. So much for wandering up to the receptionists and having a flirt.

Once Rick had gone and Valentine stood in his place I found he was a big fan of the WWF. Now the WWE. I grew up on a diet of Saturday afternoon wrestling and my dad often used to take me to the Granby Halls to watch. Whilst Valentine was into the Ultimate Warrior, a huge, wild haired, face painted ex-bodybuilder, I liked the Four Horsemen, a group of bad guys who went around causing mayhem. It was all good fun and I loved the idea. In my mind, I really did see us as the Leicester version of this wrestling gang. The Four Leicester Horsemen of the Apocalypse. Yeah. I know.

I made it to early April, about the time of Rick's Chinese Defence incident. Big M had quit American Football. We teamed up as training partners. My nosebleeds eventually stopped. I think I ran out of spare blood.

Back at the bar I decided that we should have two doormen downstairs and two in reception. Apart from Ricks night of Psychobilly fun, the crowd were so well behaved that having three in the bar seemed a bit pointless. No one argued. Although we were now working in pairs we changed who we worked with every weekend to minimise boredom so everyone worked with everyone at some point. For the most part we all still found it very dull in reception, but at least there were now two of us up there so we had someone to chat to.

In spite of my growing paranoia there were also some funny moments. All of us were standing around, it must have been after we had shut the bar for the night, when one of the receptionists looked a bit embarrassed. Apparently Esau, Trevor, Robert and Lloyd had all... erm... satisfied her at some point. She looked at me in hope. NO WAY. It'd be bad enough being one of your mates, but 2 of your brothers as well. In my typical nosy parker fashion I wondered at the time who was first and who was last.

I'm also fond of the time that after we'd got the bar empty Lloyd leant down to pick something off the floor, probably money knowing him, and caught his head pretty hard as he came back up. He was so annoyed that he punched a big ceramic pot that was fastened down as part of the décor, smashing it to bits with one bare handed blow. The pot was full of brown pebbles and it went everywhere. It was an important night. After that I made sure he never punched me! Poor old me had to go and get the vacuum and clean it all up. Such a glamorous life I led.

Another time it had got close to 2am. We were all hanging about in reception while a bunch of functions played out, with aching eyes and feet and gagging to go home when this chunky female appeared in the doorway. She glanced from one of us to another, a horrified expression on her face as she realised that there were 4 burly blokes in front of her, then without making any real eye contact with any of us, she just blurted out "do you sell condoms?" We nearly wet ourselves laughing. Finally I said "try the toilets." I knew there were none in there. Who do you think made sure the place was totally empty before we locked up at night? Off she went in vain hope, only to return a few minutes later, give us all a glare and flounce off into the night. By now none of us could contain ourselves and there was at least 5 minutes of continuous snorting and guffawing until our ribs ached.

The two scariest funnies I can remember were when some townie woman came down that I'd never seen before. She had two mates with her. She wasn't bad looking and had a wavy, ear length perm which was longer on one side than the other and partially covered one eye. All of them were dressed to the nines. Townie girls on the rampage. Not really what we were used to down there. In the rest of the hotel – maybe. She took one look at me – opened up her handbag and with everyone just standing there said "I want you to fuck me... I've got a condom." As much as I flirted with virtually every woman in there, I was totally, totally shocked, as were her friends, and rapidly declined the offer. It wasn't that unusual for any doorman to get offers like this but she was the most blatant that I can remember and wasn't in line with my thinking in the slightest.

There were other offers over the time I was there. Another girl practically threw herself at me as well. I can't remember whether this was before or after the townie girl. She was often in the bar, beefy with long brown hair and always had bright red fingernail paint. I especially remember the fingernail paint. I have to admit I was somewhat tempted until door bashers brother Craig told me he knew HE was number 17 for sure! In his words he told me "she likes you to use a condom... but I didn't... SURPRISE!" Ugh. Kinda put me off. A LOT.

This time though Lloyd was really egging me on. "Get what you can and then get what you want" was his sagely advice. In the end wavy perm said "let me suck your cock then" and bit hard into my jacket shoulder, like a rabid dog. I tried shaking her off but she didn't seem to be getting the message. Her mates seemed to be getting a bit impatient. I was really unsure what to do so in the end I was quite brutal and threatened her. It was pretty unnecessary on my part. She just looked at me and walked, probably staggered, away with her frustrated and bored looking mates in tow.

Lloyd and Slim, who was there at the time, were in absolute tears of laughter. I just looked at them and they shook their heads as if to say they would have. I wonder.

The other one was when the other doormen – led by Lloyd again – tried to get me to chat up some woman with long dark hair, big boobs and a scabby red dress sitting in the half light near the door. I looked across. "She doesn't look too bad" I murmured trying to sound like I could tell. I edged closer. Fuck me. Turned out 'she' was a he. I couldn't tell because I was too short sighted. They were all peeing themselves laughing again. Bastards!

On top of that a guy with a mop of curls had started to come into the bar. He was always hanging round me. In the end he told me he was from a modeling agency and offered me a job as a male model. I was very suspicious about his motives. I thought he wanted more than just a modeling job – if you know what I mean! I said no thanks. I can't remember how I found out but it turned out he was genuine. I could've been the new face of Calvin Klein but the price was far too high!

It wasn't all good though. One guy smacked himself over the head with a pint glass just as me and Esau swopped over from the Garden Room door to reception. This must have been before we worked in pairs upstairs. We didn't actually see it. I had gone through the door at the spiral staircase, just as Esau appeared coming down the other way. All we heard was a smack and a yell. We looked at each other in horror and dashed back into the bar. The bloke was right in front of us and a right mess. He'd caused us a bit of hassle a few weeks earlier when he'd arrived stoned out of his head wearing a lot of different badges on his chest. Trouble was he wasn't wearing a shirt and all the badges were through his skin! Gross. The night of the glassing he kept screaming "who hit me...? who hit me?" No one. I was there. He did it to himself. Sharon raced over and helped us calm him down and get him out. She obviously knew him. We were both covered in his blood by the time he staggered out through the exit.

Over a few months we also had to spend a lot of time searching people for drugs, I took knives off at least 3 different people in the bar – including two from some scruffy looking punks who were playing a macabre game where they were sitting on the bench seats, trying to slit each others clothes. I knew both of them. One was a well know local musician called Ajax. I strolled over and spoke with as much conviction as I could. "You'd better give them to me!" They both looked a bit surprised… conviction… squeaky voice? Ummm… but handed them over without a fuss. I didn't quite know what to do. It wasn't as though they were threatening me or anyone else for that matter and they WERE buying drinks so I let them stay and went and put their weapons out of the way, behind the bar. When they were ready to leave Ajax came up to me. "Blades" he said, holding out a dirty hand. I just nodded and went and retrieved them for him. Pretty scary stuff when you think about it. I saw him for the first time in over 25 years a few weeks ago (2013) and we both laughed.

Ever the firebrand when he wanted to be, Esau viciously broke someones nose when he wouldn't leave at night and decided to call Esau a black bastard as he tried to get him to go. He must have been drunk or very, very stupid. Esau was so brutal it made me feel sick. First he clapped the guy hard over both ears. It was such a hard clap that I swear I saw the guy go cross-eyed. Then he pulled him to the floor and let fly with a flurry of punches directly between the eyes. The bloke's girlfriend stood there open mouthed. We all did really. In the end my brain kicked in and I pulled Esau off and the guy and his girlfriend fled for his lives. I followed Esau into the loos a few seconds later. To say what? I don't know. He had his hand under the cold tap when I walked in. "Hurts… innit" he told me. Esau was lucky the police weren't called in. It would have been very hard to defend his actions.

Me and Esau we also ejected one big lad called Penny. He was always in there. That night he really didn't want to go. I can't really remember what he did. I think he was just a bit insulting to Esau. Penny grabbed hold of one of the two big oak doors that led outside. Me and Esau heaved. The door came off its hinges complete with Penny still hanging on. A modern version of humpty-dumpty. We let him back in the next week. He bought a lot of beer. He was also a fairly well known musician and a roadie for a lot of the bands who used the bar.

Another time Esau had come flying past me as I lazed by the door. He had Louise in one hand and Julie in the other. I ran up the stairs after him. "What's going on?" I asked, horrified. Couldn't miss my goodnight kisses. "They were feisty" he grunted back at me as he heaved them out into the street. I let them straight back in. Not even 5 minutes wait. Esau called me 2 faced and didn't speak to me for a month.

I also stopped a girl from using the reception entrance to the Centre Bar and she came out with an unnecessary mouthful. Despite that I directed her round to the Strikes entrance then changed my mind about letting her in because of the way she'd spoken to me so dashed down the internal stairs by the function rooms and through the toilet. The trip took me less than a minute and her about 3 or 4. When she finally made her way down to the bar I was standing there. She couldn't quite believe it. *"No"* I grunted as she stepped forward. "Why not?" she screamed at me. "You were rude to me upstairs" I replied. I was quite calm. She continued screaming… "fucking bastard." I shrugged. She carried on. "All doorman have got a fucking great chip on their shoulders. You're a fucking bastard." Why on earth she thought this would make me change my mind I don't know. In the end she just turned round and stormed off, trying to slam one of the big oak doors on her way out. That was a joke. They were huge. She basically bounced off them and then buggered off. Who had the chip?

At that time there was another guy I'd met at Sugars who I occasionally bumped in to. He was a big chap in his jacket and Coulton had once offered him a job as our 4th man. He'd turned it down. This guy worked out in a very different way to me and any partner I was training with. Before I tried to quit the gear I had been busting a gut anywhere up to 8 times every ten days in the gym. This guy was training two or three times a week for 30 minutes a time at some place in Leamington Spa. I'd been with him once the previous October, mainly to shake down the Samba after someone had pissed in the petrol tank and it had broken down. The training was similar to my, then, favourite bodybuilders, Mentzer. I didn't really take to it there and hadn't been back.

Me and Big M bumped into this guy by accident in the city. We went for a coffee. I thought he looked bigger than ever. Hey, I was off the steroids and feeling and looking like crap. Me and M listened to him blathering on about the way he trained. Later M told me he thought he was a bit of a bullshitter but he was interested in trying out the training method. I wasn't convinced but we had nothing to lose really. We both made the effort to read up on that type of training and, despite my reservations, started doing it at Sugars.

All the hardcore regulars were laughing at us and then − miracle. With absolutely nothing ingested or injected in me I started to look and feel more like my old self. One or two guys even asked me if I was back on the gear. I wasn't. A top, world class American bodybuilder called Christian came over to do a seminar tour. Sugar based him at the gym. I never saw him lift a weight. One night he came over and asked me how we were training. Mr. Universe. **HE ASKED ME**. I told Big M. We were both astounded. The die was cast.

Life in the bar carried on but over time Louise pretty much stopped coming down. On top of that Joy had moved to the coast and Maria had disappeared. I later learned that she had contracted spinal meningitis, highly contagious. When you think how many times I got a goodnight kiss. The Nana girls had grown up and were also long gone. The bar wasn't doing at all well. By the end of the night it would be pretty much deserted. It was so bad that we even closed at 10.30pm occasionally because of lack of customers. Sharon was still hanging around though and Julie still used to make an entrance from time to time. By this time she'd changed boyfriend and was seeing a tall, clog wearing Geordie guy we all called Dave Man because everything he said ended in "man."

Dave Man was the bootleg king and mostly wore a cap that covered hair that was dyed white on one side and black on the other. He once got me to quite innocently hold his tape recorder at a live gig for an up and coming Goth band who were playing in the dimly lit Garden Room. It was a rare night off for me and the rules were that we weren't supposed to go in but I'd still found myself down there, agreeing it was okay with Coulton before saying hi to my door buddies and then hiding out of the way until the band started and then finding a nice spot standing on a little wall at the back where I could see what was going on but wouldn't be seen by too many people in the dark. I soon noticed Dave Man. Who could miss him in the blackness with that hair? I saw that he had the recorder in his hand but I was so naïve that I just thought he was recording the gig for his own enjoyment and would be listening to it again later. Being a good soul and knowing I was in a better position than him I decided to 'break cover' to ask him if he needed any help. He looked a bit surprised 1. To see me there and 2. To volunteer to hold his recorder, but he handed it over and there I stood, recording the gig for him. Oh, poor still innocent Jeff.

About 10 minutes later it was my turn to be surprised when the bands manager came up to me. He looked a bit red faced and flustered even in the darkness. "Oi" he snarled at me. "Stop that!" I thought he was joking and just laughed at him so he threatened to get me thrown out. I grinned, jumped down from the wall and moved closer all in one fluid motion. Well, I like to think it was one fluid motion.

I was massive at the time. He gulped and went white in the gloom, a funny smell coming towards me ☺. Look, I was VERY scary looking. Dave Man saw it all and came rushing over. I was slow, but the penny had suddenly dropped for me so I gave him his equipment back and wandered off. I was bored anyway. I looked for Sharon but she wasn't there so I was soon chatting to the other doorman before finally leaving for the night. I think they were glad to see me go and, to be honest, I was relieved to be leaving early for once. Mind you – thinking back – it would've been funny for Lloyd and Esau to have to ask me to leave.

Sadly Dave Man got glassed one night at another place in town while he was trying to protect some girls. His neck was pretty badly chopped up and I've been told he had about 80 stitches. This was a few years before I got a similar injury myself and was pretty cutting in my comments to him about getting involved, even criticising him for letting Helen, Richard Crazyheads nurse girlfriend for taking them out at home rather than going to his local doctors or hospital. He was very upset with me over the things I said and – I think – rightly so, but I'm sure it was the effect of the steroids or more realistically coming off the steroids that made me so ignorant. Having experienced the mess it makes of you personally, maybe I'm just much more sympathetic so many years later.

The last time I saw him was when me, Lloyd and Slim went to some newly opened, big nightclub near the bus station in the early nineties but I was a changed person by then and only half heartedly waved hello as he came smiling over. Lloyd and Slim were equally dismissive. He looked a bit dissappointed that none of us really spoke to him and then wandered off into the night.

That wasn't the only time I acted like that. About a year before I'd been in Toronto on holiday. As I was walking across the city, wearing a bright red training top and snazzy bottoms designed by Mr. Universe Christian himself, I bumped straight into a blond spiky haired Canadian lad that used to go down to the bar for a while when he was living in the UK. I recognised him instantly. After all he was dressed the same way. He looked at me. I was out of my doormans uniform and fatter and smaller but I could see the penny drop in his eyes. Although I was surprised to see him, I could've stopped and said hello. I didn't. I just smiled briefly and walked on. I have wide peripheral vision. I could see his eyes still on me as I moved away. Still shy or ignorant? I regret it to this day. Sorry mate.

As for Sharon, well I'm sure at some point that there was a genuine level of attraction between us. In the end I seemed to spend a lot of time talking to her but little else. I think she saw me as an easy touch for lifts, drinks and the odd bit of heated groping and snogging in a dark corner. One night she came up to me and gave me the most erotic kiss I'd ever had. I didn't lean against the wall that night. Rick was there at the time and saw us. I was embarrassed so it stopped pretty quickly. "See you next week" she said as she left. I didn't see her in the bar again for 5 years. I didn't have a clue what had happened. All I knew was that Richard Crazyhead came up to me one night and said "I've finally got my flat back. Sharon has gone." I probably asked him where but I'm not sure.

A short while after she stopped coming down to the bar me and the guy who trained in Leamington were having a coffee in the centre of town and he wanted to give me a phone number. We didn't have any paper and it just so happened to be the 5th of January. Guess whose birthday falls on that date.

By this time I knew Sharon was working at Ladbrokes opposite the clock tower so I made the sneaky suggestion of going down there because there would be pen and paper. I had another aim in mind. Sure enough there she was, so whilst this chap wrote down his stuff I scrawled "Happy Birthday" on to a betting slip and slid it over the counter when she wasn't looking. Then I changed my mind, turned round and, without so much as waving, walked back out. It was a very hard thing to do at the time.

By mid 1986 it was all getting too much for the hotel. By 10pm ish one time there was only me, Lloyd, the bar staff and a blond dread locked girl left in there. We spent a fair few minutes talking to her aimlessly before she let out the most enormous belch, got all embarrassed and left. Me and Lloyd just laughed. Lloyd probably farted to show me that she wasn't the only one with uncontrollable bodily functions! Frances BB was the GM by then. She made the decision to close the bar.

Oh oh I thought. Out of a job. So much so that on the last night in the bar I let people buy me a few goodbye beers and stood... well... staggered by the door legless. It was the only time – EVER – I drank when I was on duty. Hey, I never drank anyway. D'oh.

I was wrong about losing my job though. For whatever reason me and Esau were kept on and would stand by the reception doors all night chatting about nothing. Lloyd and Valentine went to Helsinkis. Coulton got them the job. We used to wave at each other across the road. Through my squinty short sightedness I watched a fight on the doorstep once. I didn't know. I couldn't see. It was Nick. Whoops. Good job it was only fisticuffs at dawn.

Nick found out later that I'd 'seen' everything and wasn't too impressed with me despite my protestations of bad eyesight. He was less impressed with Coulton and Esau who, in his boredom, had left me alone and had wandered across to have a good time with the boss while Nick was being thumped. He never did moan about Lloyd and Valentine who must have seen it all as well. We were closed for about 3 months and then Coulton came up to me as I milled around in reception. He was all animated with arms and head awhirl. "I don't know whether to laugh or cry" he told me. "We're going to re-open and try and attract the same crowd." So we did, and we did. Well, mostly.

Lloyd and Valentine came back from their brief stint at Helsinkis and we started again. We didn't advertise – just re-opened the doors one Friday night. Sure enough, the crowds slowly came back. Gays, Goths, Punks, a few skinheads, some students. Most of them had grown up since my Helsinkis days so there were a lot of new folk. I was back to memorising names and faces, smiling and saying hi.

Business was slow though and I was bored as much as anything. I was looking round the room when I noticed a great looking arse in tight silver spandex trousers standing near the door. 10 minutes passed, twenty. I screwed my eyes up and had a good old look. Eventually I tore my face away from the arse. There was a person attached to it. Her name was Claire. She was 17. What is it with me and seventeen year olds? She worked as a machinist at Corahs in the city, had a pretty, oval face, blond, crimped hair and tattoos on both her upper arms. I asked her if her tattoos had hurt and she replied "you couldn't take the pain." Then she laughed. She laughed a lot. A sort of raunchy hawing that I loved. She'd been there the whole time. 1984 to 1986, which means she was about 14 or 15 or even younger when I was at Helsinkis, and I'd never noticed her. Not once.

The Goth magnet leapt into action. It sure as hell didn't take long for the kissing and hugging to start again. God, what a womaniser I must have been! I have to say, there were lots of kisses goodnight, although more than once I had to get Claire to take her chewy out of her mouth. Kiss, saliva and chewy. Yuck.

Lloyd sighed at my antics. Esau said "yes Jeff" and Valentine grinned a gap toothed grin. More of a leer really. Valentine told me he'd heard all about me and the women in there. I genuinely didn't have a clue what he meant. It was just me still being just me. He even convinced me to walk round with a packet of condoms in my pocket, just in case, and later begged me to sell him one because he felt lucky. Hey 30 pence is 30 pence.

Claire saw the exchange, grabbed the packet from my hand and pissed herself laughing. Me and Claire had a lot of laughs really. About a year later I even volunteered to work with Valentine at Reflections after the bar closed for the night just because it was her 18th birthday party and gave her a birthday present of a calendar with movie monsters on every month – except one! I replaced September, Claire's birthday month, with a photo of me messing about in the gym.

In truth I had been sitting on a shoulder press machine waiting for my mate Kev, who I'd persuaded to go just for the day to take some snaps of me in return for me training him, to get ready to take a photo on the same old clunky SLR that Esau had used. I know it was July. Kev probably felt I was using him and I was getting more out of it than him so was a bit pissed off and being very slow at taking photos. I had got so bored that I was sticking out my tongue and putting my finger up my nose to put him off. It was amusing me anyway. Suddenly he grinned and took the shot just as my finger was there. Sod it! When I printed them up I didn't know what to do with it. Then I figured it out. That was the one that ended up the calendar.

Mind you, I did piss Claire off that night at Reflections. Whilst Valentine stood downstairs and pretended to be 'scratching' along to the sounds of MARRS and "Pump Up the Volume" that we could hear from the DJ in the Studio I did my job and wandered around upstairs, finally clearing the place at 2am. I much preferred the music and the people up there anyway. Claire was last one out that night. It was her party! I was in a good mood and followed her down the staircase with my hands pressed firmly on her shoulders. I wanted my goodnight kiss. I don't think her mood was as good as mine. "Fucking hell" she screamed at me without looking round as I pressed down. I took my hands off her, let her out and watched as she crossed the road and headed off to her flat which was a few minutes walk away. Then I inwardly shrugged and went home.

Claire had a different set of friends. I was far less shy by this time and started to talk to loads more people including Tony and Jill, a nice couple of Punks who I thought must have been in their late teens or early twenties but, again, have recently found out were even younger than Claire! Tony always looked like Vivian out of the Young Ones to me and I said that to him more than once. He just laughed. The only thing he was missing at times was the stars stuck on his forehead. I never, ever saw Jill out of full on Punk war paint replete with starched blonde hair, blue and black eyeliner, powdered white face and bright red lipstick. I was silly enough to ask her once if she ever took it off and she gave me quite a brutal "never" in response.

Through Claire I also met some incredibly skinny, flat chested girl with a bit of a mohawk and a real Leicester accent. They'd all been there the whole time but were nothing more than faces I had sometimes vaguely said hello to. I got to know them all. In jest I took over Esau's role of talking about my laggy, always going on about how small it was and if I was ever in a fight all I had to do was get it out. My opponent would then see how teeny it was and bend over in amusement to have a closer look. I could then take advantage of that and knee them in the face. Failing that I could always run away!

I even took down a plastic willie wrapped in a banana that I'd bought when I was on holiday in Spain with Ross a few years earlier and told them I'd kept it to remind myself what a proper one looked like. Claire grabbed it from my hand running around the bar screaming "I've got the doormans willie." She didn't know my name at that stage. I chased after her in vain, a big grin on both our faces. It ended up dunked in her drink for some strange reason.

I also pretending to pick my nose, copying Trevor's habit and is why I was doing it in Kevs photo that ended up on the calendar. What I used to say to them was that if I got into real trouble I could always pick a bogey and flick it at my opponent to gross him out. Just so you know – I never did that.

Tony, Jill and Claire eventually bought me a pink, knitted willie warmer. It was about ½" long, in a teeny blue box and had the instructions 'shrink to fit'. We all pissed ourselves laughing. I kept it as a memento right up until I moved to Australia.

Jeff Shaw

Tony and Jill (1987 or 1988)
Picture Courtesy Jeff Shaw

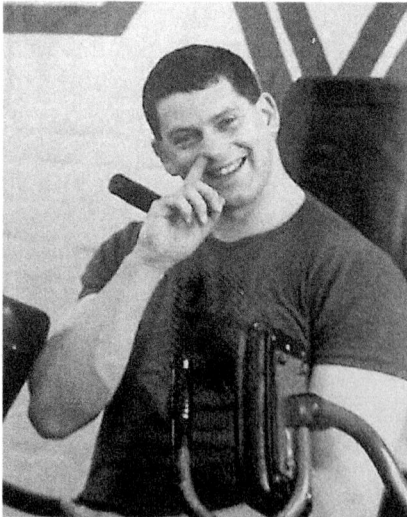

Calendar Photo (1987)
Picture Courtesy Jeff Shaw

Jeff Shaw

Claire (1987)
Picture Courtesy Claire James

By now I wasn't quite so fastidious about my appearance as I had been in my early days at Helsinkis and my jacket and shoes were starting to look a bit shabby but I didn't care. Life was back on the up. Claire even got me a birthday card and a red badge that read, "I'm the man your mother always warned you about!" in big white font across it. I kept that too.

Coulton tried hard to keep the bar going. To boost takings he organised a Red Stripe promotion night. He often added to his hotel income by DJaying at various nightclubs in the city and loved to DJ down there himself. We were all into it. It was funny that night. It's odd to see Punks and Goths behaving like townies. First he got some game lads to lie down on the little stage and chucked dry roasted nuts all over them. Any girl brave enough could then eat them. First to be nut free, so to speak, won some beer. There were plenty of volunteers – both male and female.

Big Penny, the roadie, couldn't wait. Free beer after all! I do remember that one of the Goths had a black string vest on. Must've been hard working getting all the peanuts out of that. The most disgusting bit was that after that little malarkey Coulton got the lads to remove a sock and put it over a pint of beer. Then they had to pass the pint along, drinking through the stinky sock until all the beer was quaffed. I didn't remember any of this at first but someone reminded me. I suppose this sort of stuff is pretty funny to watch at the best of times if you're in the mood, but hilarious to see it being done by the crowd that went down there! I would've been in stitches.

Another time I turned up and there was a coffin just lying outside the Garden Room. It was another Coulton promotion but no one ever really knew what for. The thing was full of dried leaves and stayed there for weeks. I never really got it. One weekend it wasn't there, then it was for several weeks and then it wasn't. Months later some people I didn't really know came down. They smiled at me on the way in. "You used to have a coffin here didn't you?" one of the men asked me as he entered. I just smiled back and nodded.

During this time I became extremely chatty with anyone who walked past. There was Colin who was always down there with a variously yellow, blue or pink mohican and a sweet faced girl in black leather and chains who liked to be called Animal. Apparently her real name was also Sharon. Animal had variously, a skinhead or a mohican and, above all else, a big tattoo down her back. There were lots of people. Residents would be astonished if they walked into the bar by accident but I'd be there, soothing things, making sure they weren't offended. Working away. Being the gentleman. Some stayed for the amusement factor, some fled back upstairs to the quieter, safer bars. I just continued to grin.

The hotel gave me a couple of awards 'Star of the Month' and then 'Star of the Quarter'. I'd grown a beard at the time in preparation for a bodyguard job I knew was coming up. Duty manager Fairey, of the swimmers night, took some slightly blurry photos of me and my out of focus, bearded face grinned out from behind a frame on the wall for the best part of 2 years. I guess it was a long quarter!

Me and Big M left Sugars Gym in July that year. It was the end of a 12 year period for me. We started to train at the gym in Leamington Spa. The guy who introduced me to it was long gone by this time. From what other people who knew him better than me have said I pretty much have the impression that he was one of those people who could never could stick at anything for too long.

Originally we were only going for three months. In the end I stayed there for about 11 or 12 years until it finally closed down in 1998. The place bulged with impressive and imposing big, blue Nautilus machines – all cams and chains. I loved it more than I loved the early Sugars. This type of equipment that suited our needs better than with this "Mentzer" style training, although it was already morphing into some thing better. It was at this gym that Kev took the, what shall I call it? The 'nose pose' photo that ended up on Claire's calendar over a year later.

It was a cheap place to join but expensive to keep driving there. We started off training a prescribed three times a week for about half an hour each. An hour to get there, an hours training and then an hour back. Clearly longer to travel than to train. It was always my car because Big M didn't drive. It wasn't surprising that it soon became twice, partly because of the cost of petrol and partly because we saw that as an 'advancement' in the type of training we were doing. I was still growing without any steroids.

It became physically obvious that this type of training was clearly working. I started to work at the Golf Range with Big M on a Thursday night, then the Centre Bar on a Friday and Saturday. I talked and flirted and messed around with Claire or Tony and Jill and finally, finally finished paying for the Samba. I'd taken out a 3 ½ year loan and done it in less than 2. For the first time since I started door work I had spare cash to spend on myself.

23

Comings, Goings and Gongs

By this time the Fan Club had opened and, as I said, proved popular, with lots of the Alternative crowd going there. Sue, the manager had offered me a job as the head doorman. She had known me for a while, first Helsinkis and then the Centre Bar. Her husband, Barry, had even been the DJ at both places. I thought about it for a few days but eventually went into a little shop she owned or managed in St. Martins Square in town and turned her down. I was comfortable. I felt safe. Trouble in the bar was at an absolute minimum, although we still got the odd bit of hassle in the function rooms, and I was having some fun again.

The Fan Club was in Abbey Street which is on the other side of the city to the Centre Bar. To enter you went through a small door and then up a long flight of stairs before emerging into a very dark, long thin and claustrophobic room. I'm glad I didn't work there. I've heard since that the doormen Sue eventually hired, two stick thin rastas with flowing dreds, were vicious and were often using the old tried and tested 1980's doorman method of teaching people a lesson. A common trick was supposed to be throwing people down the stairs and watching their heads hit the door at the bottom. Again, I have no idea how true this is. I never liked them. They tried to turn me away the few times I appeared but I always got Sue to step in and got in free. It's a proud fact that I NEVER paid to get in anywhere. One night the rastas turned up at the Centre Bar. I guess they were checking it out. In retribution I wouldn't let them in. "Now do you recognise me?" I screamed at them.

As far as I can remember the other Alternative venue that had sprung up, Sector Five, was virtually next door to the Fan Club. Often referred to by the alternative crowd as Septic Dive,

I don't think I ever went inside, although I do know that Robert of the 'F' clan was on the door there.

It wasn't all plain sailing and a return to happy days though. In February 1989 manager Susan had the bright idea of organising a satellite dish hook up so that boxing fans all over the city could watch the Bruno / Tyson world championship rematch. Bruno had been mashed up badly in the first fight and this was pretty much being seen as his last chance. The press were pushing it. HARD. Everyone was trying to cash in. The hotel was no different. Unfortunately for us, okay, from my point of view it was a disaster.

The guy setting up the satellite got pissed, pointed the dish in the wrong direction and the crowd got humpty dumpty or some other such cack. We were packed. The place went up in a riot. I was the Head Doormen. We'd hired an army of others for that night. I was supposed to be in control. The whole place erupted. So much for 50 Hells Angels at Helsinkis 5 years earlier.

There were bottles and glasses going everywhere. I co-ordinated the defence. No Chinese stuff that night. Lloyd and Coulton were there too. As far as I can remember so was Valentine. Esau had taken the night off. Even the police backed off. I dealt with everything and everyone. This time I didn't really have time to stop, think and be scared.

The next week Frances BB gave me a letter commending me for my "… somewhat brave actions… ". Got that at home too. Lloyd was pissed off he didn't get a letter. He really should have done.

If anyone thinks I'm over playing this, two guys I knew from a distance, Lincoln and Winston, both met their deaths doing this job and one of the Studio doormen I knew ended up getting life for killing some guy with a kick to the head after he was threatened by him on the door. Even the great Khachik claimed to have been stabbed once and hit by a passing car. Another doorman exaggeration? Couldn't tell you.

BTW: It cost the hotel a fortune in paying back punters from that night.

That particular episode was very unusual though. We did still throw the odd person out of the bar and got the odd bit of abuse inside but it was very tame.

One of my most vivid memories is of Animal deciding she was going to bite my hand one night. I have no idea why. Maybe it was a sign of affection! It bloody hurt and she would not let go. In the end I squeezed her boob VERY hard. So hard that she had to gasp which set me free. You can still see the scar on a cold day. I liked Animal but she was very, very underage, 14 or 15 at the most and probably younger. I was told she is another one who died a few years ago. I had no idea when I first wrote this. Now I know the truth. She's alive and well.

I took a knife off the girlfriend of some chap called Kenny. Not as tame as it sounds. They started having a barny as they stood there, out came the knife. I was only a few feet away, stepped in and took it off her. She was a tall, blond haired Punk with mean eyes. I'm pretty sure she didn't quite know how to react to some guy just asking her to hand over her 'blade' so just left. I didn't really do a thing. At least it wasn't me she was trying to stab. Kenny followed her out seconds later. I let her back in after a while and Kenny was always reminding her about the knife incident.

I think they eventually split because, after a while, I never saw her again. Years later I had to chuck Kenny out after I caught him buying some drugs in the toilets. I'd seen him and another bloke I'd never seen before, and who looked totally out of place, walk off together. I was suspicious so I followed. They were just doing the deal as I opened the door. His dealer went white and tried to leave. I was firm but polite. "Don't worry" I told them. "I'm a doorman not a policeman… just not in here." I never saw the dealer down there again. Kenny also stopped going down there after that.

I've heard that, allegedly, the place to go for your gear was the toilets or in the Fan Club, although other than Kenny I never saw anything and it was part of the job to look. Maybe the rastas at the Fan Club didn't know anything either.

Animal wasn't the first girl to bite my hand. I know they're small, no bigger than my mums, but I never realised they were so tasty. Maybe it's the salt from the sweating they always seemed to do when I was nervous. At the peak of the bars popularity I'd caught a lad called Ant filling up a pint glass from a bottle of cider he kept producing from under his jacket. I liked him but that was a bit of a no, no, so I had to ask him to leave, just for the one night. I let him back in the next day. He was with a very short, feisty girl by the name of Michelle who I knew from Helsinkis. She had long, curly blonde hair and pouted at me and tried to convince me to let him stay. I wasn't having any of it. Her response? You got it. She told me not to throw a wobbly and then bit in. Still got the scar from that one too. Someone later told me she was a 'bit feisty'. Soon after she left Leicester for good. Maybe she didn't like the taste after all.

By now I had time to notice Lloyds farting much, much more. I couldn't miss it really. Good job Stand Up Straight Claire from HR never saw us. Lloyd was a most impressive farter. I was with him in reception when he farted so hard... I swear... he left a stain on the wall that was there to the day we left. As we both laughed our socks off he started to walk across reception. With every footstep was a squueesh, parp, pip. Yuck.

Lloyd – I bet he's just farted
Picture Courtesy Jeff Shaw

Each night the doormen met up our clenched right fists would go out and would all touch for a second. I thought I was an honorary West Indian! More than ever before we became a team. Most employers talk about teamwork these days. I swear they have no idea. After the bar emptied and everyone went off to the Fan Club the Four Leicester Horsemen used to stroll around town or go off to the Travellers Rest at Griffydam. Me, Esau, Lloyd and Valentine. Large and in charge.

We'd usually go all over from nightclub to nightclub, standing in a dark corner being avoided by most people in there. I had an orange juice while the others sipped their drinks and quietly smoked the odd cigarette. Only Valentine was a really heavy smoker. I'd stand there and people watch. It's fair to say that by this time I loved going out. So far from my origins. I loved it so much that one summers night when everyone but me was tired and just wanted to go home I wailed "can't we just go out, even if it's for a walk round town?" They all looked at me and laughed. Valentine eventually caved in and we went for a quick wander into the Studio just to satisfy me. They all took the piss for weeks.

By now, once we'd finished work I'd wear my glasses so I could see what was going on. Sigh. The 3 horsemen and the one with the glasses. It doesn't sound quite right now. Trouble was they were always steaming up and I would spend the first 10 minutes in any club constantly wiping them clean only for them to steam up again. Brannigans, a small joint in Churchgate would be the worst. Former Centre Bar doorman Abdul was there by now and, after a quick glance over his shoulder to make sure the boss wasn't around, would always let us in. It would be heaving in there. Instant steam up every time.

I was busily trying to clean them up when we were in there when some guy approached me. "Can I borrow them?" he asked jabbing at my face with his finger. I was instantly suspicious. Most people never spoke to us. "Don't worry" he smiled. For some odd reason I just handed them over and watched in amusement as he used them as a magnifying glass on the teeny boobs of some girl he was with. We all laughed and then he handed them safely back. What was I thinking?

One of Esaus mates latched on to our wanderings. I didn't like it. It was the Four Horseman not the Four plus a stray pony! He was a Pakistani guy and I vaguely knew his face from Sugars but nothing else about him. What annoyed me was that he was a mouthy git and was blatantly using us to get in free everywhere as well. The gang and the pony buggered off to the Travellers without me one weekend. Coulton was DJaying. My old mate Kingsley was on the door. He would have been in his mid fifties by this time. Lloyd asked the King if he knew me. He denied all knowledge. Lloyd saw me the next weekend and told me I was full of shit about my history and that Kingy had no idea who I was. I was miffed. We went there again that same night. All of us. I went up to Kingy and asked what was going on. "Oh yeah" he said. "I thought about that after I said I didn't know you." Doormen and old age. Not always a good mix.

Mostly it was a good time during this period but it wasn't as trouble free wandering around the city as I would have liked it to have been. Is it ever? In the end we saw plenty of action around us, including one doorman creeping up on an old enemy and smacking him over the head with a glass. Turned out he was a doorman too, but from some other club. The guy who got glassed ran for his life which I thought was strange at the time. I was sure I'd have stood and fought and – as I later learned – that's exactly what I did do.

We also witnessed one poor West Indian guy having the crap kicked out of him by a gang of wild bouncers in the Studio doorway. They just dragged him to the floor and laid into him. About 4 of them. He rolled around on the floor like a croc dragging its prey underwater in a death roll but they didn't stop. In the end he somehow broke free and ran for it. It made me feel sick and I left seconds after he did. There was no way I wanted to be involved, not even as a witness.

We also learned that Khachik's agency Unit Control were looking to expand their territory. There were wild and unsubstantiated rumours they wanted to take over the Centre Bar door. Allegedly Luke and some other guy had been sniffing around and had even been into the other Alternative venues and caused a bit of mayhem. I don't think it was true. On reflection, even if it was, the Unit and the Goths in the Centre Bar. I don't think it would have worked somehow. In the end nothing materialised. Maybe that confirmed it was all just rumours and exaggeration.

There was still some humour as we rampaged around. One incident involved a young kid who came up to us as we walked up to a bar whose name I can't remember near the market. He was only about 13 and filthy dirty. Maybe he lived on the streets. It was nearly 1am. He looked us up and down and then said to Phil, who had left the agency that ran Helsinkis door and joined us as by then, "hey... son... Got a light?" Big

Phil, all 6 foot and then some eyed him up and down and dismissed it with a wave of one of his massive arms and a "who do you think you're calling son?" The kids eyes opened wide. He then tried the same with me and I was rude and aggressive but he didn't take a blind bit of notice. Phil came to my rescue and turned round and glared at him. The kid stopped in mid sentence and legged it. We all laughed. The others mostly at my failure to impress. Somehow I was perplexed. Maybe, despite my physical appearance the Goth magnet just didn't have the 'look' to scare a 13 year old street kid.

A few months later we saw a fight outside this same nightclub between my old pal Trevor, who was now there, and some other guy as we hovered in the background, trying to skip the queue. Trevor knew we were there and was pissed off we didn't help and wouldn't let us in so we just shrugged and went somewhere else. No big deal. According to Lloyd, Trevor didn't speak to him for about a year after that.

Writing this, I guess I seem to remember more of the trouble than the fun. This includes a vivid memory of the time we got threatened by some yob with a knife who stopped us as we were walking from bar to bar with a chant of "I think I've just seen Cilla Black... I think I've just seen Cilla Black...." Lloyd hesitated at the sound of this at first and was about to walk on but seemed to change his mind and slowly turned round. I just shook my head at him. He looked at me and then, in silent agreement, we all ignored it. The knob stood there, knife in hand looking quite disappointed while we all filtered by him.

I also remember all of us going round to the Fusion. It had been renamed many times and was now "The Aviary". Daz, who had got slashed on the back there had, unsurprisingly, never gone back after his injuries. Old training partner Ross had left for some other place years before outside of town. I found out much later that Cefus and Big Phil were working with him at the time. Steroids had got to him as much as they'd got to me. Apparently he had gone from a non-drinking, no smoking, martial arts champ to an untrained guy with long fluffy hair and a penchant for women.

Ross shared a flat with Big M for a while before M met Carol. Big M had forearms and hands like anvils. On the journey to Leamington he related a tale to me about the time he taken a girl he had met back to their rental and had found Ross stark naked apart from a pair of grey socks, comatose and face up on the floor. He had a lit cigarette in his hand that had burned a hole in the carpet.

M gently kicked him awake at which point Ross started puking everywhere and calling M all the names under the sun for disturbing him. According to Big M, he and the girl stepped over Ross who then settled back down in his puke and went back to sleep. I have no idea if any of this is even remotely true!

The last I heard of Ross was in the late eighties. He had been working as a security guard at Butlins or Pontins or some such place. He dropped by my house, out of the blue, with some guy I didn't know in tow in the September and we had a bit of a natter for a couple of hours and then they jumped in a car and were off. He phoned me a few weeks later. He sounded excited. "I'm in Manchester" he ranted. "I'm taking horse steroids now. I can't believe what my calves look like." If we'd have stayed training partners and mates would I have gone down that path? Probably.

Another night we arrived in our usual group of four, plus the pony, at The Aviary. I remember seeing a big, grey BMW parked nearby. It had the number plate RAM1K. Guess who? Khachik was standing there. The head of the Unit himself. It was a hot night. We walked in. The stray pony tried to come in with us. By this time I was seriously pissed off with him. "He's not with me" I mumbled. Khachik gave me an odd look. A mixture of uncertainty, disdain and boredom. I felt there was a great deal of tension between us. There wasn't. To him I guess I was still a nobody that he'd had a bit of a row with a few years before. I was creating something that didn't exist. He let us in, but not hanger on. I was pleased but didn't want any trouble with him or Khachik so stayed inside for ages. It was so hot in there and I was inside for so long that I started puking up orange juice. Valentine had to revive me in the loos. We got some good old stares. Two very obvious doormen. One big black guy, nearly 7' tall throwing freezing cold water over a tough looking, big white guy who kept thanking him every time he got a dousing.

It's fair to say that by now Khachik was becoming the new Mr. Big of Leicester. They eventually made a TV programme about him and his exploits. The guy who played him was a pock marked, weedy, very Arabian looking guy. Khachik sure has Arabian features but I would never describe him as being pock marked or weedy the whole time I knew him.

Another time I'd damaged my finger. I'd accidentally pushed it into the wall at the Centre Bar as I was messing around with Claire. It bloody hurt. The next weekend the Centre Bar DJ of the time, Tony, had got all arsey after I asked him to start to wrap it up. I knew him from my Helsinki days and thought he was well out of order. I was in charge. You didn't speak to me like that. I thumped the wall in frustration. Ouch. My poor finger. We went round to The Aviary again. I was in a bad mood. Coulton was there with some guy I didn't know. I spent all night with a pint glass full of ice and my hand stuck in it. Coulton laughed and tried to make out to his mate I was some sort of Mr. Hard Man who worked for him. I frowned at that and winced at my finger. Trust me. I never did that again.

Tony the DJ from came up to me a week later and apologised profusely. Apparently he'd just split with his girlfriend. I just let it go. Perhaps he was okay after all. It had served me right really. My bloody finger hurt for weeks.

1986 came and went. Me and Big M were joined in the gym by Haigh, a chunky guy and another one with a stupid moustache. Haigh was in his mid 20's although he was already starting to lose his hair and I thought he was a great bloke but as time went on his personality started to change. I was immediately suspicious. Then I managed to confirm what

I was thinking. Unbeknown to me, Big M had introduced him to steroids. I probably just asked him straight out. Apart from the personality changes from Haigh I **thought** they were both suddenly getting much bigger and stronger.

I watched dismally as the steroids took hold and saw more changes in both personality and physique over the next few weeks. I was very sensitive to it because I had gone through it so often myself. I must admit that I felt left out but there was no way I wanted to go down that path again. The main problem now though was that I was becoming jealous and didn't like them suddenly getting so much bigger and stronger than me. I moaned. A lot. They put up with my moaning for a short while and we even talked about setting up our own door agency. I'd already written a whole load of processes and procedures we could use to offer our services.

It never materialised. We were moving in different directions and I could still be very difficult to be around, especially once I started moaning. Big M eventually ran a very successful sports shop for a while. Haigh seemed less fussed than me about the whole thing and wanted our agency to have a jokey, light image. I argued that it didn't fit in with the views that most people had of security being serious and tough. We argued and argued about it. Hardly surprising it never got off the ground really.

Oddly enough there was only one night where we all worked at the Golf Range together. We were very late and came flying down the motorway from the gym in Leamington at over 140mph in Haigh's souped up green Ford Capri, with me bouncing about in the back without a seat belt. Plenty of skid marks that night, just not on the road. Yes. I know. It's an old joke.

Not long after that I stopped working at the Golf Range. For me, there was too much trouble there and I was becoming increasingly frustrated with the two of them – although it was me who was moaning – but I couldn't see it. Ultimately it was all too much for all of us and we all went our separate training ways after a brief, but heated final row as they stood in the doorway at the Golf Range. We never teamed up again. I don't know where they went to train but I do know that Big M and Haigh also split up as a team a short time later. I have never seen Haigh since. These days Big M will have nothing to do with me after I made some unsolicited and jealous remarks about his physique.

Back then? I continued to stay out of the way in Leamington. Away from the steroid crowd. Off the gear. For a short while after that I trained with the guy from Leicester who had the reputation of not sticking with anything. The purpose of this was mainly to try and lessen the burden of the fuel costs more than anything but he proved the comments I'd heard about him to be true. He was coming back after a long layoff so I wasn't too surprised to find he rarely trained hard. It is very difficult. He was always far more interested in planning my workouts for me – something which I didn't want him to do – than finishing his own workouts. He often used to tell me he was amazed at how focussed I was in the gym which I found gratifying, but a bit of an odd thing to say and would've preferred to train with someone who wanted to train hard themselves. Instead of that I carried on going with him and just as I felt we were finally synching a little as a partnership he blurted out in a broad Leicester twang "I've got summit to tell ya. I ain't training wiv ya anymore. I'll train ya like, but I ain't training meslef." I thought about it for around 10 seconds. Fuck him. He obviously didn't feel we were fitting together either. All he had to do was say. We continued the journey in muted silence. He tried ringing me for a short while but I wouldn't take his calls and I don't think I ever spoke to him again.

I carried on going to Leamington by myself. I've never trained with a training partner since.

Eight or more years later I wrote an article based on his approach to training and my thinking at the time. It was for an international writing contest and was intended to highlight the fact that neither of us were open minded enough to realise something was wrong. I got about 6th place. He found out 10 or so years later, long after I'd forgotten I'd written the bloody thing. I had been busy. He took it very personally – even though events had moved on by nearly 20 years by then and despite me contacting him to discuss it, was somewhat abusive to me over the internet for quite some time. Nice. I did retaliate at first, but just let him get on with it in the end. I have no idea where he is now.

As all this wandering around town was going on Coulton got himself a part time job as the DJ at the Studio. We often went in there too. He had shaved off the dead caterpillar by then. He would take the piss out of us over the microphone as we strolled in and we'd all laugh. It was on one of these trips that Esau and Valentine pulled two very tarty looking women. One was chubby with a crappy, bleached blonded perm and the other was very tall and thin with long dark hair and bright green nail varnish. I especially remember the nail varnish. As far as I know nothing much happened between them the first week they met but Esau managed to convince them to come down to the Centre Bar the next. He was seemed set on sex with them – either one. He didn't seem to mind. He spent ages trying to convince me – rather than Valentine – that I should join the 'party'. "These are experienced women" he proclaimed. I was very, very uninterested. Valentine was more than happy to step into the breech. I found out later Esau's enthusiasm for me to... er... partake was because he knew my house was empty that weekend and so it would have saved him trying to find somewhere.

As part of clearing the Centre Bar the night they were there I walked into the ladies loos and there they were, adjusting their make up and getting ready for a good night. They were surprised when I walked in but even more surprised when I backed out at about 100mph! I think Esau had been building up their expectations about me. In the end Esau, Valentine and the two of them went off to the Studio and I went home.

The week after Valentine was first to arrive. "How did you get on?" I smirked, being as nosy as ever. He grinned. "They were good fucks, but I think they wanted us to spend more on them." "Where did you go?" I asked, pushing for info. "Oh... we went to the Studio for about an hour and then back to their place" he told me. "I had the dark one. Trouble was" he went on "that the walls were thin and all I could hear from the other room was Esau going ugghhh... ugghhh... ugghhh."

About 10 or so minutes later Esau arrived. Valentine had wandered off somewhere. "How did you get on with those two birds?" I asked him, wanting his version of efforts and remembering some of the stories about doormen and women I'd heard over the years. "They were a good fuck" he told me. "Trouble was" I could sense what was coming "the walls were thin and all I could hear from the other room was Valentine going ugghhh... ugghhh... ugghhh."

I never saw these two women again. I don't think Esau or Valentine did either.

I don't think it would be a great surprise to realise that during this period we were now getting very well known as a team and getting other jobs. This was sometimes through our own efforts, but mostly through the boss. In early 1987 he got me a job working security at a Sigue Sigue Sputnik gig at the Powerhouse in Birmingham Anyone remember them? They were the epitome of soft Goth. Mohawks, black makeup, black string vests, the lot. I think one of them used to go down to the Centre Bar.

Bizarrely they had a bad rep. Someone had been in contact with Coulton. There was a cry for more men to cover the gig. Word was they were hiring doormen from all over the Midlands. Coulton asked if I was interested. More money. None of the other Centre Bar guys were interested so I enlisted Big M to help.

The boss enlisted 2 or 3 Psychobillys from the bar including little Keith that Esau had used as a ping-pong ball and his brother, Adie. We all went in one car. It was a tight squeeze. Two big doormen, Mr. C and some quaffed up Psychos. Apparently one of them had some billy whiz and pretty soon everyone but sanctimonious me was a bit happy, including the driver. It was an interesting drive. Big M was in good spirits but he had broken his hand on someones head the week before at the Golf Range and had a couple of stitches in him here and there. His hand was still in plaster but with him in the lead and me puffing and panting behind him we worked hard that night. We were right in front of the stage. Threw tons out.

Overall it was great fun. I was standing next to some good looking girl who looked about 15 when a lad came up to her, grabbed her by the hips and spent the next 3 minutes of one of the songs... how can I put this? Thrusting himself rhythmically into her. She looked at me with mock indignation and I asked her, over the thumping of the music, if she wanted him removed. She giggled and shook her head violently. After it was all over he just wandered off, presumably to find another girl to... um... dance with. Got to say, she looked quite contented. So did he!

In my memory I was back to being a nice guy and a gentleman and was coaxing people to leave but I seem to remember that Big M was a bit less patient than me. Having said that, he got a personal thanks from the Head Doorman that night so he must've impressed a lot more than I did. I do remember that Adie also spent all night rubbing his groin into the rear of a girl standing in front of him so I suppose he had a good night too! Strange 'dance' that. Must try it some day.

A few weeks later and M was out of the plaster when he broke the same hand again on someone else's head. I don't think he had any stitches this time. I met him at his flat and saw his swollen hand. It was obviously broken and he hadn't done a thing about it. I offered to run him to the Leicester Royal so him, Carol and one of their kids hopped in. I was so busy gabbing away that I drove up to the hospital, past it and about a mile down the road before Carol shouted at me "where are we going to get out?" In my own world again.

Dirty Den, Leslie Grantham from Eastenders, mania was also at its peak that year. In the middle of the year Coulton got us all a gig as security when he went to do a signing at the Studio. It was summer but it poured and poured that night. Despite the weather the place was heaving with women. The

Studio staff got us to turn some tables on their sides and use them as makeshift barricades to keep the crowds back. They were heavy so I tried to push one with my foot, missed and whacked my shin hard on the edge. Bloody hell!!! I hadn't really wanted to be there but Trevor had covered when actress who played Dot Cotton had done a similar event in the same club. In the end I had only agreed to work that night because I had wanted to see a flash of boobies. I wasn't a fan of Eastenders. At the time the Sun newspaper was happily reporting that Grantham was signing any boobs that were thrust under his nose at these events.

After we got the tables set up, I was happy enough to stand in the background and nurse my leg but the manager, a skinny Scottish chap knew us and me in particular. Well, we did go in there a lot. He caught my arm and, despite my squealing, asked me to work as Granthams personal bodyguard. Now – as I said earlier – when Fairey had taken my 'Star of the Quarter' photo I knew that I had this job coming up and had grown my thin, red beard, but I thought I would be one of several general security men. His personal bodyguard indeed!! The purpose of the beard was to disguise myself. I was determined that no one should recognise me. Looking back, how the hell I thought a red, scruffy beard was a good disguise, I have no idea.

Grantham had arrived through the back entrance and me, the Studio manager and one or two others had to get down to the main bar so we could get close to the ladies. The idea was that we went out of the nearest fire escape, down the soaking wet street and then back in through another fire escape about 30 feet away and get behind the bar. I led the way. I peeped out. The street was pretty much deserted. One lone woman was standing there looking miserable. I decided we could go. She saw us emerge and looked absolutely shocked but, as soon as she realised what was going on, rushed up to hug the actor. I got in between and she gave a big cry of "awwww!!" I looked at Grantham and he shrugged so I wordlessly stepped back, she got her hug and then we dashed the remaining few feet into the next entrance. Less than a minute from start to finish.

We got in behind the bar, a bit sprinkled with wet and breathless. The DJ got a signal and announced him and the house lights went up. The crowd rushed forward but there was absolutely no trouble. Despite my throbbing shin I was a bit amused really. All those doormen for that.

I stood behind him while he signed every type of boobie known to man for about half an hour. With my eyesight I had a shit view. In the whole of the time I was with old Grantham all he actually said to me was "let's go" after he'd had enough. Of course, later it turned out he'd been inside for murder and even later he the Sun exposed him as an internet pervert. No wonder he didn't mind signing boobs.

I shaved my red beard off the moment I got home. Today I tell people I once worked as his Minder. I suppose it's true in a way but I don't tell them it really was only the once, unplanned and for a maximum of 30 or so minutes, including less than a minute in the street.

About a month later Coulton got us work as security at the Studio for a sexy lingerie show. The girls doing the modelling were from an... ahem... gentlemans magazine. In fact, for some strange reason I recognised one of them. Well okay then, parts of her anyway. Magazines like that regularly made their way around at work in those days. It wouldn't happen now. We'd all be fired.

I was supposed to be keeping the crowds back. In the end I think it worked a bit the other way! I felt someone tugging my trouser leg and looked down. It was another guy I'd been on the holiday to Spain with in the early 80's. He had a big, cheesy grin on his face. So did I. I grinned back.

The one girl I recognised stood less than three feet in front of me, looked me in the eyes and stripped completely naked. The crowd cheered. I squinted as hard as I could for a better look. It made me look like a perv. Not a pretty sight. She turned around and I watched her bare arse wiggle away. Now that WAS a pretty sight. Not as good as Claire's of course but not far behind. There's a little joke there somewhere. Later I was told that she'd 'got off' with one of the other doormen, or, as it was put to me. One of the other doormen 'got off' with her. I bet it was another doorman exaggeration.

With the car now off my back and no steroids to buy I was starting to earn a small fortune for all my hard work. What's the phrase? The harder I work, the more successful I become. Funny that.

24

The End of Christmas Nights

Over the years, especially after I moved to the gym in Leamington, the traditional Sugars Gym Christmas outings had started to fade. I think a lot of that was due to the ever changing faces in there. I'm also pretty sure that the mass steroid use that was going on behind the doors had resulted in more and more of the crowd I knew turning to door work. The reason? Same as me; to supplement their incomes from their day jobs to pay for the gear and make ends meet. The result of that was at Christmas most were out working, or in my case, usually too exhausted or aggressive to want to go out.

The first sortee had been in 1981 when a very small number of us – maybe 4 or 5 including Khachik and Kingy – had wandered up to some pub on London Road, not too far from the gym, for an hour or so. It was wet but not too cold. We sat there in a little huddle laughing and joking and I sipped my orange juice whilst Khachik called me a puff. Even in jest that wasn't a good term to use with me. Kingy must've seen something in my eyes and took on the fatherly role that I suppose he always had towards me. Eventually Kingy diverted Khachik enough for the piss taking to stop. I was pretty relieved.

I think that Kingy and Khachik were great rivals in many ways. Over the years I heard talk of them lining up for a battle but it never happened and was probably complete bullshit from someone's colourful imagination.

After a short while in the pub someone jumped up and we all left. I remember being a bit reluctant. It was so unusual for me to be out like this. I can only assume that both Kingy and Khachik had to go to work on the doors that night.

We wandered back in a group to the gym where my car was. Everyone started to make their way off. I was left alone with Khachik. He rewarded me for being there by pissing up the back of my car after and calling me a puff again. This time I shouted but this WAS Khachik and there was just me and him so I didn't shout too much. He just laughed at me and told me to grow up. I suppose I smiled but I bet it was a grim one. He didn't drive then. I don't think he passed a driving test until he was well into his twenties. Guess who was dumb enough to give him a lift home. It was something my dad would've done. I thought I was being his mate.

I was one of the main drivers to set this up as a regular event. Like I said, I hardly ever went out so it was an opportunity for me to see what nightlife was all about. I mean, once a year. Hardly the king of the swingers. I waited a whole year between nights out. Twelve months without going out once. Not once.

By the second time round Khachik was in prison. I desperately wanted to go out, so did some talking. Even then I could have a fast mouth when I wanted to. In the end a few of us agreed to meet up on about the 23rd. For me it was even more fun than the year before. Rather than just go to one pub for an hour we rampaged around town – Trevor was there – dick out and rubbing it up against any unsuspecting women. I'd never seen anything like it before.

Training partner and buddy of the era Ross was also there, along with his terrifyingly skinny mate Terry who lived opposite him. One or two others were there as well but I can't recall their names or faces.

I didn't like Terry. He had had been on the holiday with us earlier in the year. I thought he was a complete knob the whole time we were there but tolerated him for the two weeks and even went with him and Ross to a similar thing the next year. Apart from being stick thin Terry had a massive nose, a monobrow and a VERY, VERY big gob. He clearly disliked me as much as I disliked him.

On our night out I got pissed on half a pint of Guinness at our first stop which was some nameless, trendy wine bar which sat under a car park opposite where the Fan Club would eventually be. The others had led the way. I only had the Guinness because I was so innocent that I didn't know what else to order. I know I asked for a pint of beer but because it was a wine bar they didn't sell whole pints. Everyone looked at me a bit bemused. Hey. I didn't know.

I sat and sipped my drink and pretended I was enjoying it. I hated the taste and the smell. The others were far more used to town life and led the way. I just trailed, drinking or pretending to a pint here and there. Although I got a little jolly the truth is I left most of it undrunk on some table or ledge everywhere we went. The others were getting more and more pissed and I laughed, amused at their behaviour. They couldn't really tell I wasn't *that* drunk. In the end we were all getting tired and lost Trevor and his dick in some place in Silver Street. I asked him a few days later where he had got to and he just grinned.

Eagle from Sugars Gym had been on the door when we had arrived. He had moved from the Fusion. He smiled when he saw me and let us all in. This place was right next to a trendy pub where I stood on the door myself 10 years or so later. Later on I often wondered if all the guys I knew, met and worked with were all around town then. They probably were. Leicester is a relatively small place.

I guess we all enjoyed it enough to make it an annual event. Well, okay. I enjoyed it enough to make it an annual event.

In my mind the biggest and best years, in terms of fun and friendliness, were probably 1983, when Roy was with me and I asked Lee for the job in Mr. Kiesas and 1984 when I found myself crawling on the floor in Tipplers.

By 1986 or 87 I didn't really know anyone from Sugars anymore and absolutely didn't know anyone from the Leamington Gym. My workouts were too brief and infrequent and I would never stop to chat. I just wanted to get there, train, get in the car and drive home. Even these days I don't really talk to anyone when I'm training. I just find it too distracting.

Because I'd got the taste for going out by then and, if I wasn't working, me and Coulton would go out at Christmas. It was usually at my insistence. His favourite trick was to get me steaming and then phone up on Christmas Day to make sure I was still alive. I complied quite happily. It didn't take a lot of beer.

He did it one year when we bumped into some other guys we didn't know at all and Mr. C convinced them they should come and work with me at the bar. I was so drunk I don't know their names or where we were. All I can tell you is that the boss led the way back to the hotel and jumped over a big wooden fence in the process. I looked at one of the guys with us. Even in my state there was no way I was going to do anything as stupid as that. Who knows what was on the other side or where we were. The guy looked at me. Neither of us were willing to do it.

About 5 minutes later an anxious looking Coulton appeared from around the corner. *"Where were you?"* he asked. *"No way"* we said in unison. Coulton just grinned. *"This way"* he cried and we unsteadily followed him the long way round. I still didn't have a clue where we were.

I remember we made it back to the hotel. The plan was that Coulton would show them round and they were due to start the next weekend. They never showed. I think they were too drunk to remember as well. Apparently, and I don't remember this, I was so drunk I was crawling around on the floor trying to chat up Andrea who was sitting there with a few of the hotel managers. I don't think I impressed her too much that night.

I have no idea how I got home but that was pretty much the last time I ever touched alcohol. It would've been 1987. I do know that in June 1988 I'd got very pissed in Helsinkis. I didn't know where else to go and I felt safe there. I was so drunk my lips went numb. I got a taxi home from Jim in the hotel reception, managed to stop myself throwing up in the car but fell over in the drive when we arrived, went arse over tit on the ottoman in my bedroom and then spent all night, in between running to the loo to puke and clawing my way back to my bed, trying to stop my bed spinning under me. I was still in a bad way two days later as I stood on the Centre Bar door. Roche saw me groaning and eventually came to call me the only man to say never again to alcohol and mean it.

When it got to Christmas of 1988 I wanted to go out again despite other events that were going on around me but had now lost all my ties from Sugars. On top of that Mr. C either couldn't make it or didn't want to go. In the end I worked Christmas Eve dinnertime. I didn't want to drive in so took a taxi. The taxi driver called me a gentle giant. Not really.

When I finally got home I stayed in all night and watched a movie starring Jeff Bridges and Glenn Close called Jagged Edge. I thought it was superb. I suddenly realised that I didn't miss the boys night out or the alcohol associated with it and I have to say I still don't.

In late November 1989 my grandma died. She was 90 or 91. By the time we got her buried Christmas of that year was nearly on us. For a Christmas break and a chance to get away me and my mum took a coach trip to my old haunt – Paris. It took us longer to get there than the time me and Ross made it by train. The damn coach we were on broke down and we were stuck for hours on the motorway. I wasn't the nicest person to be stuck with for hours on end at this point in my life. When we finally got there I showed her around, took her on the Metro and up the Eiffel Tower on Christmas Day. I told her where I used to get my drugs from. It was no secret.

After that I took her past the house the Honey Monsters lived in. I had wanted to say hello to them. Unfortunately they weren't around but their dad – universally known as Papa – was sitting by the window painting. That was his full time occupation. I recognised him from my previous visits and waved. I wanted to ask him where his sons were but he was engrossed in his work and ignored me. Oh well.

I found that year was a refreshing change and, overall, I enjoyed doing something so different, although the group that we were with probably found me a little strange. After asking if there would be anything formal when we booked up and being told no, I hadn't taken a suit or tie so turned up for the Christmas meal in a sweatshirt and jeans.

My mum had warned me but I hadn't taken any notice. Everyone else was dressed to the nines. I was pretty embarrassed but no one dare say anything to me. My mum was embarrassed too – not just because of the way I was dressed but also because of my behaviour. I told her I didn't give a shit but that isn't true.

In the end it became a holiday of being stuck in lifts. First we were stuck in a lift on the Eiffel Tower and next we got stuck in the lift in the hotel. It was good though because these incidents allowed me to tell little funny stories. I like to tell tales about myself and the way I react to things. It's something else I used when I gave lectures in Australia. I suppose I have a fairly self-depreciating humour.

Fortunately being able to relate these tales that Christmas the way I did made some people realise that there was a human side to me and I had a few, brief chats with them but such was my steroidal behaviour that when we weren't out and about I mostly sat by myself in a corner and glared or sulked. I probably glared at people when we were out and about as well. I don't know. Look at me. I'm a doorman! Nearly 16 stone at the time with cropped hair and Rolex on my wrist. Stay away unless you want trouble! It worked.

It was so different for both of us that after that we made it a bit of an event to go away every year for a while. For me, it was away from door work and it broke the, somewhat bad, habits of the previous few years. I managed it for quite a few years in a row, always with my mum for company. Maybe not quite the image I paint of myself is it? Perhaps my mum was just being extremely tolerant. As far as I was concerned the others could keep an eye on the bar and the hotel if it opened and it allowed me to take my mind off other events that were going on in my life.

Over time I like to think that my behaviour was improving and I even started to relax and have a little bit of pleasant fun with the people around me but there was always something lurking in my mind. In the end my mum got too frail, I didn't want to go by myself and I emigrated anyway.

When I lived in Australia I missed company. I also missed the cold Christmas weather and spending time at home opening presents or going away with a small group for a few days.

Christmas on the beach or alone and an ever growing chance of skin cancer – not for me thanks. I enjoyed Christmas 2009 in the cold and wet with my family and my long time friends around me, although I supposed Lloyd and Phil were working somewhere – as always.

I've never seen a Christmas Eve film that I've enjoyed or have been engrossed by as much as Jagged Edge since. In reality I don't think it was that particular film. I think the time for me to change my ways had just come. Sometimes these things are conscious decisions. Sometimes they're not.

25

Incessant Chatter

Sadly, by now, the Centre Bar had become only fractionally busy compared to its heyday. Coulton still kept getting bands down to the Garden Room but they were getting less and less popular and sometimes that stayed closed while they played on the little stage in the Centre Bar which made it very claustrophobic and hugely noisy. Occasionally though we had great success and the place would be back to brimming if someone nationally famous like the UK Subs or locally well known like the Hunters Club or Crazyhead played.

Having said that, sometimes the band would be the only one in there and the first time the Hunters Club played I was the only one in and out of the room all night. We were all bored shitless. The night dragged on. Me and Esau wandered in one last time. It was last orders. Just as I asked their lead singer, Ian who I knew quite well, to wrap it up a few people wandered in, maybe 5 or 6. Ian got all excited and they started to play as ferociously as they could. The growing noise attracted a load more. There moment of stardom had begun. They didn't want to come off. This was their chance. Esau started to get a bit grumpy and there was a kind of musical stand off. In the end Ian just laughed, played a few more notes and they packed it in. The growing audience couldn't believe it. Neither could I. Sod's law I suppose.

I recall the UK Subs, a very, very popular Punk group being booked more than once. The first time weird Johnno, from the Alternative Miss Universe night, had jumped on stage to join in, while another punter had grabbed the mic and sung along. It was great, the only downside was when their table of saleable goodies ranging from orange coloured 7" discs to T-Shirts collapsed under the load just as I drifted by. Lloyd asked me if I'd kicked it over on purpose. I just looked at him gone out. Of course not! I loved nights like that. Unfortunately it wasn't so great the second time. The bar was bulging with people as we waited for the band to arrive but there was no sign of them. Nothing. Coulton was there very early on but did a runner when he realised things were going to be problematic, leaving me to explain to a very disgruntled crowd that we had no idea what was going on. I had to be very smooth that night. Some people had traveled a long way. About midnight, an hour after the bar shut and just as I was leaving, a car pulled up in Rutland Street. A very stressed looking Charlie Harper, the lead singer, got out. I looked over, made eye contact than smirked and then ambled off to my car, got in and drove home without saying a word.

The lack of lots of customers most nights left me with more time and space to speak to the people that still wandered in, so much so that Red Cap Kevin even came over and spent ages with me and Lloyd discussing how best to read a complex engineering drawing!

The bar struggled on. Julie, the final third of the Helsinki trio still appeared from time to time. Of all the girls I'd ever hugged and kissed I never hugged and kissed her. She grabbed me as she was leaving. "It's my 21st birthday" she pleaded. To say she got very close would be an understatement. Basically she... er... mounted me, clamped on like a limpet and, with Esau watching in amusement from the other side of the corridor, started to gyrate up and down. I assume she was pissed but I'm not sure. I... er... had a little bit of a reaction.

The thing was I simply didn't fancy her. Not in the least and never had, even though she'd made it obvious over the years that she had some interest in me. That's why I'd never got close to her before. I thought she was a nice enough girl but just a bit chubby and plain for me.

Might as well make it the hat trick I thought. We had a bit of a snog, just the once. After a few minutes I guess she realised that, despite what she could clearly feel, a kiss was the best she was going to get. In the end she looked a bit embarrassed and vamoosed, leaving me pointing, so to speak, in equal embarrassment at a grinning Esau.

She never mentioned that night again and neither did I. At least she didn't smell like an ashtray. Not that I can remember anyway.

I'm positive she rode past me on a pushbike in mid 2008 when I was visiting my family on a sojourn from Oz. I was looking for an internet café in the city when this woman rode by, saw me and nearly fell off. It was either Julie or her twin sister.

By now Valentine was becoming more and more unreliable. I do remember trying to phone him when he hadn't turned up again. I rang... and rang... and rang... and rang... and rang... and rang. I was pissed off with him. There was no way I was hanging up. After about 5 minutes of continuous ringing this voice screamed down the phone at me "WHAT!!!" "Have you been shagging?" I asked. I know. Just call me subtle. In the end me and Nick, the bars manager got so fed up with it that we sacked him. Valetine came back a week later, dressed to the nines, and pleaded for his job back. I was all ready to relent but Nick, rightly, stuck to his guns. Valentine seemed to blame me and didn't speak to me for many years.

Over at Helsinkis, after Lloyd and Valentine had rejoined us, Mel and Tony had gone back to using an agency. Their doormen changed a lot as a result. I soon saw, as best as my eyesight would allow, the appearance of a massive West Indian I got to know. This was Phil.

I didn't know him at all at this point but from what I could see of him I reckoned he was in his mid twenties and easily as tall as Valentine but, while Valentine was skinny, Phil was built like a tank. I later discovered that his brother, Robert, was a barman at the hotel. I assume that with the help of Robert, Coulton offered him a job as our new man because I got there one night and he was there.

Phil was a very experienced doorman even then and really looked the part. As I shook hands with him I discovered he had a pair of mitts like a bunch of dry bananas. Funnily enough I've always liked shaking hands with Phil. I've got small hands. His engulf mine.

A guy called Teddy joined Victor to replace Phil at Helsinkis. Another of Cefus' brothers. The odd bit is that, as far as I know, Victor is still there. I don't know what happened to Teddy.

Now the Centre Bar quartet consisted of me, Lloyd, Esau and Phil. Sadly me and Phil had a bumpy start. We were still swopping who we worked with every weekend but Phil hardly spoke to anyone, including us, the clientele, the bar staff, Coulton and Nick. Even my attempts at exuberance didn't work. In the end I found I didn't like standing with him because he never made any attempt at conversation and casually told Esau I was beginning to think about getting rid of him when Phil trapped me in a corner and demanded to know why I was such a bastard to him and that he'd never done anything to me. He was very upset. So was I. I was slow but even I realised something about myself that night. We both stayed and became very, very good friends. We still are. Turns out he was just careful about who he got close to and was fundamentally shy as well. Isn't it odd that doormen can be shy?

Me and Phil often used to find ourselves sitting in the hotels residents only bar being served by Judy, who had sewed the sleeve back on my jacket. We would sit there and sip orange juice until the small hours, chatting away about our lives, his kids – he had at least one young daughter who would be well into her twenties by now – the future, our different training regimes and more.

Phil liked running and always spoke about it until he made the mistake of telling us all the story of how he had stepped in some dog shit as he pounded round a field. After that there was too much piss taking for him and he never mentioned it again. Unlike me, Phil also loved being out in the fresh air and was variously a postie, a bus driver and a long distance driver. Ultimately we all got a bollocking for using the residents bar and were told we weren't allowed in there. Time to find somewhere else to go.

I still spent my nights messing around with Claire, Tony, Jill and any number of other people in there. I chatted incessantly to Roche, a beetle eyebrowed guy with a black spider tattooed on the back of one hand and his older para brother who went down there when he wasn't on tours. At one time Roche the younger used to wear a white woolly hat permanently fixed to his head. It became as dark as his hair. I inevitably spent time with his skinny girlfriend Alison as well and their pals. These included Mandy, a dark haired girl from London who I best remember for coming in one New Years Eve begging someone, anyone to take her virginity. Also in this group were roadie Penny, Kip, a shaven headed local lad, Chaz, dirty looking with dreads, black fingernails and scruffy jeans and Megs, a lanky geezer who was another of Louise's former boyfriends. I'd known them all for years. In fact Roche was the guy with the Doc Martins who I'd asked to hang around for a few minutes years earlier at Helsinkis.

Mandy's cry for someone to take her virginity was very funny. Maybe it was to fulfil her new years resolution to herself. Just to let you know, I declined. I suppose I could have but I thought nah. No thanks. I didn't fancy her and she was very young, no more than 16 and also pretty drunk at the time. I think a chap called Colin did the honours. She certainly gave him a good caress right in front of me. More accurately she gave a small, but growing part of him a good caress right in front of me! Embarrassing. He didn't seem to care.

More than anything, I chatted to and hugged and kissed lots and lots of different girls. There was Caroline, in my eyes a tiny, pretty mousy blonde with her crimped hair often tied back in a pony tail that had been going down to the bar for ages – I spent a lot of time holding hands with her – and her dark haired twin sister, Nikki.

Nikki had been pretty open in coming over and chatting before listening to me blather on about nothing before calling me "too lary" and backing off. Caroline was much more careful around me. She always smiled and I smiled back but we hardly said a word to each other, then I overcame my shyness and sat next to her in the Garden Room as she struggled to adjust a knee length boot she was wearing. She looked warily at me as I grinned at her as she struggled on. We were the only two left in there. Finally she pulled the damn thing off to reveal a black woolly sock. I absolutely wet myself laughing. That was it. No longer scared of Jeff.

Caroline (1987/88)
Picture Courtesy Lisa White

There was also Catherine, an Irish nurse with red hair who was always commenting about my sweaty hands. Maybe I was nervous around her. Earlier that year Catherine had been in the Centre Bar with some of her mates one Thursday night when I wasn't working and had got attacked by some random bloke in the doorway. Apparently she was screaming for my help so much her attackers ran off. How's that for your reputation preceding you?

Catherine had an on / off Irish boyfriend called John, a Fergal Sharkey look-a-like, who had once worked at the bar. I liked him but I never sussed out the full extent of their relationship. She asked me once if I'd seen her with him to which I replied "well... there's been so many" and her replying "oh yeah" ever so slightly sarcastically. I even went to her 21st birthday party after we'd stood together in the bar a few weeks earlier while, with a bemused Lloyd looking on and one of her friends in the background, she sucked at my fingers. Her friend shrieked "that looks a bit personal." It sure was. God knows where John was that night or what he would have thought.

Coulton was DJaying the night I went to her birthday party. Dave Man was helping, which he did quite a few times in those days, and I saw Catherine, Caroline, Nikki and a whole host of others I knew. Catherine was with John. I gave her a pretty pink card my mum had picked out for me but the best I could do, after Coulton asked me why I wasn't at the hotel, was to stand moodily at the back because I'd had a bad night. I went home alone.

Another girl who let me get reasonably close was Erica. Reasonably close was let me squeeze her arse. Pretty, with a long face, she had big hair and a big tattoo of a horse on her back. She was always going on about stroking her pussy. No double entendres there then! I used to stick my hand up the rear of her dress while we both stood with our backs very close to the wall, then put my hand on her bum. What can I say? Sorry Erica.

One final little blond that I can remember is Julie. I remember sitting there one night stroking the side of her breast for ages. She didn't move an inch. Julie was another one who had lived in Australia but I went off her when she told me she drank mini vodka bottles all day long.

I have to admit, there were many, many more whose names, sadly, I can't (or won't) remember. It was all reasonably platonic with most of them, although I suppose it's fair to say that I had my moments. Deep down I suppose I missed the heyday of Louise and Sharon but I knew that was all over by then. One good trick I did learn was to cut my feelings right of, so although I got reasonably close to some of these girls, in my mind I never really got too deeply emotionally involved ever again.

Erica
Picture Courtesy Ellen Wells Symington

Typically of me at the time I got friendly with Adelle, the head bar woman and April, a pretty flame haired, but very shy girl who worked behind the bar with her mate Mags, a friendly but a tad rotund half caste girl.

April had appeared one Sunday night. I'd got a phone call. "Could I get someone to come in that night? There's an 18th birthday party in the Garden Room." I didn't like to work Sundays. I was already working six days a week and had been for years but that weekend I had nothing better to do. I roped in Lloyd. We both turned up in our jackets and ties for about 8pm. I was tired and hadn't even bothered to shave.

Lloyd was pretty much in the same state. The whole place was quiet except for the party. It was just getting going. Me and Lloyd peeped in. There weren't that many people in there. Suited me. The night went on. No trouble. Nothing. In the end we just sat in the empty bar and nattered away to each other. Every time Coulton wandered past we jumped up and pretended to be on patrol. In the end we couldn't be bothered any more and he came and sat with us.

Out of the corner of my eye I spotted this young girl sitting on the other side of the empty bar. She had a lad with her and was trying her best to flirt. I could see she was having some problems. April had arrived. I didn't take too much notice. I never thought I'd see her again. I was astounded when I walked into the Centre Bar the next weekend and this same girl was standing behind the bar. Years later I took the piss out of her early attempts at flirting in an empty Centre Bar. April was equally astounded that I'd seen her and remembered.

Mags was really nice but she could talk really fast. She had short-cropped black curly hair and always wore a white shirt that was never tucked in. I seem to recall her shielding April from me a lot but that may be imagination.

There were still a lot of functions upstairs, the odd function in the Garden Room like Aprils party and jobs outside the hotel and enough trouble to keep us busy, and employed, including the night of Claire's 18th.

It was very late 1987. I wasn't happy with my physique. My bodyweight had dropped with my continued attempts to stay off steroids and I was much lighter and smaller than I wanted it to be. I started to bulk up, a very 1960's bodybuilding method. I was eating anything that wasn't nailed down. I started to get really fat. Oh dear. There's another photo of me taken by one of the guys that regularly used to come in at Christmas functions, take snaps of people at the functions and then sell them later at night. My head looks like a potato. I keep that one to remind me. I was huge though. I got so big I had to go to a special shop to get shirts that would go around my bulging neck.

Jeff Shaw

My jackets, once so tight across the back and loose at my waist began to get tighter. Problem was it was now at the front around my waist! I started to look like a beer barrel. Never-the-less I was pretty happy in terms of being back to a gentleman.

By March 1988 I'd been off the gear for just over a year. I decided that I wanted a record of my training. For my kids. Yet to be born. Still waiting. Maybe someday. I tried to talk Esau into doing the same. He wouldn't. I hired a video cameraman, took a Wednesday off and we filmed me training in Leamington Spa. I went home all happy. My dad was there, so was my mum. He was on the phone. I was sitting there. He just had a major stroke and collapsed at our feet.

They turned the life support off the next day. It's hard to be light hearted about this bit. I only watched the final video of me training once. I never talk about that day, so I'm not going to write about it. Good soldier. In floods of tears I went to work the following morning. So did my mum. Both of us got sent home. I had the Friday off from my day job and played "This Corrosion", which is a pretty depressing Sisters of Mercy track, over and over while my dad lay being assessed in ITU. Then I went to work at the Centre Bar that same night.

It was obvious I was very unhappy. It showed in my face, my body, my energy. Two Goth girls I knew quite well walked in and saw me. I know one was Ellen but I couldn't remember the name of the other for a long time. I eventually found out it was Nadia. They sat opposite me for a few minutes watching intently. I half looked back under shaded and reddened eyes. I didn't smile or say a word. MOST unusual.

They looked at one another and called me over to ask me what was wrong. It was very kind of them. With a quivering lip I told them my dad had just died and they uttered some words of sympathy. I thanked them, turned round and leant my elbows on the bar with my head down to my chest. Just then Esau walked in. I had my back to him but saw him out of the corner of my eye. My head was still down. He said something to me which I didn't catch and I grunted in return. He called me some name. I heard Ellen and Nadia call him over and tell him my news. He came back and put his arms around me. I cried.

I really, really appreciated it but it must have been odd to see two bouncers, one crying in the others arms.

Nadia
Picture Courtesy Ellen Wells Symington

I should never have been there that night. Mr. C found out about my dad. I don't know who told him. He told the others to keep an eye on me and I made it through the night and the next. After we shut the bar on the Saturday I went to the Fan Club looking for someone to hit. Anyone. Little Caroline waved shyly and vaguely at me. I ignored her. Somebody threw a bottle at me. It hit me on the back, gently, softly but I was way beyond redemption that night. I know that Lloyd was with me, keeping a watchful eye. He made me go home before I got myself into bother. It was a good idea. That sort of stuff though is why me and Lloyd are still friends a million years later.

Shortly after my dads death my mum hired a clairvoyant and who told me that my dad was now my guardian angel. I clung on to that. I even wore his wedding ring for a short while, but I don't like rings so soon stopped. It was too big anyway. Then, in a heap of emotion, I left the steel industry and Metallurgy less than two months later and got a job that I thought was my future. I became a manager at a small assembly factory on the outskirts of Leicester. That was when I met a man I will always call "the bastard."

26

Down the Slippery Slope

I'd been so upset when I'd been interviewed that I hadn't used my doorman skills and sussed "the bastard" out properly. He simply made my life hell, literally from the very first day. Looking back it was all too soon after the death of my dad for me to cope. Because of his behaviour towards me I don't think I really had time to grieve.

To try and put some of it in perspective, I'd already had someone take my wing mirror off my parked car about a week after my dad had died. My car had been brand new. So new that my dad had never even had the chance to sit in it. I'd just parked and was still sitting in it when – wham! The other driver did get out, but I couldn't believe it. Then I had a car crash the weekend before I changed jobs. Someone just rammed me from behind while I was stationary. Added to this someone else had kicked in front door while I was working in the bar. Neither me or the car were doing too well.

I shakily turned up for my new job. I was smartly dressed with a shirt and tie and a little briefcase I'd bought. Not like being in the steel industry where steel toecap boots and ear defenders were the order of the day. "The bastard" gave me a dirty, down the nose look. I was a bit unsettled. The death of my dad was very much on my mind. I needed my guardian angel. I smiled nervously. To start a conversation and get to know him I showed him the triple damage to my car.

I was totally shocked by his reaction. It was as though I was the shit on his shoe. Here was his new boy and in the first hour of the first day he showed his true colours. His behaviour towards me from then on was absolutely disgraceful. I was truly a turd in his eyes. His whipping boy. Slowly at first, then more rapidly, under a continual barrage of sneers, bullying, condescending comments and the effects of my dads death I began to spiral downwards.

I found myself returning to steroids. I still had plenty left over from my visits to Paris. I guess it was all related to the stress he was laying on and I wanted my size back as my defence, but I had an internal battle. I really didn't want to take them. The result was that I then went into a very rocky bit of on-off low level usage with all the steroidal moods and ups and downs that came with it. Ultimately my mind was set though. No matter what, I was finished with the gear.

I finally broke their grip forever in July 1990. It had taken two and a half years of massive effort but by this time I was as used to "the bastards" abusive ways as you could ever be and being big hadn't stopped them. He even made some sneering comment to my mum about "your big son." I'm happy to say I never took them again. Whoooo fucking hoooo!!

I really don't know how I was being viewed by anyone at this stage. At night in the bar, flirting away I was pretty much my usual self. I was good and disguised the way I felt the same way I disguised how steroids used to affect me when I was at Helsinkis but sometimes I could be 'odd' and just stood in the shadows or watched what was going on in the bar through reflections in the mirrors behind the bar rather than turn around. If there were occasional fights, more often that not, I flew into them without considering the risks to me or my crew. Phil told me once that I should be more careful, but all I said was "I'm protected." An oblique reference to my guardian angel. The effects from "the bastard" were so bad that I even remember standing in a cupboard just to keep out of the way. I just couldn't take anyone talking to me. Coulton found me. He asked me what I was doing and I had no answer. He was just bemused. Not surprising.

I still had some humanity though and would chat away in the bar or leap out of reception anytime Caroline or someone else I fancied went past. I wanted, and needed, to be hugged. Other times though I could be, and was, a complete monster. Once the bar emptied and I stood and worked the rest of the hotel or at any other time during the day I was a total c*nt. People were talking about me behind my back and it wasn't good! My poor old, confused brain.

There are times I know I didn't contain myself when I was in the bar either. In September of 1988 Claire came in with one of her other mates, a skinny horrible thing none of us liked. Skinny told us it was her 18th birthday, although it was really her 16th. I began to get nasty and just took the piss. Lloyd thought I was joking and told me he'd got a good idea. "Let's make a birthday card out of toilet paper" he said enthusiastically. I went along with it. We gave her the 'card'. Not surprisingly she got quite upset. Part of me felt guilty. So did Lloyd. We ended up buying her a Southern Comfort to cheer her up. It was my fault. I still feel guilty over twenty years later, although I have since met this girl and apologised profusely. She told me she didn't even remember.

Around this period I had an argument with a crop haired regular called Heath. He was a buddy of Roche's and had only just got over a car accident of some sort where he lost a middle finger so hadn't been around for a while but he had been going down to the bar for ages. I can't remember what the argument was about. I threw him out in a "bastard", and probably steroid fuelled, temper tantrum. As he went, kicking and screaming he threatened to come back that night and firebomb the place and especially me. According to him he spent loads of money there and should have been treated better. I'd heard that one before by now. He was drunk so I let it go. I was so far gone I don't think I cared anyway. Then he came out with the "I was a dead man" crap. I laughed it off. I was so changed by now that threats like that had no thumpity-thump effect what-so-ever. None. I just got more aggressive in getting him out and he went like a little lamb.

As usual nothing untoward happened from his threats. No sign of Heath and no firebombs. Typical. The next week Roche came in. His horizontal eyebrow was in full animation. "You were lucky" he said to me. "Why?" I asked blandly. Apparently Heath was coming back on his motorbike when the police pulled him over for riding erratically. They found the bomb under his jacket. I can honestly say I wasn't bothered one way or another.

Another time I lost it was after I'd just bought some designer glasses from "For Eyes" in St. Martins Square. Black frame, trendy. Nice and expensive! I left them behind reception for safekeeping. I didn't want any harm coming to my new specs. I couldn't have coped with the stress. At the end of the night when I picked them up I found that manager Sally had tied a ribbon around them in fun. She hadn't seen the other side of me at that point. Out of the blue I went berserk. Poor Sally, she didn't know what had hit her. I don't think I ever apologised for that one. If you read it now – sorry Sal. After that I left my glasses behind the bar. In the end even Nick managed to put a pile of optics on top of them and bent the frame. Great. I went mad at him too.

About a year after my dad died my brother and his family came to see my mum one Sunday. His kids were very young then, about 7 and 5. I was there. He'd hardly been round since my dad died and I thought his behaviour was a bit off. Of course, I didn't take into account my own. We ended up having a massive row and I physically manhandled him out of the house while his wife was screaming that she was going to call the police. We didn't speak for about 10 years after that. Insane? Just disturbed.

Just to drum the point home one last time. I was standing in reception once sipping a coffee. It was in the wee hours of the morning, the function rooms were in full swing and there was no one around. I was exhausted. Andrea was on duty and saw me. She took one look at me and yelled "stop!" I was startled. "There's no way you're standing in reception drinking coffee" she shouted at me. I was instantly enraged. So what? I thought. It wasn't exactly unusual. I didn't say anything – just stared her down. A 17ish stone, full on out of control doorman verses a tiny little lady I'd once been quite close to. She moved away. I never, ever spoke to her again.

Ultimately Andrea left and became General Manager at a big hotel near the motorway. I went there one night a few years later looking for a room for a few nights after a row at home. I genuinely didn't know she worked there. We bumped into each other in reception. She tried hard but I still wouldn't speak to her. Shame on me. Unsurprisingly, she never did get it. After all, it had been me that had been on the edge. Not her.

I was being turned inside out in my day job and turned upside down from my on / off drug use. I grew colder and colder and I know some of the hotel staff saw me as brutal and cruel and vile. It wasn't a good time.

27

The Last of the Crew

Towards the end of 1988 Esau had begun to tire of it all. I suppose my moods didn't help. He started to get unreliable himself. Slim, the barman, had been standing in for him on the nights he failed to appear. Once he turned up 3 hours late in his little comfy cardie and had an argument with Coulton in front of us all. The boss sacked him on the spot. As I said before, he appeared a little later with the dog and had a brief chat but apart from that I only ever saw him one more time.

Around Christmas of that year Slim finally moved from the bars and took Esau's place full time. I would consider Slim another good friend. He may also read this – who knows – but I have to say, for the first time ever in public, I didn't see him as a doorman. He was an excellent barman. First class. To my befuddled mind he simply wasn't a doorman. He was also already in his late thirties or early forties and in my arrogance, despite Valentine being a similar age, I thought that was much too old.

It was the end of the Four Leicester Horsemen. Course, they only ever existed in my head so nothing really changed. It was just four different blokes that kept going round town.

In comparison to the rest of us Slim was massively inexperienced. He'd never worked as a doorman in his life but was pretty chunky so looked the part. Slim made no pretence at being a hard man like some of them and his main method of doorwork was to stand there and pout or grin depending on who he was confronting. Much like my favourite method really!

Like many of the staff Slim was married with a couple of young daughters. He worked as some sort of metal fabricator during the day but he had had some questionable personal behaviour and habits. I remember every time a woman with a big arse walked past he would come out with something that sounded to me like tir-wu-ak-birra. It wasn't long before Lloyd was saying it as well, followed by... well... you can guess. He said it so often that it really stuck and I still say it to myself today when anyone with a big bum waddles by me.

One night I was sitting next to him when his nose started to itch. He grabbed hold of some nasal hairs and started tugging. His head went up and down like a yoyo until – eureka – he pulled them free. He then rubbed them in this fingers until they were all dry and casually dropped them, right on to my leg. "Slim," I said. "We no do that in England." I used that line on him a lot – anytime he did something I found remotely disgusting. Yeah. As subtle and out of control as ever. In return he'd greet me with "Jaffraaayyy" in a piercing shrill every time I pissed him off. It's fair to say there was a lot of "We no do that in England" and "Jaffraaayyy" that went on. Looking back I'm amazed we stayed friends. I was out of control. These guys must have been incredibly tolerant of me.

Funniest Slim moment was when some teeny black leather clad girl got a bit gruff with him in the ladies loos down in the bar over nothing that I can remember. Slim tried to throw her out. We'd both gone in there under the impression that there was some sort of trouble. As I stood and watched she held on to the wall with her tiny little fingers and he pulled for all he was worth on her ankle. Amazingly she was winning until I thought enough is enough and casually tapped her fingers loose one by one. I was shocked when both of them flew across the room! Whoops. Didn't mean for that to happen. She was a regular and I thought she was quite pretty. That automatically meant that I liked her. Never saw her again after that.

Shortly after Esau had gone there was a young Doctors do. There were hundreds of them dressed in evening wear. Word had got out that they didn't need a ticket. Wrong. On instructions from yet another manager, Linda, we started to turn those without tickets away. The whole hotel wasn't doing so well at that point, never mind the Centre Bar. The heydays were over. Mr. C came up to me. He wasn't very pleased. He told me off and that I should use my brain a bit more. Look, by now my brain was pretty fucked from my day job. What did he expect? In his view, if I let them into the Centre Bar we could get revenue off them and still keep them out of the function. The function was downstairs. The bar was downstairs. Both groups used the same toilets. I honestly didn't give a flying fuck.

It didn't take long. The two parties met as soon as they all started to have a leak. Two became one. We gave up in the end but not before some guy tried the reception door and gave it all the eyes, flaring nostrils and threats that, by that time, I heard so, so many times before. It's sad, but a cold, cold, sullen and uncaring Jeff took over that night. Sweet, naïve, shy, quiet, polite Jeff was gone. Was I ever really like that?

This guys flaring nose looked like it had been bitten off at some point and then sewn back on – badly! This was the same door that I'd had my first fight in back in 1985. I'd learned. I trapped bitten nose in the doorway. There was no way he was getting into reception. He started to hit the glass panes. I just stood there coldly and let him do it. After about 2 minutes of door bashing, which is quite a long time, he gave up. I turned my back and wandered off, satisfied he'd hurt himself sufficiently. Like I said. Caring was not high on the agenda at that point.

Because of his inexperience Slim let him in about 20 minutes later! I had a go at him. Slim told me in no uncertain terms what I was really like. I deserved it. Even Lloyd questioned my approach, saying to me "you're a fucking Scorpio aren't you?" as my behaviour became more and more and more obsessive. Silent, massive Phil was the only one who didn't really say much about the way I was acting. He'd been trained by Cefus.

A few months later there was an Elvis tribute night. Me and Phil were upstairs when Coulton came charging across reception towards us. Apparently one of the crowd had gone down to the hotel car park and tried to break into one of the cars or steal a bike or something like that. He'd been seen by one of the bar staff and done a runner back into the function to hide. The boss wanted us to find him and grab him while he called the police. We wandered into the function. A dozen Elvis' looked at us.

We found this tiny guy behind a 1950's version. He claimed all innocence but there was no doubt it was him so we… ahem… gently escorted him to the kitchen behind the function room and I took up position on the left of the door that led in and Phil stood on the right.

The guy was petrified. Guilt, two hulking doormen, a stomach full of beer and a promise of the police. He made a dash for it and dived right between the two of us. Me and Phil were bored, snoozing. He went right through the middle like a piece of paper sliding under a door. We jumped alert and went after him, both turning into the doorway at the same instant and promptly bouncing off each others chests. That, of course, is why they call us bouncers.

Can you imagine the scene? Shaven headed, sullen, moaning, obsessive Jeff and massive, silent Phil charging across a room, chasing a tiny chap past an Elvis for every era. I leapt across chairs, Phil did a version of the jive around them. Elvis would have been proud.

The guy was fast. I'll give him that but he was also stupid or drunk. Very. As he ran he looked over his shoulder to see how far behind we were. He nearly made it. He was right at the door that led into reception. We were huffing and puffing away miles behind. He looked again and ran… bang… straight into the mirrored wall. He went down like he was pole axed. Just then the door opened. Slim saw him lying there and without a seconds hesitation jumped on his chest. Ouch.

Not long after me and Lloyd worked a private party in the Centre Bar on a Thursday night. All was going well until the organiser came up and told us that there were two guys at the bar who hadn't been invited and could we ask them to leave please. Both of us strolled over. The two blokes looked normal enough i.e. not townies or part of the Baby Squad and I just thought they were residents that had wandered in by mistake.

In my politest possible voice of the time I told them it was a private party and asked if they could use the residents bar. To my utter amazement one of them started to give me some real lip. He only half turned towards me and grunted. "I'm a senior guy at Penguin Hotels[6]. I could get you sacked at any time." As he spoke I could see his teeth. They were all brown. Like they were dead. I shuddered. "I'm not interested" I told him. "This is a private party and the organiser would like to you to leave. Please can you make your way out and use one of the other bars." He still didn't turn round fully and half looked at me, a dirty disdainful look. It was just like the one "the bastard" was giving me all the time. I felt my moody hackles rising.

He just stood there looking down his nose at me. His mate seemed happy to go. "Time to leave" I repeated more coldly. He looked me up and down. I was expecting, and probably wanting, to have to grab him by the arm, shove him out and probably get sacked the next day. Suddenly he turned round fully. I noticed he was swaying slightly. You're pissed I thought. He looked at me again and just slowly staggered out. His mate followed. Me and Lloyd just stood back and watched them go. I never heard another word. Odd that. Maybe he woke up the next morning and felt a right twat. Maybe he was never part of the hotel management. Maybe he couldn't even remember.

By the end of the year I was ready to pack it all in. I was still training in Leamington but was tired and jaded and, even though I'd only just turned 29, I was regularly thinking that I was getting too old and too fat to keep standing there. I was still stuffing myself with food and financially I was now very well off so no longer needed the money. Nick convinced me to stay.

At my day job we'd hired a nice chap called Simon but he left after 6 weeks to be replaced by a girl called Tracy. She only lasted four days before she mysteriously didn't appear on the Friday. One of the part time bar staff at the hotel knew her from her previous day job and, that night, told me that Tracy

---

[6] Owners of the International Hotel

had turned up and asked for her old job back. I was shocked. On top of that she told me Tracy could be a bit weird and unreliable. "The bastard" had quite viciously and unnecessarily blamed me for Simon leaving so quickly and for her Friday absence so I was pissed off yet again. I also didn't want to be standing on the door. The functions were in full flow so I went to stand outside for some fresh air and to calm down a little when I spotted two lads trying to break into cars. I didn't want to know. Not my business and then, with my poor eyesight, I saw them trying to break into what I thought was mine – the very same Escort I'd already had the crash in and that already had the door kicked in once before. Whoa. I chased down the road after them.

I like to think I was so fast that none of the other doormen saw me go. More than likely they were working and I was skiving. I caught them kicking in the door of the car next to mine. I screamed at them "get away from my car." One of them screamed back "I don't give a fuck whose car it is" and gave a big whack with his foot into mine. Another dent! My poor old car. Old! It was still only 8 months old at this point. Screamers next action was to punch me in the face. I hadn't done anything other than shout at him. That was it. A big battle ensued. One huge, weight trained, irate, steroidal, moody, aggressive and punched doormen against two squirts. They didn't really stand a chance. I flattened them.

I gritted my teeth so hard in anger and frustration that one of them snapped. I was so aggressive. My hate for "the bastard" was coming out in a level of viciousness that even surprised me. I tore the shirt off the one who punched me. Some bloke stopped me in the middle of the battle and asked if I was alright. Hah… Oh yeah. He must've seen two onto one and thought I was in trouble. I remember some girls screaming at me to stop and that I was far too big to being taking on these little guys. I shouted back "they attacked me" which was true. Then I lost sight of them in the heat of the battle and as I struggled away. I presume they just walked off. Slim, in all his

Jeff Shaw

inexperience was there. Luckily for me he eventually pulled me off.

I don't know where he came from or how he knew what was going on. One minute I was wrestling with these lads and the next I was being pulled backwards off my feet. He got me back into reception. I was raving. At the end of the day – all I'd done was go outside for fresh air and look what had happened!

Red Cap Kevin, our former occasional doorman, was in there on crutches. I didn't know. Apparently he'd been inside the place at a function but had been having serious problems with the ligaments in his legs. I'd not seen him for months. He wanted to know what was going on. I told him. Words poured out of me in a torrent. Then I went to put my right hand in my pocket to get my car keys out so I could move it to a different spot and found I couldn't get my hand inside my trousers. I didn't know until that moment – I'd broken it and a couple of my fingers during the fight and it was already swollen to about twice its normal size. Bugger. In the end Slim crammed his hand in my pocket and pulled them out and lurched off to move my car. It would've been funny if the whole thing hadn't been so unnecessary! I still don't know exactly how the breaks occurred. I do remember being thrown into the wall at one point. Maybe it was then.

As I dismally looked at my hand one of my attackers wandered past outside. It wasn't the guy who had punched me and kicked my car door in but it was good enough for me. Me and Slim dashed back outside, Kevin hobbled behind us. I grabbed the little bastard and dragged him into reception. He came without a fuss. All he kept saying was "I don't want any bother." Too late mate I thought. I looked outside. I couldn't quite believe my eyes! His shirtless buddy was wandering by so we all dashed outside again, well... okay... Kevin still hobbled... and grabbed him too. His best line was "I don't know what you're talking about... nothing to do with me." Comedian. I'd been 2" from his nose. Even I can see that far without my glasses. Who did he think he was kidding?

By this time the other doormen had idled up. Bloody Lloyd. He never did hurry anywhere! Two of them and four of us, well – three and three quarters if you count my hand – plus Kevin, albeit on his crutches. They weren't going anywhere. Someone called the police. I think I was shouting at reception to get them but they were probably jittery enough to do it without my desperate encouragement anyway. People from the functions were standing around. "What's happened?" I heard some woman say. "Don't know" her mate replied, "but something has."

The police arrived a few minutes later. I don't know how much later. Not long. Perhaps it wasn't a busy night. There were two of them, male and female. Normally I'd have fancied the WPC. Hey. Uniforms. She listened to me babble on, wandered round the corner with me to look at my car and arrested the lads. Then she told me to go to the station and make a statement.

Satisfied with the arrest, I decided I needed to look after my hand first, which now I knew was broken was throbbing like mad, so ignored what she'd told me, got Jim the Night Porter to get me a taxi to the Leicester Royal and zoomed off for a patch up which involved the usual 4 or 5 hours of sitting around, x-rays and repairs during which they uttered the immortal line that "I'd lost some knuckles, but that didn't matter'."

I finally made my way to the police station at about 3am where I ended up talking to a very nice, bearded sergeant. He didn't seemed to mind that I was hours late. It must REALLY have been a quiet night for them. My hand was still throbbing and the Royal had given me a sling to wear. Maybe they thought that fixing my hand to my chest would stop me trying to thump people! The sergeant was very, very kind to me. He clearly didn't like these two car thieves. They must've been well known. I took my hand out of the sling and wistfully showed him the damage. "I've been doing this job 30 years" he told me. "Let's think about how we word this." He was good at his job. I got a police award for bravery. I ducked out of work one day when "the bastard" wasn't looking. He didn't even notice I'd gone.

I got a nice letter and some money for making a citizens arrest. My right hand still shows the scars of that night. I have two permanently depressed knuckles and some lumps on my fingers where they were broken. The Royal was right. It never did affect the use of my hand. The guy who hit me in the face admitted assault and criminal damage that very night. Seems he did know what we were talking about after all. His mate pleaded innocence but the case was strong enough for him to go to court about a year later and he pleaded guilty to common assault. Not a strong charge I know, but I did feel it was deserved. I was a witness and nervously sat in a waiting room in the back reading and re-reading my statement. I never got called.

"The bastard" came round to my house the Monday after the fight. I was sitting there nursing my broken hand. He came in, perched himself uninvited on the edge of my coffee table and then proceeded to tell me everything about me he didn't like. IN MY OWN HOUSE. Apparently it was an appraisal. I never really got over that.

I unwrapped my hand and fingers after about 4 days after reading a nursing book in the corner of WH Smiths that said you shouldn't keep broken fingers wrapped up for too long. I waggled them. They worked. I went back to work.

Tracy, who had been on my mind when this whole episode erupted, re-appeared in the office the next week and stayed for about 6 months before she could get herself another job. Apart from that first week and her last day when she just walked out at about 11am I never found her to be weird or unreliable. Just goes to show. "The bastard" was relentless though and even blamed me for letting her disappear early on her last day. As if I could have prevented that!

Despite convincing me to stay at the hotel Nick left not long after the hand incident. I think he went back to Yorkshire for a better job. He was replaced by a lad called Terry.

About 30, sandy haired and scruffy, Terry was always a bit unsure of himself. He only lasted a few weeks before he was replaced by Adelle. a tall Goth with tiny boobs and a big tir-wu-ak-birra arse (she'll love me for that), also from Yorkshire. She had black hair, tied up in a sort of spiral and I liked her a lot.

Coulton had basically poached her from Helsinkis which was a bit naughty really I suppose, but back then no one seemed to care. She had an accent as thick as Yorkshire pudding and used to make me laugh. She was very down to earth and wasn't afraid to fart or curse in anyone's presence. In fact, she let rip a snorter as I was standing there. I don't know if she ever knew that I heard her. It was pretty funny.

Adelle
Picture Courtesy Jeff Shaw

We talked a lot. Ernest, the brother of Franklin from my early days at Helsinkis, was working with us from time to time. He was only there a few weeks and was filling in for anyone who couldn't make it. I can't remember him being a regular member of the team but do remember ringing him now and then to ask if he was available. I didn't know that he was Franklins brother at first. Ernest had some facial resemblance to Franklin but wasn't the same sort of trouble maker. He was much quieter. It was also now many years later.

It was only when I was talking to him and Franklin appeared, speaking in a strained patois that he hadn't had when he worked with me, that I discovered the truth. I was more than a bit surprised. Ernest also got on well with Adelle. I think she knew him from somewhere else.

During our many chats Adelle told me an enormous amount about her background, including her battle with anorexia, that she was the daughter of a very senior policeman and the fact that she'd once gone out with Andrew Eldritch, the lead singer from the Sisters of Mercy. Apparently Eldritch had noticed the finger of a glove she'd stuffed under her corset when she first met him in an attempt to make her boobs look bigger. Adelle hadn't stuffed it in properly and the finger was sticking out. "What's this?" he'd asked in amusement as he tugged.

She even went on about Ernest carrying a holster under his jacket and how it had scared her to death when she'd seen it. I can confirm he did. It was a wallet. I laughed. I knew how quiet he was compared to Franklin and told her it was okay for Ernest and her to have a holster as a wallet. "As long as there was no gun in it" I told her. There wasn't!

I never told her about my days carrying the rounders bat under mine and, as you'll discover, I had my own views about carrying a pistol around in my own pocket about then.

Ultimately she had a big row with Coulton about some minor crap that I didn't hear a few months later and walked out, passing a somewhat startled me on the way, and screaming to me "no one talks to me like that!" Even in my selfish and disorientated state I was sad to see her go. I never did ask Coulton what he said. I wasn't that far beyond my selfishness.

A slightly built, mousy haired guy called Chris, who had been working in the catering department took over. He was a massive Leicester City fan had a little pointed face and big, sticky out ears. He was pretty shy himself but seemed desperate to go out with bar maid April and tried very hard. Well, as hard as his own shyness would let him. Her equally red headed – and about as far from shy as you could get – brother Dale also used to work at the hotel as a Night Porter and thought Chris would be good for her but April wasn't having any of it.

April was growing up herself and losing her own shyness and often used to flirt with me. I really, really liked (i.e. fancied) April and would madly flirt back. There was one time when she'd hurt her back and pulled the bottom of her shirt up in front of me to reveal her pale, bare back and then started to rub it. I hesitated. She turned her head and looked at me with a bit of a pout. I didn't budge. After a few seconds she pulled her shirt back down and I walked away before any inevitable reaction took hold.

I thought she was a lovely girl but I always felt she was too young and sweet for my persona by then. She hated to be called sweet. Added to that, the fact that I was becoming so remote and was so full of moans and groans made me think it wouldn't be fair for either of us to take it any further than flirting. Privately I was also bothered about how fat I'd now become and I think that was playing on my mind too. The closest we ever really got was when her dad died. We all got to hear and she was standing sullenly behind the bar by herself when I arrived for my shift. When my dad died I may have got sent home but no one from work really ever came up to me and offered any words of sympathy. It hurt and still does. I couldn't do the same. Part of me was still a nice guy.

When I arrived in the bar that night the first thing I did was call April over, she looked uncertain and sad. I briefly held her hands and offered my condolences. She smiled her thanks and went back behind the bar. I hope what I said to her helped in some small way.

By now the others, including Coulton, weren't at all shy in telling me I looked like a dumpling. I guess it was their retribution for my foul moods. Coulton came in one night. I was standing in reception and hadn't seen him for quite a few weeks. He took one look at me and stuck his arms out to the sides and puffed out his chest in some sort of mimic of me and told me "you've put some beef on." Yes. I knew. And it sure as hell wasn't solid.

The last time I saw Chris was after I'd just finished compulsory Jury Service for the morning, some 10 or so years after these events. I was making my way around my old haunts in the mid afternoon sun. He was just coming out of the Grand which is virtually next to the old Sugars Gym. Chris had been sacked from the International Hotel years before while I was still there for nicking a set of optics for his bar at home. Stupid man. Apparently he'd been pissed when the police had stopped him. He was carrying a black back so they asked him what was in it. Allegedly his garbled reply caused enough suspicion for them to ask him to open it and his excuse for having the optics was incomprehensible. The rest is history.

At first glance outside the Grand both of us had to do a double take but once we recognised each other we had a little chat. He's much heavier now and married with two kids but he isn't married to April. Not as far as I know. He's still a massive City fan. Fool.

Chris, in turn, had worked for Mick when he was at the Centre Bar. Mick was a former head chef with a bushy beard. At least he didn't have a funny looking moustache. The night way back in 1984, when the skinhead girl had kicked the pane of glass in and nearly severed her leg, it had been Mick who found her bleeding and in a state and it was him who administered first aid until an ambulance came.

Typical of my views of my ignorance around then, I thought Mick was incredibly fat. He probably wasn't. Never the less I thought he was a nice guy. Gay, but a nice guy. I liked both

Mick and Chris but they couldn't control me. My day job had screwed me up. Well "the bastard" had. My fading physique was playing its part and my attempts at steroid withdrawal had finished the job. My internal and external image was not good. I suppose my descent to the sullen bit was pretty much complete.

Good job I had, and still have... oh yeah... you're reading this... make up your own mind, a sense of humour.

28

Some People Turn to Drink

As my depression spread even I could feel it eating away at my soul. From the number of people who happily or sarcastically told me, I knew I was not coming across well. I just couldn't seem to break out of it. I tried and tried though. I was then – and still am now – a very determined man.

I had holidays in far flung corners of the earth to try and leave it behind. That was when I met Khachik in LA, but it didn't really work so I started to re-read my collection of James Bond novels at night to occupy my troubled mind. I used to own the entire set.

I was fascinated by Bond – not the character in the films – the hard man of the books. There's a scene in the opening sequence of Quantum of Solace – which is one the few films that portrays Bonds character as close to the books as you can get – where Bond is walking away from a series of violent explosions. Debris and percussion from the blasts is flying all around, occasionally hitting him. Bond just keeps walking. Completely oblivious to the carnage and the flak bouncing off him. Unafraid, determined and uncaring of the consequences.

The more I read the more I decided that I desperately needed to split my brow beaten day persona away from my door persona. I decided that the doorman was a separate entity. An alter ego and, for me, that alter ego was the calculating, secure, confident, brave and womanising James Bond. All the things, except the womanising, that I felt I was losing. It allowed me to paint a picture in my head of someone else. At least I didn't hit the bottle. I can understand why some people do and for anyone who has, they have my sympathy.

I can't emphasis enough that once I pulled on my doorman's jacket in my depression and mental state that image of Bond is how I often saw myself. By this time, in my world, I was born to be a doorman. I think I even said it out loud a few times. As much as I'd pictured never losing a battle when I gave my grandma a lift, I often pictured riots and violence and crowds running past me as I stood there and faced it, also unafraid. Alone. Uncaring. Ready to die in battle.

Despite my mental imagery, I just found it was impossible to leave my day job troubles completely behind. I think that part of my problem was I was overwhelmed by the stress that "the bastard" put me through and part because I was getting into the habit of moaning all the time but not taking the right actions to get out of the situation.

None of this was helped by the fact that many of the girls who worked at the assembly factory had learned of my 'secret' and knew I was a doorman. They would ask me where I worked, how long I'd been there, what it was like down there. Had I been in any fights?

Because of this intrusion I found that it was getting harder and harder to move into my Bondian mindset so I invented a sort of in-between. What did I call him? Er... told you I wasn't too good at the imagination thing. I called my incarnation Norman. Norman the Doorman to be precise. Sadly it's the best I could do at the time.

Unfortunately I unwittingly let Norman the Doorman's persona spread into my day job and my door job. Part of the problem was that more often than not I would wear the same trousers, shoes and shirts to both jobs. The only difference between the two sets of attire was the jacket. I just couldn't separate them.

It got so bad that some guy I used to call Nielson, because he told me his name was "Neil, son," when I asked him, found out from me where one of the Goths worked and phoned her up, pretending to be me. My bloody big mouth. I was incredibly embarrassed when Nielson told me with a leer. I took her to one side in the bar the next weekend and apologised. From the look on her face I think Nielson had taken her in and she was sure I was going to say something else. Despite everything my shyness was still there.

So there you have it. Norman was far from being the James Bond of the books. More the James Bond of the films. Cartoonish. A bit of an oaf. A caricature. A git. Shit. There goes that image then, just when I was on the verge of convincing you. "Norman" would've looked ridiculous on my old name badge anyway.

I started to flirt with the girls at work as much as I did in the bar. Flirt king was enjoying it at the time but I guess it wasn't a good idea. I've never gone out with a girl I worked with in my life. It stems from my chronically shy schooldays when I avoided the girls in my classes. I hated to think what would happen if it went wrong. Girls in the bar or behind reception – fine – I could spend the night flirting with them, more if it happened but then I could just walk away. When you spend 8 hours a day with someone, 5 days a week it's not so easy for someone like me.

Suddenly, without intending it I found my two worlds colliding with a nasty bump. There was a young girl at my day job. I chased after her like the doorman I was but on permanent heat. Fortunately she was a bit enamoured. Well, I hope she was and we had some fun but I could've got myself into so much trouble. Lucky again.

With the overtness coming out of me it wasn't too long before "the bastard" got to find out about my second life. It just gave him more ammunition which he freely used against me. "Security" he sniffed. It came out as "sac-your-arty." He said some funny things. "Thee-ay-tare" (theatre) was another, although "Spakin" when he answered the phone was my personal favourite. I thought he'd said "spanking" when I first heard it.

I presume I was supposed to know what he meant by the snivelling "sac-your-arty" phrases. I used to get so, so out of control. More veins throbbing away in my temples. I'm sure everyone at work thought I was a madman. Dearie, dearie me. What would James have done? I got no counselling or help or guidance at all. I was truly lost. I know I avidly watched a programme on TV once. Some old guy gaily said that if you didn't understand something, in a two way conversation, the best way to get a common position was to repeat back "so what you've said to me is…." I tried it on him A LOT of times. It never worked. He was always changing what he wanted and blaming me if I failed to understand or did the wrong thing – which I would always do. It left me continually flatfooted, confused and worse – **permanently enraged**.

In the end I couldn't keep a civil tongue in my head at work, to anybody. Of course, it's possible, probable really, that I was going through massive steroid rebounds as I continually went on and off them.

Many years after this was all over I had a long conversation with the younger brother of my bodybuilding hero, Mentzer. He had also been a top-level bodybuilder. Our conversation got around to modern day bodybuilding and the amount of drug use that must be involved to get to the serious levels of development the guys these days have and our own drug trials and tribulations. "Can you imagine what these guys are going to go through when they have to stop?" he asked me. Yes mate. Oh yes. I sure could.

A nice lad by the name of Dean, was working for me at the time "the bastard" was ranting on about me being "sac-your-arty." Dean was only about 18 or 19 and had a cleft palate so suffered with a bit of a speech impediment. It never bothered him or me but "the bastard" was such an ill tempered, badly behaved piece of work that he had even criticised him for not speaking clearly. Dean was pretty forgiving but even he struggled to cope with the constant changes in direction and lack of leadership and man management skills and ended up calling "the bastard" by his own nickname of "Mr. U-Turn" more than once.

I wanted this book to be humorous. It is in parts. It's also quite sad here and there and this is one of those bits. Helsinkis changed me, the steroids changed me again, my time at the Centre Bar developed my confidence but this also had a massive influence. I should've left but I took it and took it and took it. In the end I knew I had to get out before I ended up in the same state I'd seen my dad in so many times. My assertiveness, nerves and self-esteem were being shredded. Daily. Hourly.

What people like "the bastard" do is pick on your strengths and then start telling you they're weaknesses over and over and over. It's was bullying all over again. Just like Keith at school and you know what I think of bullies.

17 stone, aggressive, sullen Jeff bullied by a weedy little prick. Given my history as a kid is it that hard to believe? I think my shyness had something to do with it. In my mind I was trying to be respectful as well to a degree. After all, he was the boss. At first you deny these so called weaknesses but when these bullies persist, in my case for years, a part of you starts to question yourself. Coupled with the steroids this self-doubt took a grip on part of me like nothing had ever done before or since. To say that I was on a short fuse would be the biggest **UNDERSTATEMENT** I could ever make in my life. My rage continued to spread and spread.

Looking back, it's no wonder I didn't know what was happening to me. This guy used some key phrases on me – no matter how false, unnecessary and vicious – that, if someone says them in passing, I still get upset 20 or more years later. I can't even write them down here and I have had to purposely avoid thinking of them as I put all this down. After it was all over I had to undergo assertiveness training. These days it amuses me when people tell me I lack assertiveness – and it does happen from time to time because I'm now a very quiet chap. I make myself behave that way. It's a purposeful act. They **seriously** have no clue.

At the hotel it was now so obvious that something was wrong with me that everyone knew. I didn't see Frances BB, the GM, that often by then. There was no need for her to be there at night but she did occasionally turn up with a young daughter in tow. John BB had long gone by this time. Her daughter came up to play with me and Lloyd. I was unhappy about my life and irritated. Sorry Frances. I couldn't help it – I was out of control. I was aggressive and rude – to a 5 year old.

Lloyd, whose own kids were about the same age gave me yet another look. I suppose I was used to receiving them and didn't give a shit. The kid went crying off to BB. She came over. To my amazement she was all smiles. I went home that night and wept for my lost self. There. Said that too. I cried a lot in the end.

I think I didn't leave the assembly factory long before I did because I was scared of losing some sense of financial and personal security. All I had other than that was door work and the gym. No woman would stay with me in that state. Like I have said. I was getting desperate. I didn't know what to do. Outside the bar hardly anyone was giving me the time of day. Even my mum was well beyond tolerant with me.

One day I miserably shuffled into WH Smiths and saw a tiny little book called "Situational Leadership and the One Minute Manager." It was cheap, so I bought it. No other reasons apart from being desperate and the price. Good job I did. It started to help me change my life.

I devoured it in one session. First person I started to try and use the techniques on… Slim. I saw an instant change in his reactions to me and I had another life changing moment. I tried it at work on Dean the next week and my eyes were opened. I will never forget the techniques in that book. I may not be the best person in the world at applying them but, again, I try. I went out and bought the whole of the "One Minute Manager" series and read them one after another. I went to my day job and applied the techniques some more. I met up with the other doormen and applied the techniques.

More than any memento from the Centre Bar, I still have these books. That's really when a period of intense retrospection started. I spent a lot of time studying – mainly leadership skills, technical skills, communication skills, positive thinking and, of all things, philosophy. I began a success journal. Every day I didn't lose my temper was a "Successful Day." I've had LOTS of them since but it wasn't easy.

I'm very happy to say that some people remembered the gentleman I'd been before all of this and were very sympathetic. Frances BB was one of them. In 1992 she very kindly offered me a job as a Night Porter with Jim, still working as a doorman at the weekends. My behaviour had really given her pretty good grounds to sack me but she didn't. I was wrong before when I talked about why me and Lloyd, Slim, Phil and Coulton are still friends all these years later. They put up with me during this entire time. That's why we're still friends. I owe them – big time.

I didn't really want the Night Porter job but was going to take it. By that stage I would've done anything to get away from "the bastard." The day I was going to accept I went to a supplier on a routine visit. I was still going in the right direction but very, very down. "Have you got any jobs going?" I asked sullenly and hopefully. "My engineer George just handed his notice in this morning" was the reply. "Can I have his job?" I asked. I had an interview at 6.30pm that night and started the next week. I drove home in tears of relief.

I tried to let Frances BB know at the weekend. I did everything I could to keep her in the picture but, in the end, had to leave a message and she didn't get it for a week which upset me when I found out and frustrated her but she was very understanding.

When I handed in my notice "the bastard" grunted at me "your loss" and walked off. He was very bow legged. It came out "yar-lace." I remember his hands were shaking in rage. Pathetic. At the time I gave my usual extremely aggressive response towards his comment and his behaviour. It was hardly my loss, in any way, shape or form.

Looking back I now see his behaviour as extreme, petty jealousy. I suspect he was desperately brow beaten himself either by his wife or his own boss. Probably both. His boss was a complete bastard himself and had no people skills at all. He had called me into his office one early afternoon and took great delight in trying to skewer me to the wall with his words. I was at my worst but I took it. I should've told him to stick it up his fucking arse with a red-hot poker. Considering how I was behaving at the time, it's a wonder I didn't. "The bastard" even told me off later in the day for not answering back. Some you just CANNOT win.

After I left I found out through some contacts that "the bastard" was planning to try and sack me. I wouldn't have been the first or even the second that he had done that to. It was clearly impossible to satisfy him. He even made an unsolicited phone call to my new boss and told him that he should never have employed me, that I was a bad-tempered, unwilling worker and that I had no place holding down a job. If he had tried to sack me or indeed had sacked me and he never did. **Let's be clear about that**. I would have taken him to court for constructive dismissal and, from the advice I've been given since, would have won quite easily.

Norman the Doorman died a natural death in the end. He could've been a good idea but I think he did me more harm than good in terms of my internal and external image. I like the Bond image much more.

29

Incidents in the Street

What with steroids, Hells Angels, the Meteors and my own Bette Noir in later years, there were times during my entire life as a doorman that were far from fun. What I've not really talked about is anything outside the bars I worked in. Sure, I've spoken briefly about reception and some of the functions we worked and, like I mentioned, the place was huge but one of the biggest problems was protecting our cars from any stray passer by. It could be a real pain in the arse. I'm sure this is true for any and all doormen.

Personally, I was always devastated when I found some damage to mine, particularly during my descent. I was working so hard to be able to buy nice ones and tosspots that I didn't even know or never saw were taking chunks out of the things. There's an oldish film called Road House starring Patrick Swayze which is supposedly about the life and times of a doorman in the US.

All I can say is that someone had a pretty good imagination but there is a scene in it where the lead character gets to his car after a nights work to finds all the tyres slashed. He just grins, opens the boot and starts to change them. If only. I think we all had car issues before we learned and started to hide them on the hotel car park and even down there.

From the night the police caught some git trying to steal the Samba during my Tipplers days I used to change where I parked mine every night. I'd park up in a variety of different spots, take long looks around to make sure no one had seen me and then lock the thing up and creep into work. I kept this up long after I moved to the hotel. All in the name of avoiding getting my car damaged. I even came out of Helsinkis more than once only to find my car gone and panicked that it had been stolen! Shit!!! Every time it was because I'd forgotten where I'd left it and – every time – my tired old brain would eventually kick in and tell me to stop being a twat and look in the next street. Overall I was reasonably successful at keeping it out of sight but I'm still sure people used to spy on me.

My spying fears were almost confirmed very early one evening when I was working at the hotel when the youngest of the two Roche brothers came dashing into the bar. "Quick… quick!" he yelled. I was taken aback. "Where's a fire extinguisher? Alison's car is on fire!" I dashed to the light switches, expecting to find one in there. Nope. I ran to the Garden Room. There was one in there. A red one. Water. Roche trailed. "Where's the car?" I asked him, heart doing the usual. "Just outside… right next to yours." How the fuck did he know which one was mine? Never mind. No time for that. We dashed out into the street. It was dark and wet. Alison, his girlfriend, had a little mini and sure enough, it was there in flames. What was worse, even with my poor eyesight it was clear to me it WAS right next to mine. I ran across the road… okay waddled… with Roche hot on my heels. I don't think I was too bothered about the mini.

As I ran I noticed Alison was standing there, open mouthed and pretty much looking like a cat caught in some headlights. I didn't hesitate. Now this is very foolish and I wouldn't do it again. I just pulled the car door open, closed my eyes and sprayed. Of course, the fresh air fanned the flames and they got a lot redder. So did my face. The whole of the steering column and steering wheel were alight. This was an electrical fire and I had – bollocks. A water extinguisher. Not good.

I screwed up my eyes even tighter and squirted. Fortunately I got the fire out in seconds. Black smoke and stench came from inside and me and Roche gagged but then we realised the engine was still running. We couldn't shut it off. There was no way we could get to the ignition key. It was still smouldering so, really in desperation, Roche popped the boot and disconnected the battery.

The thing died a slow and painful death. Never mind my thumpity-thumps. I'm sure he had them as well. God knows

273

what was going through Alisons mind. We stood back and admired our handiwork. Me and Roche exchanged glances and I nonchalantly strolled back to the bar and put the fire extinguisher back where I found it. That's not a good idea either but I didn't know. I should've gone to more safety talks. I never did find out how he knew which car was mine but he was one of the ones I trusted so I didn't mind too much.

Alison's dad turned up a bit later and I helped as we all made sure the thing was towed away safely. I got my usual orange juice and a thank you for my efforts which was fine. I didn't tell the hotel I'd used one of the extinguishers though which turned out to be not so fine and eventually got a mild bollocking for it although I don't think anyone was really too bothered.

I think one of the worst events I experienced was time the someone pissed in the Samba fuel tank. It was more than pissing really. It was 1985. Long before my descent but well into my steroid use. I just know I got in and drove off – no problem – but got less than a mile or two before it started coughing and spluttering like crazy. I had to stop. It wasn't going anywhere. I was frustrated. It was October and I wanted to go home but was forced to call the AA. Good job I was a member.

It didn't take too long for them to turn up. For some odd reason there were two of them in their little brown jumpers and berets. Usually you only get one. One of them popped the bonnet and the other cranked the engine. I watched over their shoulders and saw water and shit come out of the fuel line they'd disconnected. "Someone's put something in your tank" was the solemn view. Christ! Thanks a bunch.

The thing was so crap that they hadn't bothered to design a locking petrol cap and some nice, unknown person had taken the time to take mine off and fill up my tank with piss, water, stones and crud. It was already a bad car. Did they know it was mine? Probably.

It was never the same again. I ended up having to be towed to the nearest garage and leaving it there for a couple of days while I got it repaired at great expense. As I was being towed I'd forgotten to make sure the key was on in the ignition so as we took a sharp turn the steering lock got activated. I banged the horn as quickly as possible and we slid to a stop before I hit anything. The AA guys got out of their yellow van and looked at me and smirked. "A lot of people make that mistake" one of them told me. What a knob I felt.

After we left it at the garage they took me home. When I finally got in the house it was nearly 3am. I looked at my tired and drawn face in the mirror. I had lipstick from kissing one of the Goths smeared all over my lips and cheek. No wonder the AA guys had smirked.

I picked the thing up on about the Wednesday and used it without any issues. A week after the incident was that first ever trip to Leamington Spa. I wanted to give the thing a good run just to blast the pipes through. It was the time I went with the guy who never finished anything and was my first introduction to the place. I picked him up from an empty town at about 9am on a Saturday morning and got there roughly an hour later without any real problems, the odd bit of jerking but nothing unusual for that heap of junk. The other bloke then did his training, we went for a coffee and a chat and started back about 1pm. Neither of us gave the Samba a second thought.

Half way home it cut out. We got out and just stood there in the October cold looking at it for a few minutes. I suppose we were waiting for a miracle or something then I jumped back in and tried the ignition. It started. I had no idea why it was playing up like this. As far as I was concerned I'd taken it to a garage and it was fixed. All I was doing was giving it a good run.

I got on to the motorway and off we went again but, suddenly, it started jerking horrifically, like when you're in a train carriage as the train pulls off but with a lot of starting and stopping and starting again. I was getting worried. The motorway was only about 18 miles long – but that's still a long way to walk on a busy and cold October Saturday afternoon. We jerked and heaved all the way down that damn motorway.

At the end you either turn left towards Leicester or right towards where I lived. I turned right. My passengers mouth dropped open and I could see fillings at the front. He was unemployed at the time and had to use buses to get everywhere. Even Leamington. Consequently he thought I was going to turn left and run him all the way home but I wouldn't. There was no way I was risking driving into town on a busy Saturday afternoon with my car behaving like that when I had to work at the Centre Bar at night. Fuck him.

The next weekend, after a week of jerking and heaving, I went back to Sugars and asked ex-Para Chris what to do with it. Maybe I saw him as the font of all solutions for things that happened to Jeff. He was grunty at the best of times. Everything he said started with an empty noise that sort of sounded like "harrrrrr." It was almost as if he was getting his brain into gear.

When I told him about my car he replied by saying to me "harrrrrr... pour some Redex down there. That'll shift anything..." and it did. Right to the carburettor.

Fuck me. The jerking got worse and worse. I didn't know what the hell was going on and spent many a time fiddling with what I thought was the screw that adjusted the rev speed in the carburettor. Turns out it was the one that adjusted the mixture which just made things a damn sight worse. Eventually the thing was so clogged up with muck that petrol couldn't get through. I had to have a new carburettor in there. That didn't work well at all. It was still always cutting out and I got stuck right on a busy junction near where I lived. I was furious, late for work and stuck in a damn dangerous position.

One of the Goths I knew and spoke to walked by and looked over and I looked towards him for some sort of help but didn't offer and carried on walking. I'd been at school with him. Years later he came into the Centre Bar wearing outlandish green and black striped trousers. I wouldn't let him in. I told him his trousers didn't fit in. He looked so confused. I found it funny. Lloyd was with me and asked what was up. "That one was personal" I told him. Bear a grudge? Who? Me?

The carburettor repair was so bad I had to take the car back to the garage several times. Each time with an ever increasing level of steroidal snarl and aggression. I even asked the mechanic if he *was stupid*. He was from Cornwall or somewhere and shouted back at me in rounded vowels "darn't carl me stuwped." We didn't get on.

One idiots night of fun cost me hundreds in repairs and even more in effort and frustration that lasted at least 2 years. In the end I had the replacement carburettor taken back out and the original put back in. It didn't help.

Another really bad time was a few years later. I had just got back to one of the many Escorts I owned, after the Samba had danced away, to find my two nearside tyres slashed. I hadn't even been working that night and I'd only gone in to sort out the roster. When I got back I saw a leaning car and found big cuts that went half way around the side walls. Somebody had spent a lot of time doing the damage. Mind you, somebody had even slashed the Samba tyres once so it wasn't a new event, just VERY annoying.

The time the Samba was damaged I was back in town for my workout by 10am but was too pissed off to train. Instead I wandered away from our usual coffee haunt on London Road, getting as far as a popular place called Brucciani's - about of 10 minutes away. When I walked in Adie, brother of Esau's ping-pong ball Keith, was serving. Got a nice free coffee out of that one!

It was about 11.30pm when I had discovered the damage to the Escort. It was even worse than the night of the Samba. I was tired, hungry and pissed off before I even started. I opened my boot and started to get the spare out. Now, those of you who are being alert will realise that I had two tyres slashed. How many spares do you carry? Not only that but to my horror I found the boot was full of water. Fords. Wonderful machines.

To top this off I soon discovered that the bolt to release the spare had rusted up and completely seized because of the water in the boot. In other words, I was fucked. I didn't know what to do.

Barmaid April drove past me and waved merrily. I was fuming about the car and probably glared in return. I do know she quickly drove on. Poor girl. Then it dawned on my revolving brain. Who was still in the AA? I walked back to the hotel. No mobile phones then. I made a call and waited and waited and waited.

About 2 hours later a patrolman turned up. Good job it was a mild night. "Ohhh you've had two slashed" he told me. "Uh huh'." "I'll tell you what. I'll help you get this one out of the boot, lend you a second from my van and then you can get home." "What next?" I asked. "Oh... then I'll take mine back off and you can sort it out from there." That would've meant three wheels on my wagon. Of course, it also meant that I could have got home at a reasonable time and sorted it out the next day but that wasn't good enough for me. I refused his offer. He looked at me. "Okay then. I'll call out a tyre service and they'll come and sort you out." I probably thanked him, although it's hard to be sure. I was now furious. He made the call and I waited and waited and waited.

About another 2 hours later up pulled some grey beared geezer in a flat bed truck with a heap of tyres and a fuel fired compressor on the back. It was now roughly 3.30am. My brain was on fire and steam was coming out of my ears. He looked at me. This massive, hulking, angry and miserable bastard and quickly offered me two crap Czechoslovakian no name brands at exorbitant cost. I took them and he put them on and started to inflate them. Then, just as I was starting to calm down, his bloody compressor ran out of petrol. Fuck me. This is all true. I often used to tell it on training courses but with the aggression deleted.

Now I had two new tyres, equally as flat as the slashed ones. The bearded guy took one look at my face and went white in the streetlight. Next thing I realised, he'd jumped in his truck and was off. Shit.

Jeff Shaw

Several things went through my mind. Kill was probably the first. Leave the car there and find a taxi was the second and crawl to a nearby garage and pump the things up was the third. I chose that one and on creaking rims drove at about 3mph to the nearest place and put some air in them. I finally got home at about 5am. I also probably warped the rims.

The hotel car park then. A safe haven from all this? Pretty much. Bearing in mind that over the years we were there Lloyd and Phil also experienced problems with both having their cars stolen. Phil had even, at one point, thrown some kid out – bang – straight into his own car, denting the door. Nothing much could happen down in the roller shuttered door carpark eh? Ummm.

That car park was nasty. Hard to get in to. Down a very steep descent. Hard right to get round a sharp corner and then find a spot. It was equally hard to get out of, lots of pillars, tight reversing and sharp turns. If you got stuck down there it was very hard to manoeuvre around with all the other cars. Even the great Phil managed to hit my car down there and put a small dent in it. I hated the damn place and only used it to save me from even more car dramas but once took a turn too tightly and completely caved my passenger door in. Ho hum.

In Road House Swayze goes to work in a clapped out old banger he buys for peanuts and keeps his 'day' car hidden away. That would've been the best idea by far. I never did it.

30

The Pool Table

Between 1988 and 1990, as I coped with "the bastard" and steroids, the Centre Bar carried on opening up. Limped on more realistically. Amazing really. It was very boring at times. I would practise karate chops and kicks. I've never had any proper training but it was something to do! More NLP. I still never lost an imaginary fight.

Me and Lloyd would stand there and have 'mock' battles because we were both so bored. It also allowed me to let out some of the aggression caused by "the bastard." Roche used to sit there with Alison at his side, watching and laughing because I would always pretend to cower in the corner once Lloyd upped the ante. Hey, despite my fucked brain during that time I STILL wasn't stupid.

I guess they'd seen me have to do so little for so many years and chat to so many women that they had forgotten some of the action I did have to take and thought I was a big softie. I know both him and Kip were staggered when, some years later, Slim had casually told them how I'd acted on the night of my car in December 1988. I ended up telling Kip the tale about three times. His eyes got wider every time. Mind you I *may* have exaggerated, just slightly.

My age was bothering me so much that in 1989 I added a year and, starting with Irish Catherine and ending with everyone, I became 30 when I was really 29. I don't know why I did this. I really don't. There were a lot of people out there who thought and probably still think I'm a year older than I really am.

By 1990 business throughout the entire hotel and particularly the bar was incredibly bad. In my view the standard of a lot of the managers was going rapidly downhill too. A few of the old brigade were still there but some of the new ones. Sheesh!! Now that the place was doing badly the chance of getting a staff taxi home evaporated. I asked if I could have one over the Christmas period. Just the once in about 5 years of Christmases. The response came from a red haired lady named Sue. Apparently there was no way. She'd only been there a few months.

This wasn't the same Susan that had been there when my sleeve was torn off. I asked, probably screamed, "why not?" and her actual words to me were a sneery "you're not worth it." Almost the same level of management skill as "the bastard."

When we still had the odd incident she would rush over to the melee to 'assist'. A bit like the actions of the goatee bearded GM of a few years earlier. Perhaps she thought she could sort things out herself. Riiiiggghhhttt. As a result she then got threatened so badly by some idiot that she went white as a ghost. She was pretty pale faced at the best of times. Her first resort was to look to me for help. Guess what phrase went through my mind. Slim was with me that night.

I let her stew for a few seconds and then we strolled over. The bloke doing the threatening took a look at me and Slim gave us some nice words of encouragement. He demanded to know our names. Sue started to tell him. "This is Slim and this is..." I cut her off. "My names not important to you" was my cold response. "What is important is that the doors over there." I pointed. He left.

I can't remember Sue ever saying to me again I wasn't worth it. Again, this sort of incident didn't happen very often so the majority of my time was spent wandering into functions when I had to, standing on the door in the bar and doing the odd search for drugs but mostly I fought boredom by flirting and holding hands with and hugging many, many, many different girls.

Despite my growing coldness, I had my favourites and Claire and Caroline were right up there, although Claire repeatedly told me she wasn't interested. I even went up to her one Christmas Eve dinnertime as she sat by herself on a barstool in an emptying bar. I was muttering something incomprehensible about not getting a present off her. "C'mon, I've got a special present for you" I grinned as I looked into her eyes. "I don't want that" she replied with a grimace and then jumped off the stool and flounced off.

I used to make a point of going over and holding Caroline's hand when Claire wasn't there and probably when Claire was there. I also had great fun squeezing her bum at every opportunity. It's probably safe to say we both loved it. Similar to the kisses from Louise, I made sure I was there when Caroline left for my little squeeze and she would stick it out so I could grab it. It was a nice bottom! Funny thing is though, I seem to remember squeezing a lot of different bums.

I do remember squeezing horse tattooed Erica's bum a lot as well. An awful lot. Later on Slim regularly used to chide me that I had a thing for small blondes. He was wrong. I think I liked looking at and squeezing arses. Certainly feels and reads like that now. I constantly thought about Caroline and what I could say to her at night as I went through the motions during my day job. I suppose I was a bit infatuated.

Once we met in the bar I would grab her by the arm and we would sit down next to each other on one of the bench seats, gently stroking hands, faces, thighs. She kissed me on the neck a lot and, in case you hadn't worked it out, was easily more than a replacement for Louise or Sharon in many ways.

One night I sat stroking the back of her neck while she gently massaged my thigh. I'm pretty sure she had some feelings for me at the time, even in my fat, moody and sometimes unpredictable state, although she did say to me many years later that she "didn't think I was interested."

I even went to see the New Model Army at the De Monfort Uni with Coulton one Sunday night. As usual we got in free. Even the DMU had doormen that I knew. We'd gone to see the band, true, but to also surreptitiously hand out flyers to try and boost the dismal takings at the Centre Bar. In the end I didn't bother with the flyers and spent most of the night hanging around Caroline who had gone with twin sister Nikki.

I'd been surprised to see her there. Her poor sister was pretty much left in the background by herself all night.

Mind you, there were times they both shocked me. I did catch Nikki full on knickers down having a pee in the street outside the entrance next to Strikes one dark winters night. Not the most pleasant of memories! A giggling Caroline was meant to be keeping guard. She obviously wasn't that good. They just laughed it off as Nikki pulled everything back up just as I arrived. I made sure I stepped over the spreading puddle.

We also had a period when I had to search bags after a spate of people smuggling in their own booze. I remember stopping the twins and looking through Nikki's first. "Tampax" said a smirking Caroline as I felt my face going bright red. I was so surprised I asked her what she'd just said. Mistake. "Tampax" she smirked again.

Twenty years later the three of us shared a black cab. Nikki was wearing a skin tight dress. As we got in I got a full on flash. "Have you gone commando... **again?**" asked Caroline. Nikki didn't even blink. I felt my face going bright red.

We tried everything to get the Centre Bar business back on its feet. We had a guy called Tim DJaying. He had long, straggly hair that was thinning at the top and told me he was paranoid about going bald. I looked. Better get used to it I thought. He didn't last long. After Tim left we alternated the DJ's between an oriental guy from Kettering and a long haired chappie universally called "Anarchy" Andy. Andy always wore one of those fluffy jumpers that were around in the day. His had red and black stripes on it and was stretched below his knees. I can't remember too much about the other guy except that he got his mate to ring me from Corby and ask if there was any doorwork going. "Have you got transport?" I asked. "No" was his response. Strangely enough I couldn't find any work for him.

In my opinion both Andy and the oriental guy were pretty poor in comparison to some of the others we'd had and really only played Goth stuff all night which was too limiting in my eyes. If I've heard the opening bars to "She Sells Sanctuary" once I've heard them a million times. Still takes me back though! In the end, we inevitably only had Goths and Punks down there. They loved it but takings were now absolutely dire. The rest of the crowd stayed at Helsinkis.

Ultimately even the bands stopped coming because no one turned up to watch them and eventually, as you might imagine, even the Goth and Punk crowd stopped coming. It was too much. The Centre Bar finally shut its doors in December 1990. We simply closed for Christmas, sacked the DJs, put a pool table in there and never really re-opened. None of the remaining clientele knew it was going to happen and none of the doormen or bar staff knew either but I don't think it was a big a surprise to anyone.

Claire, Tony and Jill, Caroline or Nikki. None of them ever came back to say goodbye. I was still coping with "the bastard" and had been off the gear for 6 months. I was quite low. Nobody even coming to say goodbye upset and disappointed me. As you might imagine, after all we'd said and done I particularly missed Claire and her arse and Caroline and her arse. They would've been so close and easy to find but my mood meant that I never tried to track them down again.

We didn't shut the doors completely though. April and Mags donned red T-Shirts, stayed behind the bar and would open up as usual but without any DJ. The hotel put a crap jukebox down there. It was pretty much permanently empty but every so often a few of the old regulars like the members of Crazyhead, Red Cap Kevin and his mates or Roche, Penny and Kip and their other mates popped in, put a few coins in the jukebox and played pool for a couple of hours or so.

I was amazed by the ragged sight of Richard Crazyhead. All I will say is that there must have been a few illicit substances going into his body. All of our customers would challenge us to a game of pool and, in spite of constant warnings from the various managers that filtered through, we would give them a quick game. I was useless. Lloyd is a shark. He's very good at snooker too. The odd thing about all the warnings is that sometimes I'd walk into the bar and some of the managers – particularly Debbie who was a very tall lady with a mass of red curls – would be playing too. One rule for one.

The Olympic swimmers turned up again. This time, rather than throw stuff out of the windows they decided to run a pool tournament. Roche was in there. So was Kip and roadie Penny. Me and Lloyd watched from the sidelines. Penny, big mouthed as always, started to argue with one of them over the rules. There was a bit of cue grabbing going on and I had to step forward. Penny, of course, knew me well enough to stop arguing. The other guy didn't. He followed Penny's eyes to me and, I suppose, realised that it was in his best interests to shut up. They got along just dandy after that. A few days later one of the guys Kip had played was on A Question of Sport. I watched in amusement. Kip re-appeared in the bar a couple of weeks later. I asked him if he'd seen the episode and he said no, but seemed to go away happy with his brush with fame.

For the most part though no residents came in and no crowd came down. It was always odd down there now it was very, very quiet. And odd.

One night, as I stood there bored, red eyed and tarnished, my old fixation Sharon appeared out of the blue with Irish Catherine. My heart did a flip-flop. Thumpity-thump… thumpity-thump… thumpity-thump. Good ole boy me. I hardened it. I was very good at it by then. I didn't speak to her. She couldn't understand it. "Look" she cried, "I haven't changed." I looked at her legs. Oh my god I thought. You really haven't!

It took me about 3 weeks before I even said hello. I learned that she'd spent some years living with a Goth called Craig who'd been there the night Esau had one punched the guy into the street. She told me that Craig liked to beat her up but, in the end, she left him and was trying to re-start her life. I felt some sympathy for her but pretty much I soon realised that any lust I had for her had dissipated years before. The thumpity-thumps over her never came back.

Sadly, I have been told that Craig committed suicide shortly after Sharon left him. Again, I don't know if this is true or not. In the end we got a final verbal warning for playing pool. By this time the manager that gave us it had got it in for us anyway. I suppose she had the best interests of the hotel at heart. It was starting to spread. Another told me off for slouching on one of the bench seats when the place was completely empty apart from me and a very bored April. I suppose it was inevitable. Finally the bar slithered to an end.

For quite a while there the hotel kept us on in our part time security role. I guess they hoped business would pick up again. Coulton was constantly going on about re-opening the bar and trying to attract a different crowd. It never happened.

I took our new role seriously. We all did at first, standing to attention in reception. Stand Up Straight Claire from the early days would have been really proud but, ultimately, we all took to counting down the hours before we could all go home for the night while lounging on a nice, comfy sofa.

31

Spencers

It was 1991. I was alone downstairs in a busy and smoke filled bar in a place called Spencers. A popular haunt in Silver Street in Leicester city centre and directly opposite another very trendy pub.

Working at Spencers had come almost by accident. With the Centre Bar closed and the hotel only retaining us as sort of security guards we had begun taking the weekends in shifts. 2 one weekend, the other two the next. Despite maintaining the roster every week my doorman income had dropped by 50%. Re-enter former Centre Bar doormen Valentine.

A dark and dangerous man
Picture Courtesy Jeff Shaw

Valentine was a quietly spoken guy. I never knew much about his life away from the doors. He never let on. I can tell you he told me that Valentine wasn't his real name, he was adopted, that he was a fairly heavy smoker, mean faced with blazing eyes and a missing molar that he told me he'd lost in a fight one night. I can add his appearance which always included a scruffy beard and a tie he never did up properly and I reckon he was nearly 7 feet tall – but that may be because I'm a short arse – and he was very skinny.

Like a lot of these guys I do know he had served time. He never told me why but he did say he to me "I don't take as many risks as I used to." Who knows what he meant by that?

After he lost his job at the Centre Bar, Valentine eventually found himself at Spencers with two guys, Mouthy and Mikey.

Mouthy was a white guy, late twenties and chubby with blond hair and a permanent mouth sore on his top lip. He came across as your typical loud mouth doorman often claiming victory in door battles that the real tough guys would never tell you about.

Mikey was a different. A thin West Indian, also around his late twenties, he saw himself as a fantastic women magnet which ended up with him hardly ever being there and always being in trouble for well thought out and politely articulated comments such as: "you look like a stick of rock. Can I lick you?" Not Classy. Surprise, surprise, a lot of women found this offensive and complained so Mikey, to his continuous amazement, often found himself suspended.

It was during one of these suspension periods that Valentine took the opportunity to boast that he could get someone else to cover really easily. I didn't know it at the time but he was trying to start his own doorman agency. Good to his word, he rang around. I learned later that most people said no. My guess is that Valentine must've gone down his list until he got to the one's he didn't want to talk to. He still blamed me for getting the sack and I'd had no contact with him since he'd departed from the Centre Bar. I was his last chance. He rang.

I started that weekend, working there the weekends I wasn't at the hotel. Hey. I was bored and I was missing the money. Because I was the new guy I got the shit job. Down in the basement. Alone. Every so often I'd emerge for fresh air only to be sent downstairs again by Helen, a mid thirty ish, heavy smoking, broad nostrilled, fair haired lady who was the manager.

Sometimes Mikey would be suspended, sometimes Valentine. Occasionally Mouthy wouldn't turn up. Generally 3 of us to cover two floors and about 125 – 150 typical townies.

I was still down after the loss of the Centre Bar and the loss of the group of people I'd thought of as friends. I was also still coping with "the bastard" and my final quitting of steroids. As a result I was much quieter when I stood on Spencers door than I'd ever been. I didn't say hello or goodbye to anyone who came in. Nothing. Totally cold. I recall one girl trying to flirt with me and getting zilch in return. In the end she said "you don't say much for a doorman" and gave up. Another came up and hugged and kissed me all night long. I smiled and hugged her in return but other than that I gave her virtually no response. She looked at me in confusion and eventually walked away. I didn't care.

At the end of a particularly smoky and boring stint there was a West Indian girl still in there with drink in her hand and boyfriend by her side. I tried again and again to get her to finish up and leave. She just ignored me and wouldn't stop talking. In the end I touched her gently on the elbow and she went mad at me screaming and shouting about how rude and ignorant I was. My eyes must've told her the story and the next thing I knew they were dashing for the door. Afterwards the bar staff took the piss out of me and I smiled a grim, cold smile. I was so bad that I hardly even spoke to people I knew from the hotel or from my Helsinki and Centre Bar days who had moved on from being part of the Alternative crowd and occasionally went in there. They always came over to speak. Usually it was "what are you doing here?" The best I could do was a grin and a shrug of the shoulders.

I will admit that I did fancy a girl called Alison and made some mild approaches to her. She smiled a lot in return but we hardly exchanged any words really. I thought she was skinny and flat-chested but very pretty with strawberry blonde hair cut into a bell shape. Mouthy told me she also lived in my village but I didn't really believe him. He was right though. Amazingly, it turned out she had lived virtually next door to me for years, closer than the guy with the fedora from Helsinkis that Daz tried to stop going in, but I never knew. She also worked with Trevor at the local paper and he knew her as well. It really IS a small world. However, my mind was completely twisted out of shape by now so I never really tried very hard. I don't think she was that interested anyway. I still speak to her dad.

Despite having a nice décor Spencers could often be a bit rough inside from time to time. It was a real townie place, shutters that opened on to the street, mirrored bars upstairs and downstairs, general pop of the day, lads in shirts and smart trousers, women in too short skirts and tons of makeup. Not surprising then that I had a lot of the meaningless hassle you get as a doorman in there.

By Christmas of 1991 I'd been there just under a year. In all that time Mikey only stepped in to help once. It was one wet Thursday night when Helen had some sort of promotion running and the two of us were on duty. I'd hardly spoken to him all night. I never liked him. About half way through the night I refused a guy entry and he came out with the "I've been coming here longer than you've been working here" shit which you often get, and was probably true. In my cold mood I didn't give a toss and started to shut the door in his face. He began to squeal and push back. I was ready to give it a sharp shove and snap his hand in two – a trick I'd learned years before at Tipplers – when Mikey came rushing over from somewhere behind me and calmed the bloke down. As usual he'd been chatting up a woman. I just looked through both of them.

In my mind Mouthy or Valentine never did help much the entire time I worked there either and I have to admit I felt like I was being used. I doubt I was in reality. It was just that I was now so different. I'd put up with "the bastard" for years. I'd lost the Centre Bar. My friends were gone. My physique, what was left of it anyway following my 2 ½ year on / off steroid battle, had now totally gone and I was mostly fat. I was losing all sense of rationale and care. I really, really wonder how anyone put up with me.

To put this into perspective, one of the doormen from the place opposite, a notorious Rasta with a dark history of violence, drug pushing and prison, used to park his car across a doorway behind which the others would park their cars. I knew him by sight and reputation but had never spoken to him.

I would stand there the few times I wasn't stuck downstairs and watch as he would jump in his car with a mysterious person. They'd drive round the block and then be back in less than 5 minutes. He'd then park it in the same spot and both he and his passenger would go their separate ways. I assumed it was drug deals going off. There was no way I was going to interfere because I couldn't be bothered.

At the end of one cold and bitter night his car was still there while he milled about in the doorway on 'his' side of the road. Mine was hidden on the other side of town. Valentine volunteered to give me a lift back to it to save me walking across the city. His car was hidden behind the gate. "Hey, can you move your car so I can get to mine?" Valentine shouted hopefully across the empty street. The Rasta gave him a sideways look and then completely ignored him. Valentine stood there open mouthed and swore softly under his breath. I could see he was annoyed. I was cold, I was tired, I was a sullen, heartless bastard. I wanted a lift. I started to blatantly look round for a brick to smash the window. Valentines jaw fell open. I don't think he expected it or wanted it. I was so blatant that the Rasta saw me too and started to walk towards me. I stood up and we looked into each others eyes. He knew me by sight too. He sheeshed at me. It came out as a low phhhhhaawwwwing sound. For those that don't know – a typical West Indian show of disgust. I just stood there, fat and grim faced and looked at him. Through him would have been more accurate. A show of strength between us if you like. More I don't give a fuck on my part. Then he just wordlessly got in his car and moved it. He shot off down the road. I assume he either realised that it wasn't worth the effort or was leaving anyway. Probably the latter.

Valentine looked at me out of the corner of his eye. From my knowledge of him, he was a dark and dangerous man himself but the Rasta was an even more dangerous character. Then he jumped in his own car and reversed it out and I jumped in and off we went. He never said a word, just kept looking at me out of the corner of his eye until we arrived at my car a few minutes later.

32

Scarface

I got my facial scar one Friday night at Spencers in May 1992. Valentine wasn't working that night, so there was me, Mouthy and Mikey. I remember I'd been in a good mood. I'd watched an episode of Quantum Leap on TV the day before, which I loved, and was feeling pretty relaxed which was so unusual at that time.

The night was warm and Spencers was packed solid. Downstairs was almost unbearable for me in my suit and tie. All the signs were there. It was hot. It was cramped. People were getting drunk. I was alone. I'd already 'floated' across the bar a few times and had plenty of stares. I'd squinted and smiled at a couple of black guys and their girlfriends who were just in front of me. I thought I knew them. One of the guys waved me over. I thought he wanted a chat. As I moved closer I could see his face was grim. So was his mates. I was puzzled. "Why do you keep staring at us?" he asked. I was absolutely gob smacked and, not wanting trouble, mumbled an apology and moved away.

Rather than look in their direction again I started to look around. There was a group of lads, maybe 8 or 10 of them, overcrowding one 4 seater table near where I was that were really messing about. First they put their feet on the table, then they threw lit cigarettes at each other. When they started to flick their beer around I decided that was more important then the black guys and time for a little warning, so I went over. The conversation went along the lines of "Hey guys. Please can you take it easy? That's not the sort of behaviour we want in here." Pretty simple, innocuous stuff. The stuff that would've worked at the Centre Bar. They looked at me with the usual disdain but calmed down at first and then it started again. Beer flicking, feet on the table, that sort of stuff. Nothing major. I asked them again. I was getting frustrated. Then I made a big mistake.

Communication is the key to being a good doorman. I had worked for years with the Centre Bar crew. We knew each other well. We knew when to react, how to react and what to do. I hadn't gelled with the guys at Spencers at all and didn't really know them that well. True to my practises I wandered upstairs and told Mouthy and Mikey that it was getting a bit lairy downstairs with the heat and that there was one group in particular that we needed to keep an eye on just in case.

Now, bear in mind that Mouthy and Mikey were real wannabes. This was the city centre and Spencers had a bit of a bad rep. They'd had some gangsters working the door there in the past. The most famous being some guy I never knew who went by the name of Moose. Even Khachik had worked there for a while.

Mikey asked me where the lads were sitting so I told him. Communication. Next thing he headed down there in a flash followed by Mouthy and, with a deep sigh of here we go again, me. There was no need for this. Mikey saw the group and went straight over and bellowed "you lot... out. NOW!" Oh shit.

I have to say that completely to my surprise and without any fuss what-so-ever, they all mumbled okay mate, got up and started to leave. Mikey didn't hang about. Presumably spurred by fear that he may have started trouble he bolted past me and dashed back upstairs leaving me and Mouthy to cope. Mouthy lived up to his name because by this time his mouth was so far agape I could see his tonsils. Because I was last down, and Mikey had passed me like Linford Christie on speed on his way back to safety I was left in the lead.

Well, even experienced people make mistakes. These guys were so passive I just thought they would go with no trouble so I turned round and walked up the four or five steps to the landing. I didn't even check they'd finished their drinks. Once there and with Mikey at the top of the stairs and Mouthy at the bottom I just stood back to let them out at which point and, **I have to be clear about this**, completely unprovoked one of them had secretly donned a knuckle duster and smacked me in the face. I was lucky, he missed my nose but let me tell you. Being hit on the cheekbone with a knuckle-duster **FUCKING HURTS**. It opened my face, just under my eye, to the bone.

I really didn't react well to being hit in the face. Who would? This was not the naïve, innocent Jeff of Force 8. No, this was a close cropped, seasoned, 17 stone doorman, pissed off with his day job and full of pent up aggression.

I don't really know who hit me, but none of them were very big. I hardly budged at the blow. Rumour is I went berserk. Apeshit is a more apt description. They must've thought who the hell is this because I could see them all running like terrified little rabbits. I let loose a massive right hand uppercut at the slowest and nearest of them, a skinny Asian guy. Bugger. Missed by a country mile. I always was so very short sighted. My face was on fire. I leapt up the stairs and grabbed skinny gently by the nearest part of his body. For some strange reason that seemed to be his head.

His mates scrambled all around me for freedom, escape from this wild thing they'd woken. At the top of the stairs stood Mikey. I glanced up and squinted. He'd pulled the push bar out of the fire exit and was busily waving it at them without doing a thing to stop them running. Every single one started to run out past him. I glanced down. At the bottom of the stairs Mouthy looked terrified. I still had my hands on the Asian. I started to thrust him back downstairs. It was then I got my second scar. The one that everyone notices.

As I moved one of the few remaining lads swung a pint glass at my head. I was moving fast and heading down. I was lucky again, rather than getting me full in the face which is what he must've been aiming for he just caught the back of my head with a swinging blow. The unlucky bit of it was that he basically took a piece of my scalp and neck straight out. A premature bald spot! I knew instantly I'd been glassed but it didn't hurt which was probably due to adrenalin. I shoved my captive towards Mouthy and screamed at him to hold him.

Jeff Shaw

He failed me totally and the bastard got away. Skinny saw his chance and dived for his life, squeezing past me and flying up and out while Mikey just stood there waving the bar around like a mini Zulu with his spear but doing nothing. I chased after him up the stairs but being that heavy made me slow. I was in serious agony from the knuckle-duster blow, concerned about the back of my head and losing blood FAST.

I pounded up the stairs as fast as my little legs would allow me. I stormed into the upstairs bar to get the police. I didn't really know at that time how EVERYONE had got away. It wasn't until after it all sunk in over the next few days that I realised how ineffective the others had been and my disgust at them grew.

The packed crowd parted in front of me like the Red Sea in front of Moses. I had no idea why. The whole place went quiet and I saw Helen emerge from behind the bar. She was goggled eyed.

Basically I was covered in blood and had a hole in my quickly swelling face with my cheekbone shining through. Helen shielded me from any mirrors in the joint and tried to usher me in the back. I resisted and turned my back on her to try and make her get the police. Then she saw the back of my head. Fortunately I didn't catch sight of the front of my face. My head was later described to me as like having a mohican of glass. I started to feel a little woozy so my resistance to being tugged away subsided. She got me in the back and tore off my jacket and tie. She always had the hots for me and was desperate to get in my trousers. That night she had her chance because she fumbled at my belt, undid my trousers and pulled them down to my knees. Sadly wee willie was going nowhere! Poor thing was so tiny even I couldn't find it.

Helen then got a massive fan from somewhere and turned it on me. I was going into shock. Good job she had first aid training. I sat there for a while, getting more and more woozy, grateful for the cold air blasting in my face. An ambulance arrived, then the police. I pulled my trousers up, stood up and grabbed my glasses from their hiding place behind the bar. In reality, I may have pulled my trousers up after I stood up but that would have made me look silly to anyone reading this so I prefer the first version.

The police started to ask me questions and I gave them a brief and, I suppose, somewhat garbled, overview. I know I asked them to keep an eye on my car and then **INSISTED** on walking to the ambulance, jacket and tie in hand. No one could quite believe it. The ambulance man held me by the elbow but I shook him off, walked through the Red Sea and got inside his vehicle, wiped my bleeding nose with the back of my hand and promptly passed out.

33

Patch Job

I opened my eyes again and found we had arrived at the Leicester Royal. It's only 2 or 3 minutes from Spencers by road so I wasn't out for long. The ambulance man helped me into a wheelchair and pushed me into casualty. After so many years I was no stranger there. Doorwork takes its toll but this time I was a real mess.

A nurse came towards us "I don't like his colour" I heard her say. I groaned. "It's only shock" said the ambulance man. I hope so mate I thought. They got me naked down to my undies. If only Helen had been there! Then again, I always did have a thing for nurses.

Lloyd had said to me once to enjoy my money and not be scared to spend it. I'd taken it to heart in my attempts to overcome my despair at "the bastard". I owned a new car, a Rolex watch and had expensive glasses but that night, I lay there on a hospital trolley, bleeding and in pain wearing nothing more than a grimace, my undies, my watch and a hospital gown. Good job I'd always taken mumsies advice to wear a clean pair.

First they X-rayed my face then my head. The big fear was that I'd fractured or depressed my cheekbone. I think they were also looking to see if I'd got a brain. Fortunately the bloke that had hit me must've been a real weedy bastard. One thing in my advantage was that he'd hit me on the head. Pretty much solid bone up there. No broken bones. Next they had to get the glass out of my head and neck. The nurse pulled my scalp apart and washed the pieces out. I yelped in pain. Then they shaved off a patch of what little hair I had on my head and sewed me up. In total four stitches in my face, 10 in the back of my head and 3 in my neck.

To fix my head they had to overlay the two rough edges of my scalp. The wound was wide so it was a bit of a tug. Like a face lift from the back! I'm sure my ears moved back a bit. It ended up with the overlay being very thick and the stitches very deep. I had to keep them in for 10 days which is a pretty long time. The ones in my face and neck were taken out after about 4.

My whole face and head were numb. I had lost feeling in the entire right hand side of my face. Even my teeth felt odd. My cheek muscle and nerves had been sliced in half. I got in there at about 9.30 / 10.00pm. I thanked them profusely for their efforts and got out at about 4am.

Mouthy came to see me as I lay on the trolley. He didn't tell me how tough he was. I think he felt a bit guilty for letting the Asian go. I thought – and still think – he should have held his head in shame. My one and only chance of getting one of them and he feebly let him go.

Mickey never apologised or expressed any form of regret what-so-ever. Not long after, I worked with Lloyd in some poxy nightclub in a town north of Leicester. Lloyd drove. Mikey was working at another joint in town. At the end of the night we all met up and Lloyd gave him a lift home. I didn't even know that they knew each other. I had to sit next to him in the back as he nodded off and drooled on my shoulder for about an hour. I wanted to kill him.

After they fixed me up the hospital was very insistent. **ABSOLUTELY NO** driving. I'd taken a heavy blow to my head. I was concussed. Good job my head is thick. I walked all the way across town to my car. A short drive in an ambulance. A long walk with concussion, a growing stiffness all over your body, blood soaked clothes and 17 stitches in your head. The car had been vandalised. Some clown had walked across the bonnet, up the front windscreen, across the roof and down the back. There were footprint sized dents everywhere. Thanks for keeping an eye on it. I got in and drove home. I went in and stripped off, hanging my blood soaked shirt over a chair and went straight to bed and fell asleep in an instant. I was exhausted.

I didn't tell anybody what had happened. My mum and brother and his family were away on holiday. I didn't want to upset them. I was woken up by a banging on the window. It was about 10am. Leave me alone!!! Naked, I peeped round the curtain. It was two policemen. I pulled on a T-Shirt and some jeans and let them in and they took a statement. I was stiff all over, well... not quite *all* over, and not a pretty sight. I looked better with a shirt covering my saggy muscles and belly but I wasn't a pretty sight at the best of times!

I told them everything I could remember and got my crime number. They asked me if the blood soaked shirt on the chair was the one I'd been wearing. Then they asked me if there was anyone they should tell. I said "no." Helen rang and asked me how I was feeling. I quit Spencers on the spot. She was very understanding. After all, her most reliable doorman had just been badly mashed up. What was she going to do? Get me to go back with a face swollen like a football and 17 stitches in my head. She never did quite finish off getting the rest of my clothes off me. I think we were both a little disappointed in the end.

My head throbbed like hell and my face and teeth were still deathly, scarily numb. I touched my nose with my finger and couldn't feel any sensation at all.

That night I hopped in my car and started to drive back to the scene, mainly to say my goodbyes to everyone. 10 minutes out of my house I drove past a longhaired lout strolling down the street. It was one of the lads who attacked me. My heart rate quickened. Thumpity-thump... thumpity-thump... thumpity-thump. I looked for somewhere to stop but the traffic was heavy and I couldn't find anywhere safe enough in time. I was very unsure. In the end I drove on and he strolled out of my sight in my rear view mirror. Maybe it was the right decision to drive on, maybe it wasn't. At that time I believed the police were going to help me like the night they'd helped me when I'd broken my hand at the hotel. Sadly I was very wrong.

I got to town, parked my dented little car outside the hotel and wandered across the city to Spencers. I took my time. I hurt. Mouthy, Mikey and another guy I didn't know were there. I suppose Valentine was suspended again. I spent a few minutes with them and then went inside. The Spencers staff had organised a collection and bought me a lovely T-Shirt and got a card. I was touched. I looked inside. Mikey hadn't signed it. I went straight outside and right in his face, with mine all messed up and his mates either side of him, took the piss. He looked at his feet. I went downstairs and – because I had to – stood on the exact spot where I was hit. Then I didn't give the actual injuries or the nights events a second thought, chatted to the downstairs bar staff for a bit and left.

I've never bothered about the scar on the back of my head since. I can't see it. It doesn't hurt. It's nothing.

Before I left for the night one of the female bar staff told me there had been glass everywhere on the stairs. Not only had I been hit but the little rabbits had all been throwing their glasses at me as they fled. Not one caused me a mark or scratch of additional damage. I was very, very lucky. My guardian angel truly was looking over me that day. If only Mouthy and Mikey had been too!

I walked slowly back to the hotel, head down and careful to avoid eye contact or conflict with anyone as I walked across town. It wasn't as easy as it sounds. As I walked past the clock tower some loon was giving two policemen hassle. "YOU" he was chanting "ain't got no bottle." The policemen were eyeing him darkly. I hurried on as best as my injured body would allow me.

I arrived at the hotel ten or so minutes later. Phil and Lloyd were working. I knew that because I was still organising the weekly roster. "Hello" I said with a painful, cockeyed grin. "Guess what happened to me."

Phil and Lloyd both looked genuinely shocked at my appearance. I must have been a real mess. Phil, never one for great conversation simply said "that wouldn't have happened if we'd been there." Oh so true.

It was less than 24 hours since the attack. The worst of the bruising and stiffness hadn't even come out yet. At that time the hotel had a female receptionist working there that I used to call the prison warder. I never knew her real name. She was a big fat thing with dark curly hair and massive, saggy breasts. I reckon she used to hang the things over her shoulders when she lay in bed to keep her neck warm. She always had a massive bunch of keys hanging off her waist. I hate to think what she used them for. I obviously thought very highly of her.

She was always hanging around with our very own, in-house overt gay – presumably because no man would go near her for fear of being smothered to death. I hated her with a vengeance. Luckily she hated me in return. Me and Slim had been there when some soccer hooligans had kicked a young lad senseless in the hotel doorway. We had rushed over, but they were outside so there wasn't really anything we could do. I had screamed at saggy breasts to get the police as I ran over, but she never even called them because she was "too busy." We had to stand and watch as the poor lad had the shit kicked out of him. After that she used to go round telling everyone that she was "the best receptionist this place has ever had." Yeah. Right.

That night she came over to have a look. I smiled wanly. I saw triumph in her eyes. Fuck. I spent a few more minutes with Phil and Lloyd, got one of them to cover for me in the roster and went home to an empty house.

I saw my mum for the first time since my injuries the next day. I heard her coming through the door, back off her holiday. "Er... I've got something to tell you" I shouted from the lounge. "Just a minute... what?" I emerged into the kitchen. She cried.

Because the attack had happened on a Friday night and I'd spent most of Saturday morning sleeping or speaking to the police I hadn't even been to my local surgery. I went there first thing on Monday morning. I was still concussed but, being a bit short on the brain capacity at the best of times, I drove.

There was a locum in. I gave him a letter the hospital had given me. He looked at it and asked me when the stitches were due out. How the fuck should I know? Whatever it said in the letter. He looked again. 4 days for the face and neck, 10 days for the head he read aloud. "When's that?" he asked me. I thought he was insane. "I don't know" I managed to say. "Did you count the Saturday? How the hell should I know?" He gave me a dirty look. I gave him one in return. Eventually we stopped staring at each other and he realised he had to take the lead. He fixed up some dates and a time. What now?

I'd been walking around and driving for about 2 days. I shrugged and went off to my daytime job. "I've had a bit of an accident" I said. "The bastard" was anything but kind and gentle. He gave me an all time bollocking for being late in. Later that week he made me go to a trades exhibition at the NEC. I drove there through the murderous morning motorway traffic and then I spent 10 hours walking around with a multicoloured face, stitches and concussion. I got some very strange looks. "You shouldn't have come in if you're not well enough" was his considered viewpoint.

The following weekend I went back to the hotel to let Slim admire my injuries. It was his turn on the roster. He was there with Lloyd. By this time my face was black, my head was swollen massively and I had even less feeling in my face. At least the stiffness had worn off.

Frances BB was standing in reception when I arrived. She came over. "It's not as bad as we were told" she said to me. She waved vaguely at her own head "we heard that the whole of your forehead had been torn open." Seems the prison warder had been talking. "That's the worst you've ever had" she said looking.

The week after the attack was definitely the worst. Because I had gone to work and then been sent to the trades exhibition I never really got over the concussion. My head throbbed, my face felt numb and I felt sick. A tall policewoman called Elaine visited me at my day job. "We need you to go and look at the mugshots" she said. "We've also got to take pictures of your head for evidence if it comes to court. Juries like to see injuries when they're at their worst." I only worked 10 minutes from the main police station on Narborough Road. Even "the bastard" let me go. I looked at the mugshots. Plenty of people I knew, most of them Esaus mates, but nothing on the assault front.

Elaine wasn't too helpful. Her advice? Go round town at the weekend looking for them and to ring her if I saw them. Right. Thanks a lot. I eventually did it with full Centre Bar crew in tow about a month later.

Apart from the night I drove by one of them I never saw any of them again. I got zero support from Elaine. I guess in her head it was only some doorman who'd taken a bit of a beating. She probably had more important cases to attend to.

They took photos of my head at the cop shop. I sat there and tried to make myself look all beaten up. It wasn't a challenge really. "Don't forget your CICB claim" said Elaine[7]. I asked her if being a doorman would prejudice me. "See a lawyer" she said. I did. He told me to organise my own photographs to attach to the claim. I booked a local guy to come round and take some snaps at 6pm. At about 1pm on the day he was coming "the bastard" told me that there was a meeting at 6pm and I was expected to be there.

"I can't make it tonight" I pleaded. "I've got a very important appointment about my injuries." My face was a terrible mess. I felt ill. "Cancel it" he sniffed, turned his back and walked off. I tried very hard but I couldn't get the guy. There were no mobile phones then. No one had an answer machine. I FUMED for 5 hours. It seemed like 2 minutes to me. My head pounded. At about a quarter to 6 I sent a message *through*. *"I haven't been able to cancel my appointment… I need to go."* "The bastard" came straight out of where he'd been hiding for all that time. "If you go now, you'll be fired" he said. I stayed. Good soldier.

---

[7] CICB stands for Criminal Injuries Compensation Board. Anyone injured in an unlawful attack was eligible to make a claim. Dependant on the degree of injury it could be a lot of money. I got thousands.

We took the photos a few days later. My injuries had faded marginally. They were so bad that I think marginal is a pretty good word.

Over the next few days I had the stitches out. I hadn't trained or worked as a doorman since I got them. Even I'm not *that* crazy.

When I got glassed my hair had been completely shaved down. Clippers come with a number of guards a one, two, three or four, with a number one being the shortest. In those days I made a lot of mistakes as I was cutting it myself and had given myself a bit of a bald patch so, to cover it up, I wasn't even using the guard and basically had a zero.

They'd told me the night of the attack that I could wash my hair gently the next day but then not at all until all the stitches were out. My hair had been so short and I was so exhausted by the time I got home that I didn't. By the time the final stitches came out my head smelled like damp wood and had dirty, crusty bits of blood stuck to it. The District Nurse pulled a face and took the last ones out of my scalp. "They're coming out quite well" she said as she tugged off a bit of scab. "I think you can wash your hair now." "When can I start training again?" I asked. She gave me a blank look. "Weight training" I explained. "Oh, you like that do you" she replied. "That's it. You're fixed." I went back to the gym the next day. As I trained I felt my whole scalp move. Eerie feeling.

My face went black. I still had no feeling at all on my right hand side and my mouth only worked on the left, kind of like a half smile. I had to learn to use the whole of the right side of my face again. Sometimes it still doesn't work and my scar burns and itches when I get stressed. I call it part of my charm.

About 8 months later I had my end of year appraisal. I hated them. I still do. "The bastard" referred to the day of the photos. He told me that he never wanted to see my face like that ever again, and he didn't mean my injuries.

I learned that you really can see red. My head went light and a red mist slowly descended over my eyes. I slowly turned my head and he got the same look that poor old Sadie had received the night she threw ice cubes at me nearly 10 years before. This time I never apologised.

"The bastard" would be in his late sixties to early seventies now, if he's still alive. It's fair to say we loathed each other throughout the entire time we worked together.

34

Feeling the Pain

Going back to the gym so soon after my Spencers injuries was probably a mistake. My face was black for days. So much for being fixed. I'd still got no feeling but slowly, oh so slowly it returned. I've got to tell you the relief was enormous. It's hard to kiss girls when you can't feel half of your mouth! I went back to work at the hotel the next weekend. I stood there with Slim, a big red mark under my right eye, severe bruising and what one guy once described as a big red faggot sticking up on the back of my head.

There was a medical conference on. The Helsinki crowd had changed too. This was 8 years after I stood on the left. There were far more townies. There was a bit of a fight. Me and Slim watched. Thumpity-thump... thumpity-thump... thumpity-thump. My early doorman nerves were back!

Slim went to stand on the doorstep, folded his arms and gave the scene an inscrutable do not enter here look. I stayed inside. Attracted by the noise some of the Doctors from the conference came to have a look. They saw my head and some of them oohhed and aahhed in sympathy. One asked me if I got that working security. I smiled. "It's only a scratch" I said. My turn for more doorman bravado. I was getting quite good at it. In retrospect I think it was the beginning of the end of my doorman career, although I could be being pretty harsh on myself.

Despite how I felt I carried on working the doors for another 6 years. I also carried on working security at the hotel. There was still the odd function but I soon found that I didn't like being in crowds. I still don't.

By the time of my final battle I'd suffered at my day job for nearly 5 years. It felt like 2 weeks to me. I finally, finally managed to escape about a year after my injuries and my mood slowly, oh so slowly started to improve. It took a long time. I was still moaning quite a bit although I do remember standing in reception with Slim at my side, arms high above my head and feeling free and whooping for joy. He laughed with me and not at me for once but inside I was still all twisted up.

I thought about getting a gun. I wanted revenge. I considered that Valentine would probably have known where to go. Whether this is actually true or not, I have no clue. I mentioned it coldly to Phil. I was deadly serious. Phil told me not to be such a tosser and get over it. Fortunately part of my brain was still functioning and I listened and EVENTUALLY took his advice and gave up the idea. For years and years afterwards though I thought of how many different ways I could kill "the bastard". I saw it and replayed it in my mind over and over. More NLP. I even had my escape route down pat. He doesn't know how close he came.

I have no humour for this part other than to say that with my bloody short sightedness I'd probably have missed with the gun anyway and shot myself in the foot or something.

We lasted one more Christmas at the hotel. I was still extremely restless. I guess I was trying to come to terms with my experiences. I started to behave a bit more normally towards people around me. Deep down there was still a quiet, shy, gentleman Jeff inside me. Sadly I also continued to eat anything that wasn't nailed down and looked more and more like a potato. This time round the hotel wasn't very busy at all and there was virtually no trouble. No real need for us to be there. We weren't really helping ourselves either by lounging about and chatting up the bar staff and waitresses... okay... me again. Guilty. Got me. Oh and raiding the kitchen pantry. Yes. All right. Me again.

One night Esau appeared for the last ever time I saw him. Several of the city doormen had been in contact. Esau walked up and looked me up and down grimly. "Scar face... innit" he said. He didn't grin. Then I showed him the back of my head. I was hoping he'd say good looking. He didn't. He chatted to the others, jumped into his car and vanished from my life for good.

Despite all of this I hadn't stopped my flirting. Women of the moment were Vanessa who took to doing the Julie ride on my leg in the Studio one night and Pauline – an incredibly skinny, flat chested girl with her hair in a bob and a bit of a big conk. She was a very nice girl though and always smelled great. For some reason she put up with my continued moaning.

Late in the year I walked into Strikes on one of my trails round and there she was. I went over and before you knew it she was all legs akimbo right in the middle of the bloody restaurant. I grabbed her and we headed for the lifts and her staff room on the 6th floor. We were both excited. She gave me her door key when I had a sudden change of heart. Bear in mind my mentality at the time and I was supposed to be working. I just smiled, waited for the lift doors to open and then just walked off. I felt my excitement wane. She clearly didn't know what to say or do.

I saw her the next night as I walked round a corner when she was striding towards me from the opposite direction. My first instinct was to try and hide. I was a bit embarrassed. Her eyes lit up as she recognised me and she smiled "ha... saw you coming" she said triumphantly. "You nearly did last night" was all I could say in return. She looked absolutely mortified. The look in her eyes changed. "What do you mean?" she asked. "Nothing" I said quietly and looked at my feet.

Looking back, it seems those lifts were pretty popular with quite a few of the hotel staff. I was dragged in them one night by another of the girl called Erica. She was a weighty girl with straggly brown hair and dark, dark eyebrows. It was before I was glassed and I'd just come back from Spencers to get my car. I was tired and cold. The smell of other peoples cigarettes was very much in my nostrils and emanating from my skin. Not the best. On top of that I always found her a bit smelly. I did a runner.

Strange thing is every time I was chatting to these women from my Centre Bar days were never really far from my thoughts and how they would react. How odd. I must've been really mixed up. All the girls I knew were now leading their own lives and almost certainly had no clue or didn't care what I was doing.

By now me and Lloyd had also got the odd job out of town. Coulton got us to work a wedding reception once for his big buddy Mark. We were in some small place near Nottingham. Lloyd was very upset. His mum had just died. I didn't know what to say. We stood on the door, mostly in silence, and I shivered and waited for trouble. Nothing happened. Phew.

I really hated being hemmed in. When you think of the early days, squeezing round Helsinkis and the Centre Bar. I knew this wasn't good. I stood at the back if we were working anywhere and trouble started. I had to force myself to move in, although I don't think I ever backed down – Lloyd may remember it differently.

Occasionally we'd bump into Valentine also doing the rounds. I suppose it was him that got Mikey the job out of town the night Lloyd gave him a lift home.

After that I think word about me must've spread and job offers started to peter out. I don't think I'd have taken them anyway.

Pretty soon after that it was the night of the long knives at the hotel. Frances BB, Coulton, Chris, Mick and a whole host of staff including us were all made redundant. I'm sure the mystified head chef breathed a sigh of relief. I've had to make people redundant myself and hated every second of it. In theory it's jobs that get removed not people but that's not been my experience and I've never really understood how these decisions are made. Some good people have lost their jobs.

They asked us all the doormen to go in on a Thursday night where the latest in a long line of GM's took us into his little office and warily broke the news to us. He seemed to focus his attentions on me. I understand why he was a bit wary. I'd only ever exchanged a few words with him and, after all, he was sitting opposite 4 burly doormen, one of whom had a earned a bit of a reputation for being a sullen short-tempered bastard.

Lloyd asked me afterwards why he kept looking and talking to me more than any of the others. Perhaps it was because I was the Head Doorman. Perhaps it was because I was the only one he'd ever spoken to. I wonder.

To be fair, I was expecting to lose my job. I expect we all were really. In the end I got a nice and somewhat unexpected payout so I wasn't that upset! I've never set foot in the place since and I have no desire to do so. Odd really considering the many long hours I was there.

The hotel later started to take in a lot of Romanian refugees to fill the rooms. I think they got a government grant for doing that although I may be wrong. Last time I walked past it was deserted and being converted into luxury flats.

35

Slumming It

After we were made redundant, and after my adventures at Spencers, the opportunities to work somewhere else were probably around for all of us. Because of my grim mood and my dislike of crowds I wasn't too fussed and, as I said before, the phone didn't ring anyway. I kept in touch with the others, mainly because of our closeness as a team, although I probably spoke to Lloyd more frequently than anyone else. He did seem to be getting most of the work, but then I because wasn't in as much contact with Phil or Slim so I don't really know for sure.

Personally I was really unsure about doing any more door work. I could've pushed I suppose. Despite my decreasing stress I still had a fair few mood swings. I worked the odd night with Lloyd – that was when Mikey drooled on me – but didn't enjoy it and I turned down the job in Leamington.

In mid 1993 I was at home, off sick with flu late when my new daytime boss, Brewin rang. Apparently there was some real mean looking, extremely tall black guy looking for me. He just walked into the factory where I was working. There was a phone number. I rang it. Lo and behold. It was Valentine. Did I want to sign up with his door agency? My mind went back to Secure-A-Door. I thought about the reputation of the Unit. I thought about my experiences at Spencers. I said no.

Brewin was a big, squinty eyed balding bloke – about the same age as me and turned out to be a bit of a life saver for which I am eternally grateful. He was happy to let me tell jokes and trust me to do a good job. I made some good friends there and even told a guy called Ken about the horrors of my dads death. VERY unusual for me to do that. He gave me a copy of a prayer that he told me had comforted him when his dad died. I'm not a religious man. I read it in private and cried and cried and cried. I never told any of them about my 'other' job. As I got over my bad experiences, and my mental and physical injuries healed more and more a better man re-emerged. Well, I like to think so. I have to admit, looking back, it's clear that I nearly, very nearly broke. Maybe I did. Sorry, not much to laugh about there either!

Of course, turns out Valentines agency really only consisted of one man. Himself. He had got himself a job at the Emporium, a small nightclub in Coalville. I didn't do any doorwork for about another year then me, Lloyd and Slim went there on a boys night out. We used to do that occasionally.

When we got there Phil was on the door as well. Valentine had shaved off all his hair. I guess he thought it made him look younger. He would have been in his early forties by this time. I still blamed him in some way for what happened at Spencers – even though he hadn't even been there that night. I wonder if that's why I blamed him? He looked at me and I shook his hand and we finally made our peace over many things between us over the years. He offered to get us jobs.

Typical of these boys nights out was the night I'd waved at Dave Man at the nightclub near the bus station when I was with Slim and Lloyd. Unusually we had to queue up to get in the place. It was their opening night. I thinking queueing was a first for all 3 of us. Slim peeped to the front of the line. The Head Doorman was working hard, keeping the line moving, chatting to a couple of bored beat cops. It seemed oh, so familiar. "Know him?" Slim had asked in his thick accent. "Sure" I replied. I'd competed against him in a local bodybuilding competition when we had both been teenagers. He had won. I hadn't even made the show at night. "That's Lincoln. He's a Mr. Universe from Nottingham."

Lincoln was yet another massive West Indian. "You used to look like that when I first met you" said Slim indicating the guys physique. He moved his hands around in a big arc. "Your chest stuck out'." I grinned. "It doesn't now" was all I said and then we stood quietly until we got in, still for free because we all knew some of the doormen who were local lads from Sugars and were milling around on the inside.

Other than the meal when I left the UK in 2004 our last as a team was a Thursday night trip to somewhere just outside Birmingham in December of 1998. I have no clue as to the name of the place or where it was because Phil drove. He just loves driving and has got the hghest level of UK licence you can get but he drives just a tad too fast for me. I'm the only person I know who sticks to speed limits like they're a life or death instruction. When we got there I jumped out of the car – glad to be alive! It was fucking FREEZING.

We all scurried inside where my glasses instantly steamed up, again, and then stayed until closing time at 2am. I finally got to bed about an hour or more later. I was out on my feet. I'm glad Phil drove back because it would have taken me a lot longer to get home. I crawled into work the next day after about 4 hours sleep and poured coffee down my throat like it was going out of fashion. 39 and still going to nightclubs. It felt odd to me. Worse. It felt plain wrong.

I always felt the Emporium was a bit weird. Not as weird as Helsinkis or the Centre Bar, but getting there. The clientele used to turn up in aprons and chefs hats wearing Wellingtons and carrying saucepans. Surprisingly me and Lloyd took Valentine up on his job offer. I don't know why I said yes. Slim knew better. It was his turn to say no. I think part of his reasons were his age and he was just over it all, but you'd have to ask him. Most of the old team were restored. The first night I turned up Valentine had been sacked for constantly being tardy or not turning up. It seems some things never change.

They made us wear these black puffa jackets with the words The Emporium embossed in white across the chest. Mine looked like someone had slept in it. Later I found out they had. I instantly felt very jaded with it all. It was odd for me to be back on a door and odder still not to be in charge anymore. I thought the Head Doorman went on far too much about the fights he'd been in. I know in his case it was pretty true, but I didn't want to know.

I stood there and thought of Kingsley, still on the doors in his mid fifties. I thought about Louise, Sharon, Claire and Caroline and where they were. I thought about lots of stuff. It was a long drive out and, by the time we'd had some takeaway, we didn't finish until about 3am. I used to get home at 4. Knackered.

I confided in Phil that I kept thinking about the girls from my younger days. In his usual few words, he just said to me "that ain't right'." After that I tried to dismiss them from my mind but was really not really very successful. I guess I was hankering for long lost days.

The Emporium was very dark with lots of long, black walled corridors and I was getting more short sighted than ever. I got to stand on the back door with Lloyd whilst Phil stood on the front. Joy! Clientele could pay to get in through either entrance but the back door was far less busy. Lloyd seemed to love it. He'd started a few weeks before me and knew a lot of the other guys. I didn't know a soul other than Lloyd and Phil. There was another guy, Ralph who started the same night as me. He was a youngish geezer, flabby looking even under his Emporium jacket and already thinning on top. He went on and on about that Swayze film and how he modelled his life on it. Here we go I thought. Another one. I asked him how long he'd been a doorman. "This is my first night" he replied. "What about you?" he asked pointing vaguely at me, Lloyd and Phil. "We've worked as a team for about 12 years" I told him. "None of you look old enough" he replied. Old enough for what? To be experienced, tough and, in my case, jaded doormen?

Maybe we didn't look like the characters in Road House. One of them is a grizzly old geezer with long grey hair and a droopy grey moustache. I didn't answer. I didn't grin. I just made sure I didn't stand too close to him. I think he only lasted the one night. They also had a skinny, bleached blond girl on the door as well. Female door staff were getting very popular by then. It was new to me. I watched and cringed as she patted people down for drugs, got far too close to them as she searched their clothes and hemmed herself in against the wall. Christ. Not a clue. Me and London Rob all over again. I wanted to help her, explain how to manage the risks but I truly couldn't be arsed.

About an hour into my second or third time there a former Mr. Universe appeared at the back door with his mate. I knew him from the magazines. He was massive. Far, far bigger than I'd ever been even in my heyday. Just as we got in free everywhere, it wasn't unusual to let guys like this in for free as well but it seemed to me that all the other doormen were cowering in the corner in case he 'went off'. Maybe my mind is distorting the facts again. "Me 'ed wor buzzing" he said to no one in particular. "I 'ad to get out the 'ouse" and off he went round the place rubbing himself up against any woman he fancied and generally being a bit of a pest. I'd aspired to that. Once. In my naïve innocence of my early days at Granby Health Club and Sugars I'd always believed that a Mr. Universe would be a good person, have some honour, some dignity. Some hopes. You'd be amazed how many have been in prison.

Mr. Universe looked at me, scowling at him under my boredom and distain and smiled. "Hi" he said. "I'm just 'aving a good time." I knew then I suppose. If I left the back door to wander round I couldn't see where I was going so a couple of nights I even worked there wearing my glasses. Not really a good idea for a doorman, even when I was at a place as quiet as Helsinkis. Much worse nearly 14 years later when trouble round towns was much greater. What a mess I'd have been if someone hit me with a knuckle-duster while I was wearing them. I didn't like many of the other doormen either.

There was a couple, Sam and Dave that were okay but some of the others were up to dirty tricks like stealing money from peoples wallets while in pretence of looking for drugs, while one was even walking around with a taser hidden in his jacket. If I had been in charge like the old days they wouldn't have lasted 5 minutes before I would have got rid of them. I tried flirting. It must be embedded in my soul! First there was another Claire, a short, pretty girl with a fantastic figure and brown hair and then Jo, a skinny girl who used to take the money, but my heart wasn't in it. I didn't know any of the bar staff. I felt old. It wasn't fun.

I didn't work every weekend. I didn't want to but some nights, when I wasn't working, I'd drive out there and chat to Lloyd and Phil and maybe Jo or Sam for a couple of hours. I'd get there for nine-ish just as they did. I'm sure they were getting a bit pissed off with me turning up but, as far as I was concerned, it got me out of the house on a Saturday night. Having said that I was always so glad to be able to say "see ya" jump in my car and drive home to my nice warm bed anytime I wanted. In total I only ever did about a dozen nights or less.

In 1998 I stood and shivered on a door for the last time. It had been fifteen years since I stood on the door at Force 8, 14 since I stepped through them at Helsinkis, stood on Louise and then walked into the Centre Bar for the first time, 11 since I got rid of the crappy Samba, 7 since I held hands with Caroline and 6 since I was glassed. It was over. All good things come to an end.

Shortly after I left Lloyd talked me into going to a strip show at some pub in Coalville. I didn't need much convincing. All the Emporium doormen except Phil were there. So was Claire. She was flirting with everyone like mad and I wondered at one stage if she was part of the show. Turns out she worked there as a barmaid. As I was sitting there hoping I'd get picked to go on stage – as long as it wasn't the girl who stuck the lit candle up your bum. I did. It wasn't – one of the Emporium guys, a bald headed bloke, jumped up and tried to beat up some poor drunk. He was the boyfriend of the skinny woman on the door and much, much older than her. He'd once asked me how I got the scar on the back of my head and I'd told him "I didn't duck fast enough." Watching him trying to beat up the drunk was sad. He couldn't do it.

The others raced over to help, led by the Head Doorman. A whole team of experienced doormen verses one old, tired and drunk bloke. I was the only one who didn't join in. Experience? Tiredness? The poor stripper was shocked. She was just lighting the candle at the time. It went out in a puff of something that came out of the bare and exposed arse of the bloke she'd dragged on stage. It was the only amusing bit about the whole situation.

Eventually this 'team' hustled the one man out. He was pretty much the last of the many nameless, faceless guys I saw get escorted from somewhere during my career. He stood outside and wept. I walked by him as we left at the end of the night. He couldn't understand what he'd done wrong. Nothing mate. It was an exercise in futility. Afterwards I told Lloyd that sort of stuff was pointless and just gave doormen a bad name. He didn't like it much and hardly spoke to me on the way home. To be honest I was very surprised he'd joined in. In my jaded eyes he'd changed too. Perhaps we all did.

In about 2005 Phil eventually got fed up and quit the Emporium too and went back to working all over the place. As far as I know he still is. And Lloyd? Last time I checked he was still there, wearing a lot of different shoes. I think he's 50 or more now. He would've done about 8 years at the Centre Bar and roughly 10 at the Emporium, plus a multitude of places in between. It makes my experience look miniscule in comparison.

My restlessness never ceased, especially at the weekends. In 1999 my employer sponsored me to go back to Uni part-time and I got myself an MSc and then an MBA. I'd already got a BSc in 1983. Oh. Didn't I mention it? I poured effort into my new studies and spent hours every Saturday and Sunday working away. I think it filled the hole. I'm glad I did them, but a doorman with three degrees?

Now, there's something different. I could've been a one man pop group. Three Degrees. Oh never mind.

36

Thirty Years Later

I re-wrote most of this book towards the very end of 2013, fifteen years since I last stood on a door and nearly 5 years after I returned to the UK from Australia. More importantly it's only a couple of weeks shy of 30 years since that first fateful night at Helsinkis.

It was an important period for me though, the doorman stuff. I have to say, I grew up a lot doing that job. I was not a hard man. I am not a hard man, but I sure became a lot tougher. Part of me really misses it and part of me doesn't. Even though my behaviour changed so dramatically while I worked the doors I'm so glad I did it. I'd never have met any of the people I did and my life would have been so much smaller. I hate to think where Marine Boy would have ended up.

Overall I had a great time working the doors. I kissed and hugged lots of girls and even Esau once but I'm convinced that job and man dangerously merged at some point – far, far more than I realised or expected. It took a lot of conscious effort to separate them again.

I have to say that I live in today, not the past and a lot has happened since those years. After I escaped from working for "the bastard" in 1993 it's fair to say that I veered about all over the place for quite a while and it took me a long time to find the equilibrium, humour, fun and happiness I now enjoy. I guess that's why I never got married, although that's probably an excuse.

I used those skills to cope with my situation when I returned from Australia. I made a plan and that plan meant coming home to the UK in January 2009. I'm not always good at using my learned skills – especially the positive thinking part but I do try. My personal philosphy was formed around my life experiences and something my old hero Mentzer was fond of promoting called Objectivism. Basically I have a view that I only have one life, one stab at this. Everything that happens to me is a result of my responses to the world around me. I stand and die by my own actions and choices. I always have.

Intrisincally, without ever really saying it, my parents drummed it into me. Never give up... never surrender. It saw me well through my doorman years. It helped me survive working for "the bastard". For those people that choose to try to steal my ideas – and there have been many in my life – I see you as nothing more than leeches. Good luck. I hope your lives have been as exciting as mine was as a doorman, has been since I packed it in and will be in my unwritten future.

In hindsight I think it was a good job I got hit on the head at Spencers. It probably knocked some sense into me. It certainly stopped me from turning into some sort of monster or ending up as a beaten up old doorman.

It's also fair to say that at the end of my door career I just didn't give a flying fuck. The guy who hit me that night in Spencers could have come at me with a gun, a rifle, a canon, a machete, a tank, an army and I'd still have taken him on. There was no thumpity-thump that night. The sulky bastard who stood at the Emporium didn't care one way or another. Such a far cry from the kid who stood in awe at the Helsinki Bar and the exuberant, fun loving, polite guy at the peak of the Centre Bar era.

The most amazing thing is – and, after everything I've said and written, this is going to surprise you all – I learned so much from "the bastard". Truthfully, I learned so much on how not to speak to people, on how not to belittle people and how much on how I should react if I'm ever unfortunate enough to find myself in a similar situation in the future. So, I choose to take the positives. Thank you very much. PS: Just make sure your shadow never crosses mine again!

When I had first arrived in Australia I decided I needed to get the Aussies to understand more about me so, on purpose, I started to let out little snippets of my background while still trying to keep that wilder part of me locked away and capped. I thought I was over it all but talking about it reminded me how much fun some of it was. That's why I finally committed to writing it all down.

As I have carried on with my life I have made a point of trying to keep that part of me buried. I thought I was fairly successful at first but there I was, walking through the offices when I worked in a posh design centre a few years ago when one of my workmates, Tim, looked up over his pebble glasses. He looked shocked. I gave him a querying look. "You came through there like a shark" was all he said. I understood. One of the other guys once said to me "you look just like a bouncer" as I crossed the room. Another guy there called me Dr. Jekyll and Mr. Hyde. One man. Two parts.

One guy in Australia who read an early version of this book told me "sometimes you can see it." Another was totally, totally amazed when he read the draft and told me he would never have believed it of me. Another wrote "Jeff, just looking at some of your... pics... Very impressive. Question... How can someone who looks like they can rip of your arms and beat you to death with them have such a mild mannered... personality? You can't fool me with the glasses, I know you're Superman!" Guess I could and did fool him.

Sometimes, when I was walking around one of the large, brightly lit shopping malls that they have in Australia, especially if they were busy and I found myself squeezing round, I could feel the two parts of me merging together again. It's a weird sensation – a bit like donning very old and comfortable armour. When I'm in that mode I find people steer clear of me. I like to think it's the only time outside of the gym it's visible, but I'm not sure.

I'd been thinking of writing this book for years. I started. I stopped. Then one boring day I played merrily on the internet. Out of curiosity I typed in Helsinkis, the Centre Bar, a few peoples names, including Ross' and Lews. I typed in Sharons, Julies and then Louises. There she was. Thumpity-thump... thumpity-thump... thumpity-thump. The first time I'd seen her in nearly a quarter of a century. She hadn't changed a bit. Part of me said don't do it. Leave her alone. Then again.

To my great surprise she said hello. We chatted a lot via email and even spoke for a short while on the phone before saying our goodbyes. She even put me in touch with Julie who in turn told me what happened to Sharon.

I set up a web page for people from those days to reminisce and have been startled by the level of response. Because I felt I needed to get back to my roots as much as anything else I tried very hard to find Claire and Caroline but failed. Then Claire joined my web group, asking me if I remembered her. Then someone posted a picture of Caroline and her sister. Amazing.

Claire is now in a happy relationship and has 3 kids but has sent me the odd message. Time went on but there was still no actual sign of Caroline for about 18 months and then Nikki, her sister appeared first. Another one asking if I remembered. It didn't take too long to discover that they both now have their own little families, as you may expect. The powers of Facebook. Fuck me. I even came across Tam the Scottish doorman of the shiny shoes and finally learned his surname.

The irony for me is that Caroline has since taken the time and trouble to explain to me that she didn't even remember spending that much time with me. Maybe that's why she never came to say goodbye.

In March 2010 we all had a big reunion, courtesy of some hard work behind the scenes by some of the Goths and Facebook so, ultimately I did get to see them all again. Loads were there. That's how I ended up being flashed at by Nikki in the black cab.

During that first one, the more the night went on, the more the music pounded – the more the two parts of me merged. While everyone else danced, drank and had a good time I sipped my orange juice, started to look out of the window and around the room, checking, squinting, waiting. They all tried but I'm afraid I just looked and behaved like a doorman... again. I'm sure they all wondered about me. Afterwards Claire told me I looked like I was really out of my comfort zone. In an odd and tired way I was completely in it.

I look like a doorman in all of the photos except one where me and Claire are grinning inanely into her camera. I didn't check her arse. Not that she saw anyway.

First Reunion – March 2010
Picture Courtesy Claire James

I like to think that my doorman courage still sits in there like a sleeping lion. The wilder bit like a caged tiger at times. In the early days, like I said, I was often scared by the way people looked at me, their appearance, their potential threat. These days I don't have those fears. I learned to be assertive and that can only be good.

As far as steroids go – the personal price just to be that big is far too high, although you have to understand. I **hate** and **mourn** the loss of my physique. I see so many kids in the gyms today. I know where they are, where they're going and where they will end.

Apart from the ones who have died, there are several other former high profile bodybuilders that have paid the price for taking these things. Probably the most notable is a very high profile guy that was nicknamed Brutal because of the intensity of his workouts. So brutal in fact that, according to bodybuilding lore, he used to regularly beat up his first wife and ended up on death row, convicted of shooting his girlfriend and her mother.

Lew, my training partner, had warned me all those years ago, but I just ignored him. Now I have old acne scars and horrific stretch marks across my chest as well as scars on my back, arms and thighs. I also have a torn muscle in my chest and had to have an expensive operation to remove a common steroid deformities caused by fluctuations in testosterone.

My personality is much better now. I hope. My dear old mum called me a reformed character recently. At least she didn't say I looked like a prostitute!

These days there is still pretty much just... me. I am still prone to bursting into tears, but it's my body's reaction to stress that does it. We all react in different ways and that's mine. It doesn't bother me although it does shock and surprise people from time to time to see a man as big as me crying. It no longer has any relationship with being embarrassed or scared.

Today no one calls me a puff. I think all that I went through with my steroid use and as a doorman proved that I never was. I still like to people watch. Piss taking of idiots who try and get away with wearing ankle snappers, drooling over cute little arses whenever I can get away with it and admiring too tight dresses are as popular as ever!

We're all 30 years older but I believe the core from our youths will always be there. We still have a shared history and the Helsinki Bar and the Centre Bar and, I suppose, the music.

I'm pleased to say that despite all my troubles and tribulations at the time some of the old clientele from those places called me the most popular doorman EVER. Red Cap Kev even called me a legend. Nice eh?

Jeff Shaw

One last thing about doorwork though. It will always nag in my mind. Did I change so much that I really just quietly asked those lads to just stop messing around in Spencers or was I a tad more aggressive than I think? When I stood back on the stairs that night in May 1992 did I give them any hint I was ready for a battle? I guess I'll never know for sure.

Ummm. The scar on my face is burning and itching.

Let me tell you something you already know. The world ain't all sunshine and rainbows. It is a very mean and nasty place and it will beat you to your knees and keep you there permanently if you let it. You, me, or nobody is gonna hit as hard as life. But it ain't how hard you hit; it's about how hard you can get hit, and keep moving forward. How much you can take, and keep moving forward. That's how winning is done. Now, if you know what you're worth, then go out and get what you're worth. But you gotta be willing to take the hit, and not pointing fingers saying you ain't where you are because of him, or her, or anybody. Cowards do that and that ain't you. You're better than that!

Sylvester Stallone: From Rocky Balboa (2006)

I was 14 when I started going to Helsinkis… and used to get drunk on pints of snakebite and black. Leicesters Alternative scene was brilliant back then. You could hop between Stinkis and the Centre Bar and then go on… to either Reflections, the Fan Club, Sector Five or hop on the Rock City bus. [Paula].

I used to go down [to] Helsinkis when I was about 14. My mum and Dad were none too pleased. One night my Dad pitched up outside… and told the door staff [i.e. Jeff] that if they saw a young lad with spiky black hair and a leather jacket they shouldn't let him in (bless his cotton socks). Needless to say I spent the next few years happily boozing away... [Richard].

I was 14 too! (1983/4) when I discovered the meaning of life (which was crazy colour, leather, tattoos, crimpers, backcombing, black eye-liner, hair extensions, spandex, punk rock, Grolsch, Voodoo, all of the above meeting places/watering holes and THE COOLEST M8S EVER!) [Claire].

Printed in Great Britain
by Amazon